THE
BAND
THAT
PLAYED
ON

The Extraordinary Story of the 8 Musicians
Who Went Down with the Titanic

STEVE TURNER

THOMAS NELSON
Since 1798

NASHVILLE   DALLAS   MEXICO CITY   RIO DE JANEIRO

Published in Nashville, Tennessee, by Thomas Nelson. Thomas Nelson is a registered trademark of Thomas Nelson, Inc.

Thomas Nelson, Inc., titles may be purchased in bulk for educational, business, fundraising, or sales promotional use. For information, please e-mail SpecialMarkets@ ThomasNelson.com.

Scripture quotations are taken from the KING JAMES VERSION.

Library of Congress Cataloging-in-Publication Data

Turner, Steve, 1949–
   The band that played on : the extraordinary story of the 8 musicians who went down with the Titanic / by Steve Turner.
      p. cm.
   Includes bibliographical references and index.
   ISBN 978-1-59555-219-8
   1. Titanic (Steamship) 2. Musicians—Biography. 3. Musicians—History—20th century. I. Title.
G530.T6T87 2011
910.9163'4—dc22   2010047182

Printed in the United States of America

11 12 13 14 15 QGF 6 5 4 3 2 1

CONTENTS

TITANIC (s).—*New York*, April 15.—A telegram received here from Montreal says : The liner Virginian reports in a wireless communication that the liner Titanic, which is reported to have been in collision with an iceberg, has requested assistance. The Virginian is hastening to her aid.—*Reuter*.

——————————*New York*, April 15.—A telegram from Cape Race says :—The wireless telegraph operator on board the Titanic reported the weather calm and clear. The position of the liner being then 41 46 N, 50 14 W. The Virginian at midnight was 170 miles west of the Titanic, and is expected to reach her at 10 o'clock this morning. The Olympic at midnight was in 40 32 N, 61 18 W. She is also in direct communication with the Titanic and is hastening to her.—*Reuter*.

——————————*New York*, April 15, 3 30 a.m.—The liner Baltic has also reported herself within two hundred miles of the Titanic and says she is speeding to her help. The last signals from the Titanic came at 12 27 this morning. The Virginian's operator says that these were blurred and ended abruptly.—*Reuter*.

——————————*New York*, April 15, 3 45 a.m.—A telegram from Cape Race, at 10 25 on Sunday evening states the Titanic reported she had struck an iceberg. The steamer said that immediate assistance was required. Half-an-hour afterwards another message was received saying the Titanic was sinking by the head and that the women were being taken off in lifeboats.—*Reuter*.

——————————*London*, April 15. — In reply to inquiry Signal Station at Cape Race cables :—10 25 p.m. Titanic reports by wireless struck iceberg and calls for immediate assistance ; at 11 p.m. she reported sinking by head, women being put off in boats. Gave position as 41 46 N, 50 14 W. Baltic, Olympic and Virginian all making towards scene disaster ; latter was last to hear Titanic signals at 12 27 a.m., reported them then blurred and ending abruptly. Believed Virginian will be first ship to reach.

——————————*London*, April 15.—A Central News telegram states : The liners Mauretania and Cincinnati and a number of other vessels are proceeding to the scene.

First mention of sinking in Lloyd's Weekly Shipping Index, April 18, 1912.

To my mother, Ivy Frances Turner,
who first gave me a love of history.

INTRODUCTION

In the old music-business joke, a songwriter is asked, "What comes first—the words or the music?" and the writer answers, "The phone call." When I am asked, "What made you write a book on the *Titanic*?" the honest answer is, "The e-mail." It came from Joel Miller, VP of nonfiction at Thomas Nelson Publishers, and after mentioning the launch of the *Titanic* in May 1911 and the maiden voyage in April 1912, he said: "I'd like to do a one hundredth anniversary popular history, and think I have a unique angle for it, one that ties into two of your areas of expertise, biography and music. Are you free to discuss?"

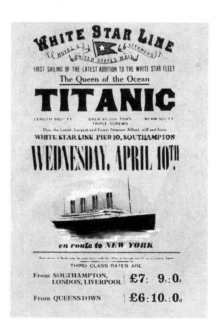

I'd never read a book about the *Titanic* and had only seen the James Cameron film after being dragged along by my wife and daughter. Biography. Music. *Titanic.* It didn't take many seconds to work out that he was probably going to ask me to write about the celebrated band on the ship that went down playing.

Despite having seen both *Titanic* and *A Night to Remember*, I still had a mental image of the band on the stage of a ballroom carrying on with their music as the dancers made for the exits and the water lapped against their music stands. In other words, I didn't know very much.

But after spending a couple of days researching on the Internet, I quickly discovered that not only was this an absorbing story—one that had once transfixed the world—but it was also a story that had never been the subject of a book, despite the floods of *Titanic* books since the 1980s. Everything that was known about the members of the band, with the exception of Wallace Hartley, could be fitted on half a dozen sheets of A4 paper. This seemed odd, given the multiple angles that had been employed over the years to open up the *Titanic* story in fresh ways. I was sure there was a book to be written about them and that the key to it would be tracking down living relatives who may have inherited photographs, documents, and anecdotes. In 2009, when I accepted Joel Miller's offer to write the book, I didn't know what I would find, but I knew it would give me the sort of challenge that I thrived on.

The Band That Played On is the result of my research. It's a portrait of eight men who were thrown together on a maiden voyage, never having played together as a band, and whose names will be forever linked because of an extraordinary act of courage in the face of death. It's also a portrait of the age in which they lived, a time when everything seemed to be going right and human ingenuity was about to surmount all the old obstacles and bring about a world that was faster, wealthier, more luxurious, and more peaceful.

I've not attempted to write another history of the *Titanic*, as such, but to focus on a group of men who were on that ship and whose biographies have necessarily been defined by what would otherwise have been another few days of routine work. I've included essential information about the ship only inasmuch as it helps the story of the musicians along. I don't attempt to determine whether the craft sank because the rivets were too short or the steel plates were too thin and neither do I spend pages speculating as to whether it broke up and sank or sank and then broke up. My assumption is that if readers want that type of detailed information they can be well supplied elsewhere.

I began the research knowing very little about the band and have finished the writing feeling that I know just about everything that can be known about them without the discovery of a hitherto unknown cache of letters, diaries, and journals. I met the descendants of their brothers and sisters and the son of the only known child of any of the bandsmen. I traveled up to Oxford, Liverpool, Dumfries, and Colne, across to Walthamstow and Notting Hill and down to Eastbourne and Southampton. I saw the homes they lived in, the schools they studied in, the rooms they played in, and the offices some of them worked in. There were times when information was so elusive I felt I was banging my head against a wall and other times when stories fell into my lap without really trying.

Why does the story of the *Titanic* continue to fascinate? There have been bigger and more costly disasters. There have been more obvious examples of human error and natural calamity. I think it's because there are not many stories where people who are neither ill nor caught up in a conflict have a few hours to contemplate their imminent deaths. We automatically ask ourselves how we would react in the same situation because we know that our choices reveal our deepest values and beliefs. Would we do absolutely anything to get a place in a lifeboat or would we gladly put someone else first? Would we stick to husband or wife, or could we live with the possibility of being parted? Would we carry on playing music, or pack up our instrument and leap overboard?

The musicians faced this ultimate challenge. I hope that I have done their actions justice. I hope that some deserving stories will have been drawn back into the light. I'd like to think that if Wallace, Georges, Roger, Theo, Percy, Fred, Jock, and Wes were to read this book they'd think I was spot on.

STEVE TURNER
London, September 2010

1

"THAT GLORIOUS BAND."

On the night of April 18, 1912, a dimly lit low-slung steamer with a single black funnel graciously eased its way up the lower reaches of the Hudson River headed toward Cunard's Pier 54. Never before had the arrival of one ship been the focus of so much anticipation and speculation. New York's traffic was gridlocked, police barriers had been erected around the west end of 12th Street, and the eyes of the world were focused on a gangway that would soon connect lower Manhattan with the British steamer *Carpathia*.

More than fifty tugboats manned by journalists had been nipping at the vessel as she made her approach, hoping to be rewarded with shouted-out answers to questions or handwritten scraps of information that would put them one step ahead of their competitors in the scramble for headlines. Reporters with megaphones made offers of $50 or $100 for firsthand reports, while photographers lit up the side of the ship with their flashes of magnesium powder. Some of them even tried to invade it when a rope ladder was let down for the river pilot to climb on, and they had to be forced back by Second Officer James Bisset.

The object of all the attention was not the ship's prebooked passengers who'd set out for the Mediterranean exactly a week before, but the more than 706 survivors of the world's worst shipwreck who'd been hauled on board from the freezing Atlantic.[1] The *Titanic* had gone down almost four days previously, and the story of its loss had dominated the front pages of newspapers around the world. But beyond knowing that it had collided with an iceberg, and that the majority of the crew and passengers had died, very few hard facts had reached the shore. An early report had suggested that all were safe, and a wrongly attributed wireless message gave the impression that the damaged *Titanic* was being towed slowly back to port.

Speculation had developed that a cover-up was being mounted, that the meager output from the *Carpathia*'s wireless room—a provisional list of survivors—and the refusal to answer press inquiries was a stalling tactic to give the chairman of the White Star Line, J. Bruce Ismay, himself a *Titanic* survivor, time to concoct an official explanation that would absolve him and his company of negligence charges. An intercepted wireless message from the *Carpathia* indicated that Ismay wanted the *Carpathia* to let its passengers off farther downriver to avoid the press.

The public naturally wanted to know how this apparently invincible liner had come to grief on what should have been a routine Atlantic crossing, but for most of the curious the explanation would have little or no immediate impact on their lives. For the friends and families of *Titanic* passengers, the need to know was vital to their peace of mind. Many of them gathered in the shed at the entrance to Pier 54 uncertain as to whether they would see their loved ones emerge. For newspapers, getting an accurate record of this event was a professional duty and an unparalleled editorial challenge.

The *Carpathia*'s arrival hadn't been expected until the early hours of April 19, so when it was spotted at 6:10 p.m. on the eighteenth, off the coast of Sandy Hook, New Jersey, the news spread quickly through the city and the streets began to fill with traffic. Limousines and touring cars sped so quickly down the newly asphalted Seventh Avenue that many of them slipped on its rainy surface and found themselves running into the curbs. Police were brought in to ensure that no one was allowed on the pier itself but the two thousand already issued passes.

Although the city was frenzied as it readied itself to receive the survivors, the atmosphere in Cunard's shed was muted. There was only a hush occasionally punctuated by sobbing. Pass holders were organized in groups behind placards bearing the initial of their loved one's surname. This was to make it easy for survivors to connect with their waiting parties. In addition to friends and relatives, there were professional caregivers: officers from the Salvation Army offering hospitality to those with no local contacts, doctors in white jackets and nurses in uniform to attend the sick and injured, representatives from the White Star Line to answer questions and handle problems. Against the walls of the shed was a row of stretchers for those too emotionally traumatized or physically damaged to make the walk.

Half a mile above Battery Park, the *Carpathia* released thirteen now empty *Titanic* lifeboats in order to deny newspapers the opportunity to photograph them. Three of the original sixteen they had picked up were too damaged to haul back, and they were left at the wreck site. The thirteen were all that remained of the proud steamer that had left Southampton on April 10 for its maiden voyage. Everything else was spread out over the ocean bed 550 miles off the coast of Newfoundland.

The *Carpathia* turned toward the Cunard Pier, where at 9:30 it tied up. The first person to emerge was a sailor dressed in a yellow oilskin. Then out came the first survivor, a fragile and unsteady woman who needed the support of a ship's officer. She was collected by her husband, who wept tears of joy and relief on her shoulder. This scene, and ones very like it, was played over and over again through the night. In many cases the longed-for face didn't appear, and there were tears of bitterness and loss.

For waiting journalists the challenge was to work out how best to use their limited time in researching and writing the most dynamic and informative copy for the next morning's papers. This was clearly a story that would win or lose the reputations of newspapers, editors, and reporters. Everything from advanced planning and breadth of coverage to shorthand skills and speedy copyediting would be put to the test. This truly was journalism as the first draft of history.

The *New York Times* had led the way in the accuracy and scope of its reportage. Its newsroom received the first Associated Press report that the *Titanic* was in trouble at 1:20 on April 15, based on a message picked up by a Marconi station at Cape Race, Newfoundland. It stated that an iceberg had been hit, lifeboats were in the water, and a distress signal had been sent. Half an hour after this initial contact, wireless communication from the stricken liner ended. Working late that night was the paper's inspirational managing editor, Carr Van Anda, who cast his eye over the facts and intuitively felt that something far worse than a damaging collision had taken place.

After telling correspondents in Montreal and Halifax to pursue the story, he trawled the cuttings library and found that there was a history of shipping collisions with icebergs in this vicinity. The *Carmania*, which had arrived in New York only the day before, had reported a field of ice. A year before the Anchor line ship *Columbia* had smashed her stern in the same area. Two years before that the *Volturne* had found itself "pinched" by moving ice, some of which ground along its side.

Other ships had reported an ice pack during the past week. The *Niagara* had been badly dented, the *Lord Cromer* and the *Kura* had both been damaged below the waterline, and the *Armenia* reported an ice field at least seventy miles long. Captain Dow of the *Carmania* had been quoted as saying: "I never saw so much ice and so little whisky and lime juice in all my life. Had the ingredients been handy there would have been a highball for every man in the world!"

Although Van Anda knew that he couldn't go into print announcing the loss of the *Titanic*—as yet there was no conclusive evidence—he used his hunch to give the story of an Atlantic collision the prominence worthy of a disaster. He spread the news over four columns, and around the core information about the distress call and subsequent radio silence, he packed stories of the other ships that had encountered ice, listed important passengers, and used images of the captain and his ship. He employed the word *sinking* in the early editions, and there are claims that he used *sunk* in later editions, although, if he did, no copy of this edition is known to exist.

The arrival of the *Carpathia* with its hundreds of eyewitnesses presented a logistical problem for all newspapers. Who were the best passengers or crew members to interview? How should the rapacious appetite for facts and truth be balanced against the need of survivors for peace and consolation? What was the most effective yet honest way of getting an exclusive on a story that would spread as quickly as a virus once the survivors were home?

Van Anda hatched a plan. He booked an entire floor of the Strand Hotel at 502 West 14th Street, close to Pier 54, to use as the *New York Times* base while it covered the arrival. Telephones on this floor would be linked directly to a desk at the *Times* where quotes and descriptions filed by reporters could be instantly hammered into stories by skilled rewrite boys. The journalists could then be reassigned to other interviews. The *Times*, in common with all other papers, was only granted four pier passes, but Van Anda ordered an additional twelve reporters to head down to the area to mingle with arriving survivors and their kin.

The most vital source, Van Anda knew, was Harold Bride, the *Titanic's* twenty-two-year-old junior Marconi operator, who had not only survived the sinking but had worked the wireless of the *Carpathia* as it sailed back to America. With the captain and most of the senior officers dead, he was the only person alive who would have been present at the heart of the drama. He had been in direct contact with Captain Edward Smith, had communicated with nearby ships, had witnessed the rescue, and would have been one of the last men to leave the ship. He also had the advantage of being able to explain what he saw in nautical terms.

But how could the *New York Times* gain access to the *Carpathia* when both Cunard and the docks authority were fiercely guarding it? Van Anda came up with a solution. He would involve the Marconi organization. Cunard might turn back a reporter, but not Guglielmo Marconi, the celebrated inventor, entrepreneur, and Nobel Prize winner, whose name was synonymous with wireless communications. It was his recently developed equipment that was revolutionizing sea travel. It was unlikely that any *Titanic* passengers would have been saved if not for the Marconi wireless transmitter.

If Bride gave an exclusive interview, it would enhance the name of Marconi as much as that of the *New York Times*. Bride wouldn't lose out either. The fee for his story would equal three years' wages as a wireless operator. The Marconi office had already sent three messages to its own wireless room advising the operators to hold their stories until approached by the *New York Times*. The last of these, addressed to "Marconi Officer, the *Carpathia* and the *Titanic*" and signed by American Marconi's chief engineer Frederick Sammis, simply said: "Stop. Say nothing. Hold your story for dollars in four figures. Mr. Marconi agreeing. Will meet you at dock." This was later assumed to be another reason for the *Carpathia's* media blackout. Even President Taft couldn't get in touch to find out whether his trusted military aide Major Archibald Butt had survived. (He had not.)

On the night of April 18, presumably unaware that the *Carpathia* was ahead of schedule, Marconi was at a party. Van Anda sent a messenger to fetch him down to Pier 54 to board the ship with Sammis and *New York Times* reporter Jim Speers. It was now around 11:30 and almost all the passengers had already disembarked. The copy would have to be ready for the printer within an hour if it was to make the first edition on April 19.

When they got to the pier, police stopped them. The reporter, Speers, protested: "Sir, we are Mr. Marconi, his manager, and a *New York Times* reporter." The officer pushed the Marconi engineer Sammis back, believing him to be the journalist in question, saying, "Mr. Marconi and his manager may pass through. The reporter can't." Speers and Marconi boarded, while Sammis had to remain behind the police line. The two men made their way to the wireless room where they found Bride still tapping out messages left for him by passengers. "That's hardly worth sending now, boy," said Marconi. Bride, his frostbitten feet still bandaged, looked up slowly and then recognized his distinguished employer.

Bride's story, which he poured out to Speers in a rambling monologue, was everything Van Anda had hoped it would be. He'd got out of bed on the night of April 14 to relieve the senior operator, Jack Phillips, only to find that the *Titanic* had been in a collision. He watched as Phillips calmly made contact with the *Carpathia* and the *Olympic* and saw Captain Smith's dawning realization that the ship was beyond salvation.

In a sensational comment, he revealed that a stoker (one of the men who stoked the ship's furnaces with coal) had come into the *Titanic*'s wireless room to steal Phillips's life jacket. Bride attacked him. "I did my duty," he said. "I hope I finished him. I don't know. We left him on the cabin floor of the wireless room and he was not moving." It was never clear from this or subsequent interviews whether Bride was claiming to have killed him or merely to have knocked him unconscious and left him to drown.

Phillips died of exposure while in the water. Bride found the last remaining collapsible boat, but when it was pushed overboard, it landed upside down with him underneath it. Bride managed to swim away as sparks poured from one of the *Titanic*'s funnels, and the ship finally disappeared from view. After some time in the water, he was given space on his original boat, which had since been righted.

Bride gave a detailed account of how the ship's band had carried on playing throughout the sinking. The matter-of-fact way he told the story gave it added poignancy: "From aft came the tunes of the band," he said. "It was a ragtime tune, I don't know what. Then there was 'Autumn.' Phillips ran aft and that was the last I ever saw of him alive."

His description of the ship's final moments suggested that the musicians didn't even attempt to escape in a lifeboat. "The ship was gradually turning on her nose—just like a duck does that goes down for a dive. I had only one thing on my mind—to get away from the suction. The band was still playing. I guess all of the band went down. They were playing 'Autumn' then. I swam with all my might. I suppose I was 150 feet away when the *Titanic*, on her nose, with her after quarter sticking straight up into the air, began to settle—slowly."

Bride ended by saying that two things about the sinking stood out in his mind above all others. One was that Jack Phillips had continued to send messages even after Captain Smith told him he was free to leave his position and look after his own life. The other was the band that played on. "The way the band kept playing was a noble thing . . . How they ever did it I cannot imagine."

The twenty-five-hundred-word first-person account appeared in the next day's *New York Times* along with fifty-two other stories about the ship. The headline was "Thrilling story by *Titanic's* wireless man." The subheadings were "Bride tells how he and Phillips worked and how he finished a stoker who tried to steal Phillips's life belt—Ship sank to tune of 'Autumn.' " The image of the lighted ship sliding under the waves ("She was a beautiful sight then"), while the band carried on regardless, captured the public's imagination.

Getting to talk to Bride was a journalistic scoop and one that would be associated with Van Anda for the rest of his life. But there was another journalist who'd been one step ahead. Unbeknown to the *New York Times*, Carlos F. Hurd, a thirty-six-year-old reporter from the *St. Louis Post-Dispatch*, owned by Ralph Pulitzer, had been with his wife, Katherine, on the *Carpathia* as a paying passenger headed for the Mediterranean when it had diverted to pick up the *Titanic* survivors.

Hurd found himself in the sad but privileged position of being a writer surrounded by eyewitnesses of one of the biggest peacetime tragedies in living memory and having plenty of time to amass an oral record. He began to speak to those who'd been rescued and found that there was no need to coax information from them. Happy to have been saved, they "found a certain relief in speech." He took notes and employed Katherine as his assistant. The *Carpathia*'s crew members, who'd been instructed by Captain Rostron to keep him away from the *Titanic* passengers, impeded his job. The crew refused him supplies of paper, banned him from contacting America by wireless, and had his cabin routinely searched for notes and transcripts. He was forced to write on anything available, including toilet paper, and to keep his material with him at all times.

Messages sent to him care of the ship's wireless room were not passed on, so he was out of contact with his editors. Despite that, he knew the New York staff would find a way to get to the *Carpathia* so that he could pass on to them this huge story. One of the telegrams that didn't reach him was sent on April 18 by Ralph Pulitzer: "Chapin is on tug Dazelline. Will meet Carpathia between New York and Fire Island Thursday. Been [*sic*] on lookout and deliver to Chapman [*sic*] tug your full report of wreck with all interviews obtainable." Charles Chapin was the editor of the Pulitzer-owned *New York Evening World* and Hurd had already anticipated what Chapin would want and had packaged his manuscript in a white waterproof bag, attached it to a cigar box, and added champagne corks on lengths of string, ready to toss it overboard. It was an unusual way of delivering copy, but these were unusual times.

Captain Rostron of the *Carpathia* tried to deceive the flotilla of tugboats that he knew was awaiting his arrival in New York waters by radioing false positions, but the *Dazelline*, which could equal the *Carpathia*'s speed of fourteen knots, didn't fall for the trick. It managed to locate the ship and draw up close to it while a reporter bellowed Hurd's name through a megaphone. Spotting Pulitzer's flag, Hurd tossed the package toward the tug but, unfortunately, one of his corked strings tangled with a rope from a *Titanic* lifeboat, which had not yet been released and was still in the spot it had been hoisted to during the rescue. "A sailor reached out, took the bundle, and hesitated," Hurd later wrote. "'Throw it!' cried a dozen persons. The sailor tossed the bundle to Chapin. With an acknowledging toot of the tug's whistle, the little craft churned off."

The drama didn't end there. The tugboat ploughed its way toward an empty dock at the end of 12th Street, but after disembarking, the *World* employees found their exit blocked by a boarded-up warehouse with no electric lighting. They had to smash their way into the darkened building and out on the other side to make it to the street. An elevated train took them to the stop closest to the *New York World* building at 53–63 Park Row. During the journey Chapin hurriedly marked up Hurd's lengthy handwritten copy and added instructions to the typesetters. A reporter named "Gen" Whytock met him at the station and sprinted the half mile to the office with the script. By the time the *Carpathia* docked, an Extra edition of the *Evening World* was already on the street with a condensed version of the five-thousand-word story on the front page beneath the headline "*Titanic* Boilers Blew Up, Breaking Her in Two after Striking Berg." The *St. Louis Post-Dispatch* also managed to run this story in an Extra that night, putting the full story on the cover the next day.

Headline from the April 18th evening edition of the *New York World*.

Thus it was Hurd's story that first informed the world about the band playing on. In the *Evening World* he wrote: "The ship's string band gathered in the saloon, near the end, and played 'Nearer, My God, to Thee.'" The fuller version published in the next day's papers, and later syndicated by the Associated Press, read: "As the screams in the water multiplied, another sound was heard, strong and clear at first, then fainter in the distance. It was the melody of the hymn 'Nearer, My God, to Thee,' played by the string orchestra in the dining saloon. Some of those on the water started to sing the words, but grew silent as they realized that for the men who played, the music was a sacrament soon to be consummated by death. The serene strains of the hymn and the frantic cries of the dying blended in a symphony of sorrow."

The *Leeds Mercury*, which would have been read by bandleader Wallace Hartley's bereaved fiancée, Maria Robinson, contained a quote from Carlos Hurd in its April 20 edition. "To relate that as the last boats moved away the ship's string band gathered in the saloon and played 'Nearer, My God, to Thee' sounds like an attempt to give added colour to a scene which was in itself the climax of solemnity, but various passengers and survivors of the crew agree in declaring they heard this music."

Other accounts that confirmed Hurd's report swiftly followed. Caroline Bonnell from Youngstown, Ohio, who'd been traveling with two aunts, an uncle, and a cousin, told a reporter from the United Press Agency that those closest to the ship when it sank heard the men singing "Nearer, My God, to Thee." This story appeared in the *Christian Science Monitor* on April 19 and was picked up by other newspapers.

By the twentieth of April, the story was widely accepted and was viewed as one of the most heartening acts of bravery in the whole tragedy. Southampton resident Ada Clarke was pushed onto a lifeboat by her husband, who chose to remain behind. "I shouldn't have done it otherwise," she told the *Cleveland Plain Dealer*. "Oh, they were brave and splendid, all the men. They died like brave men. At the last, all the men were kneeling and there floated out across the water the strains of 'Nearer, My God, to Thee.' I could hear it and saw the band men kneeling too." Mrs. Caroline Brown of Belmont, Massachusetts, told the *Worcester Evening Gazette*: "The band played marching from deck to deck, and as the ship went under I could still hear the music. The musicians were up to their knees in water the last I saw them."

Under a headline of "Band Goes Down Playing," London's *Daily Mirror* reported: "In the whole history of the sea, there is little equal to the wonderful behaviour of these humble players. In the last moments of the great ship's doom, when all was plainly lost, when braver and hardier men might almost have been excused for doing practically anything to save themselves, they stood responsive to their conductor's baton and played a recessional tune." In one edition the front page was given over entirely to the words and music of the hymn.

London's *Daily Mirror* front page featuring the words of the hymn, April 20, 1912.

On April 21 the *New York Times* devoted a story to the musicians that favored the tune "Autumn" that Bride had mentioned in his interview as the band's swan song. They had taken him to mean a tune of that name used by Anglicans in England and Episcopalians in America, not taking into account the fact that a young wireless operator would be more likely to identify hymns by their first lines than by the name of their tunes. According to a correspondent to the *New York Times* on May 12, "Autumn" was not wedded to a particular hymn and listed seven hymns regularly set to "Autumn" in America: "Guide Me, O Thou Great Jehovah," "Saviour Breathe an Evening Blessing," "Glorious Things of Thee Are Spoken," "Jesus, I My Cross Have Taken," "Hail, Thou Once-Despised Jesus," "Love Divine, All Loves Excelling," and "In the Cross of Christ I Glory." In addition, the tune "Autumn" was also known in some hymnals as "Madrid" and in others as "Jaynes or Janes."

Carlos Hurd himself later became less certain that the musicians had taken their last breaths playing "Nearer, My God, to Thee." He didn't question that the band had carried on playing and that they had played a hymn or hymns, but he couldn't be 100 percent sure that his sources could be trusted to accurately identify a tune, given their distance from the ship, the extraneous noises, and the dreamlike way that events seemed to unfold. Twenty years after the sinking he wrote:

> The endeavour to fit such a story together showed how fragmentary was the knowledge of individuals. One would mention an incident which could be confirmed or completed only by another. In the search for the other, new suggestions and new complications would arise. The job would have taxed the energy and resources of a dozen reporters.
>
> An instance of this difficulty was the incident, still remembered, of the playing of the hymn music by the English musicians in the sinking ship's orchestra. Several persons told of having heard this music from their boats, but, because of distracting noises, they could not be sure what the melody was. Two women, who professed familiarity with sacred music, said it was "Nearer, My God, to Thee." This statement appeared in my report and gained general currency. *The New York Times* later obtained a book of music said to be a duplicate of the one which the *Titanic's* orchestra had. It did not contain the tune *Bethany*, to which the

hymn already named is sung, but it did contain the hymn tune *Autumn*, which, though in a different meter, is much like *Bethany*. The *Times* concluded that *Autumn* was the number played.

Although minor details differed in the accounts of survivors—the band marched or knelt, played "Autumn" or "Nearer, My God, to Thee," carried on to the bitter end or calmly packed their instruments away before the final plunge—there was an overwhelming consistency. The musicians had played on the deck as the ship went down. They had forfeited their lives for the sake of others. They had played the tunes of hymns to induce a spirit of peace and calm. They were heroic. Admiral Lord Fisher of England referred to them as "that glorious band," and the phrase caught on.

The story of their gallantry came to epitomize a spirit of courage, duty, and self-sacrifice. It was held up as proof that manhood wasn't withering away through self-indulgence, frivolity, and lack of religion. Although the disaster itself was widely regarded as a comeuppance for the powerful and wealthy who had become fixated on speed, luxury, and the domination of nature, the behavior of the musicians showed that worthy "old-fashioned" values of chivalry, fortitude, and love of neighbor still persisted.

The names of the musicians began to appear in newspapers and magazines, although little was known about them. The *Daily Mirror* contacted Charles Black, the Liverpool agent who had booked the band for the *Titanic*, to find out more. He explained that there were, in fact, two bands—a "saloon orchestra" of five men, and a "deck band" of three. "Probably they all massed together under their leader, Mr. Wallace Hartley, as the ship sank," he suggested. "Five of the eight, Mr. Hartley, P. C. Taylor, J. W. Woodward, F. Clark and W. T. Brailey were Englishmen. One, J. Hume, was a Scotsman and the remaining two, Bricoux and Krins, were French and German respectively."

Neither the quintet nor the trio had played together before boarding the *Titanic*, three of the musicians had never before been to sea, and, not surprisingly, there was no group photograph to illustrate the stories describing their heroism. Their names were often misspelled or wrongly reported. In the *New York Times* the cellist John Wesley Woodward became George Woodward, the pianist Percy Cornelius Taylor became Herbert Taylor, violinist Georges Krins became George Krius, bandleader Wallace Hartley became Wallace Hattry, and cellist Roger Bricoux became Roger Brelcoux. (On one memorial he was permanently inscribed as Roger Bricouk.) Even agent Charles Black was confused about the nationality of Georges Krins. He thought Krins was German, not Belgian.

Almost two weeks after the sinking, the *Illustrated London News* produced a full-page memorial poster with oval portraits of all the musicians except Bricoux, whose family hadn't been able to supply a picture in time. A series of six postcards by Holmfirth, Bamforth & Co., featuring images of the *Titanic*, grieving women, and the words of "Nearer, My God, to Thee," was published. In France fifty thousand copies of the sheet music to "Plus Pres de Toi Mon Dieu" were sold in a matter of weeks. In America musician Harold Jones and lyricist Mark Beam wrote a song titled "The Band Played 'Nearer, My God, Thee' as the Ship Went Down."

> *There the brave men stood,*
> *Las true heroes should,*
> *With their hearts in faith sublime,*
> *And their names shall be fond memory*
> *Until the end of Time.*
> *And the band was bravely playing*
> *The song of cross and crown*
> *—"Nearer, My God, to Thee"*
> *As the ship went down.*

Nearer, my God, to Thee, Nearer to Thee"
E'en though it be a cross that raiseth me:
Still all my song shall be,
Nearer, my God, to Thee, Nearer to Thee!

On May 18 bandleader Wallace Hartley's body was brought back to his Lancashire birthplace of Colne to be buried in the family vault alongside his two brothers who had died in infancy. The funeral was an event of epic proportions with crowds of thirty to forty thousand thronging the streets; photographs of the procession and burial were published around the world. Just as the band had given the victims of the sinking a human face, so Hartley gave a face to the band. He was the only one of the eight whose remains would return home.

His parents were inundated with letters from members of the public who claimed to share their grief. A typical letter read: "I desire to congratulate you sincerely on being the mother of a hero and a gentleman whose name—many years after yours and mine are forgotten—will bring a thrill of pride wherever Englishmen are gathered. The knowledge that your dear son died at his post giving comfort and consolation to hundreds of others must ever be a comforting and consoling memory to you." Others wanted souvenirs of a man they had never met—photographs, samples of his handwriting, copies of music he had touched, something he had owned.

Six days later the Orchestral Association mounted a memorial concert for the musicians at London's Royal Albert Hall. It featured a five-hundred-strong orchestra composed of members of London's seven main orchestras—the Philharmonic, the Queen's Hall, the London Symphony, the New Symphony, the Beecham Symphony, the Royal Opera, and the London Opera House. Conductors included Thomas Beecham, Henry Wood, and composer Edward Elgar. Ada Crossley, an Australian soprano, sang a solo.

A century later the *Titanic* musicians' story is still known, not through newspaper accounts or even history books but through the movies *Titanic* (1953), *A Night to Remember* (1958), and *Titanic* (1997). *Titanic* societies keep their names alive as do excellent Web sites such as www.encyclopedia -Titanica.org and www.Titanic-Titanic.com. In 1997 musician Ian Whitcomb recorded an album of tunes the band would have played and was nominated for a Grammy for his comprehensive sleeve notes. His musicians for the project were named the White Star Orchestra.

Yet despite widespread recognition of the event, we appear to know as much about the musicians as was known in 1912. A book published that year had asked: "What about the bandsmen? Who were they? This question was asked again and again by all who read the story of the *Titanic*'s sinking and of how the brave musicians played to the last, keeping up the courage of those who were obliged to go down with the ship. Many efforts were made to find out who the men were, but little was made public." Although because of the Internet it's now much easier to retrieve contemporary accounts of the band's actions, the members still remain a ghostly presence. The same photographs are used repetitively, the same rumors are circulated, and other than Wallace Hartley, who entered the *Oxford*

Dictionary of British Biography in 2010, the band members remain anonymous early-twentieth-century figures.

It's not hard to determine why this is so. These were not famous performers who had given interviews, filled in questionnaires, and been profiled during their lifetimes. None of them had written songs providing insights into their concerns or even, as far as we know, made recordings. For the most part, whatever diaries and letters they may have left behind have been lost over the years. They were famous for their deaths, not their lives. As a result, we know a lot about how they spent their last moments on the *Titanic*, but almost nothing about how they came to be there.

The *Titanic* sailed out of Southampton but was registered in Liverpool. It was from an office in Liverpool that they were hired, at a Liverpool outfitter that they had their bandsmen's uniforms adapted for the White Star Line, and from Liverpool stations that most of them left for what promised to be the journey of a lifetime. And so it is to Liverpool that we have to return to start the search for the band that played on.

2

"THE WORLD'S GREATEST LINER."

It was from their third-floor office at 14 Castle Street, Liverpool, that two Manchester-born brothers, Charles William and Frederick Nixon Black, planned the *Titanic*'s music. We'll never discover what guided their choices or how they approached each instrumentalist, but we know that they had hundreds of players on their books, that they had both played for professional orchestras, and that their task was to put together two impressive groups of musicians appropriate for a first-class passenger list drawn from the top echelon of European and American society.

STREET DIRECTORY.

AS

t STREET – continued.
ncrete Construction Co.
lliam & Co. builders
thur C., A.M.Inst.C.E. con-
ig engi eer
James & Sons, Ltd.
t importers and
s men
L. No. Bank 3450
wires
graphic Address—
'Cattle, Liverpool."

Williams Roderick & Bardsley solictrs
Inman Arthur solicitor
Aldridge Ernest C. architect and
    surveyor
Thornely & Furbur quantity surveyrs
Wright Frederic architect & surveyor
Black C. W. & F. N. music directors
16 & 18 Saxone Shoe Co. Ltd. boot and
    shoe dealers
20 Collins, Robinson, Driffields & Kusel
    solicitors
Carruthers & Gedge solicitors

Sloan & Lloyd Ba
& foreign pat
consulting & el
gineers. Trade
gistration Offic
TELEPHONE
T. A. "Technica

Gilbert Frederick Cha
36 The London City &
    Ltd. (Leyland's b

Gore's Liverpool Directory showing C. W. & F. N. Black at 14 Castle Street.

17

No one could have known that they would be sending the eight musicians to their deaths by booking them. After all, the *Titanic* was the newest, safest, and most prestigious ship on the seas. Evidence suggests that the musicians may have been enticed by an above-average fee, and the tips alone would have made the trip worth taking. They were contracted only for the maiden voyage. These men from comparatively modest homes would be mingling with some of the world's richest and most powerful people in an ambience of unparalleled luxury on a voyage that would make history.

The Blacks were to emerge as villains of the piece. The tragedy exposed their unfair business practices and lack of consideration for their employees' welfare. The ire of the Amalgamated Musicians' Union had already been aroused when the Blacks became sole agents for all the major shipping lines, and the fate of the *Titanic* players simply gave the union more ammunition. They also revealed themselves as either heartless, thoughtless, or both, by asking one father to pay up for his son's outstanding tailoring bill. The garment that had been altered was the uniform he died in.

Although the Blacks argued for their innocence in the press, they couldn't shed the reputation of callousness. Three of the bereaved fathers took them to court, and the AMU continued to campaign against them, eventually advising musicians either to stay with the AMU and not work for the Blacks or to work for the Blacks and relinquish union membership. The brothers, in turn, tried to make amends by raising money for the dependents of the *Titanic*'s band and making a show of their good deeds.

Whether it was because of their notoriety, or simply because agents weren't part of polite society, the Black brothers lived and died almost without a trace. To *Titanic* historians they have simply been C. W. & F. N. Black, the name under which they traded. No one has ever fleshed them out or discovered a photograph of them. When they died within a year of each other in the 1940s, their passing wasn't even noted in their local newspaper. Their archives, which would have been of such value to researchers, must have been destroyed when the company ceased trading during World War II. They were never interviewed about their crucial role in the *Titanic* story.

Castle Street had always been close to Liverpool's center of power. In medieval times it was the street that connected the castle with the market and the river with the Pool, an area where several waterways converged into a docking area for ships. In the late eighteenth century the present town hall was built at one end. In the first decade of the twentieth century, when the Blacks began renting their offices, it was within walking distance of the headquarters of two of the greatest shipping lines of the era: Cunard on Water Street and White Star on James Street. It was also close to the newly completed landmark Royal Liver Building at the Pierhead. All of the buildings in the area announced confidence, wealth, and dominion. On the ground floor of number 14 was the Bank of British West Africa and the vice consular office for Salvador.

Albion House, also known as the White Star Building, Liverpool.

Nineteenth-century British prime minister Benjamin Disraeli once described Liverpool as the Empire's second city. Internationally it was beaten only by London in terms of the value of its sea trade. New York was third. In 1908 almost 26,000 vessels used the 418 acres of docks that spread along the Mersey. A significant proportion of its population—from the owners of boardinghouses and makers of rope to dockworkers, bar stewards, boatbuilders, and travel agents—were dependent on sea traffic. In 1906 the port listed 1,305 steamships and 914 sailing ships in its register.

Castle Street, Liverpool, looking toward Town Hall. The Blacks' former office was in the building on the left.

While the port of London handled more cargo, Liverpool dealt with more passengers. Since 1825 almost 56 percent of all people leaving Britain had embarked at Liverpool, and a surge in numbers after 1905 pushed its share to over 60 percent. The bonanza came from a wave of emigration that was only halted by the outbreak of World War I.

Most of these passengers were traveling to either America or Canada with a minority going to Australia, New Zealand, or the Caribbean. Liverpool had long established routes to New York, Boston, Baltimore, Galveston, New Orleans, Quebec, and Montreal, and it attracted passengers from mainland Europe who would travel by ferry to ports such as Hull on the east coast and then overland by train. Some of them had return tickets but the majority were emigrants. The Atlantic crossing was their bid for a better life and Liverpool was their last glimpse of England.

Charles and Frederick Black were born into a working-class Manchester family—their father William was a carpenter and joiner—and they and their sister Elizabeth learned music as children. Musical ability eased their entry into the newly emerging middle class. Frederick, whose main instrument was the oboe, studied at the Royal Manchester College of Music from January 1899 until July 1900. Between 1900 and 1904 he ran F. N. Black & Co., Musical Instrument Manufacturers and Importers, from the family home at 6 Stanley Street in the Fairview area of Liverpool. He started off selling strings, became sole agent for Becker's violin and cello pegs, and then began selling reasonably priced violins.

Charles, the older brother by ten years, was a professor of music by the age of eighteen and five years later joined the Halle Orchestra as a second violinist. In 1899 he was joined by Frederick, who became one of the orchestra's four oboists, obviously able to do this job while operating his business from home. Elizabeth became a music teacher. Charles also doubled up as second violinist for the Liverpool Philharmonic Orchestra.

The Halle, Britain's first fully professional orchestra, was founded in 1857 by German-born pianist and conductor Charles Halle. Based at the Free Trade Hall on Manchester's Peter Street in Manchester, it consisted of more than one hundred musicians, and a separate Halle choir had almost four hundred voices. Each year the orchestra would do a season of twenty concerts in Manchester and tour throughout Britain.

Another reason for the paucity of information on the Blacks is that they left no heirs. Neither of them married, and nor did their sisters. Florence died in 1905 at the age of thirty-four after a bout of influenza. Elizabeth lived until 1955 and left her estate to her solicitor. The closest living relatives are the granddaughters of a cousin, one of whom owns a faded and damaged photograph of a previously unidentified Black brother. The young man with a dark fitted coat and bow tie is holding a violin, proving him to be Charles, the older and more dominant brother.

The studio portrait contains few clues about the man who created the *Titanic*'s band. Charles stares at the camera without a hint of

Charles Black posing with his violin.

expression. Because of fading it's hard to tell whether he's clean-shaven or has a very light, downy mustache. His hair is parted left of center, and his nose has a beaked tip. The bow tie and formal jacket suggest that this was taken when he was playing for the Liverpool Philharmonic and Halle orchestras. Twenty-five years ago, elderly musicians in Liverpool who had worked for him remembered him as Charlie Black, a small dapper man with a neat mustache, smart gray suits, and spectacles, who looked more like a bank manager than a music agent.[1]

There are no known photos of Frederick Black. The only description of him comes from an army medical record six years after the *Titanic* voyage: five feet ten inches tall (taller than the national male average by three inches), 145 pounds, light-brown hair, gray eyes, and a fresh complexion. By then, although still a relatively young man, he had a perforated eardrum that impaired his hearing.

Charles finished with both the Halle and the Liverpool Philharmonic in 1907 and between then and 1909 established the agency, describing himself as a "musical director" rather than a mere "music agent." This suggests a more creative role involving assembling bands, choosing repertoire, and supplying music. A musician friend, Enos Green, became the Blacks' London representative, working out of his home on Fordwych Road in West Hampstead.

C. W. & F. N. Black became the sole agents for the Grand Central Hotel in Leeds; the Kardomah Café in Castle Street, Liverpool; and the Constant Spring Hotel in Jamaica. They claimed to be able to supply groups of between five and fifty musicians. The most lucrative side of their business was to come from the shipping lines, which all used professional bands on their major passenger routes. By 1912 they were booking musicians for American, Anchor, Booth, Cunard, Royal Mail, and White Star—lines that owned more than eighty vessels between them. Players in the employ of the Blacks were known in Liverpool as "Charlie's navy."

Although the musicians on ships played stringed instruments and were often referred to as an orchestra, they were officially bandsmen under the direction of a bandmaster. In a rare interview from the period, John Carr, a musician on the White Star liner *Celtic*, explained: "It's a mistake from the technical point of view to call a steamer's orchestra a band. The term is a survival of the days when they really had a brass band on board. On all the big steamships now the music is given by men who are thorough masters of their instruments."

Initially music on ships was provided by musically competent passengers, later by crew members. Stewards in second class were routinely tested for musical skills. When bands were eventually recruited from outside, they made their income from tips, but by 1907 the first salaried professional orchestras appeared on ships such as the *Aragon* and *Adriatic*. A 1909 White Star Line brochure for the "big four"—the *Adriatic, Baltic, Cedric,* and *Celtic*—used music as a selling point: "The cheery surroundings of the lounge make it an ideal spot for casual conversation or for the leisurely after-dinner demi-tasse, and, with the ship's own orchestra of professional musicians discoursing catchy airs in the main foyer of the steamer, just outside the lounge doors, a pleasant sense of camaraderie is certain to be developed between the passengers even though they hail from many corners of the globe."

Crew lists reveal the names of these often uncelebrated musicians who played their way around the world: people like Ernest Drakeford of Rotherham, Ellwand Moody of Bramley, Frederick Stent and Albert Felgate of Egremont on the Wirral. Some of the older musicians were in their late fifties. Some of the younger ones were barely out of their teens. Many would stay with a ship for months or even years, but others would flit from ship to ship and from line to line. On Mediterranean cruises two English musicians might, for example, leave the ship in Italy to be replaced by two Italians. It was the ideal job for travelers, adventurers, and those escaping domestic problems.

The work was long and arduous. A band could be expected to play at lunchtime, during teatime, and then again in the restaurant at night, as well as rehearsing every day. They might also perform at church services, evening balls, and at special celebratory events, such as when a ship broke the speed record. A sixteen-page White Star Line music booklet of the period lists 341 numbered pieces ranging from overtures, waltzes, ragtime, and marches to sacred music, classical music, and operatic selections. It was an extensive repertoire and new hit songs would be added as the list was constantly updated. Passengers—each given a copy of the booklet—could call out the number of any tune, and the band would be expected to play it.

The rewards of the job were the regularity of employment and the chance to travel. Musicians on regular transatlantic sailings would inevitably spend as much time in Boston and New York as they did in Liverpool and Southampton. They made friends in these cities, especially among fellow musicians, and were able to experience the music, theater, and art of America. As a result they became experienced and confident players able to turn their hands to anything from a Rossini opera to the latest music hall hit.

The standard wage for a ship's musician was £6 10s. 0d. a month (£6.50 in decimal currency)—slightly higher than that of a police constable but lower than that of a miner. Food and lodging were free, however, and there were tips and a monthly uniform allowance. As crew members, musicians were under the command of the captain and in the case of injury or death were covered by the Workmen's Compensation Bill of 1906. If they handled their money well, it was possible to accumulate decent savings after a few years at sea.

The Blacks were definitely servicing ships by 1909 and first appear in *Gore's Liverpool Directory* for 1910.[2] In August 1909, an Austrian bandsman on the *Lusitania*, Paul Schumann, gave the Black's office address in Castle Street as his contact address. Yet at that time not every ship's musician was a client of C. W. & F. N. Black. Musicians were free to deal directly with the lines or with individual bandleaders. This changed in the early part of 1912 when the brothers negotiated with the major shipping companies to become their exclusive music agents. A White Star representative said the deal was "a contract to furnish an orchestra of five musicians for a fixed sum for each ship." All future business would go through C. W. & F. N. Black.

The Amalgamated Musicians' Union in Britain reacted angrily on behalf of its members. Not only were the Blacks harming long-established relationships between musicians and ships, but they also used their power to cut wages by almost 40 percent and abolish the uniform allowance. Their contracts confusingly prohibited players from accepting tips while simultaneously stipulating that gratuities should be pooled and then distributed equally to each musician, except for the bandleader, who was to get a double portion. The Blacks must have known that the wage reduction made tips essential for the players.

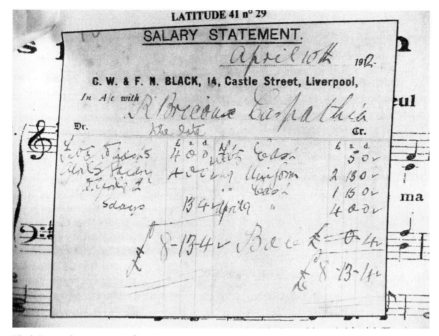

Black Bros. salary statement for musician Roger Bricoux.

In March 1912 an AMU delegation traveled to Southampton, where the *Olympic* was in dock, to confront the White Star Line's chairman, J. Bruce Ismay. Their case was as follows:

> While we admit that anyone who finds the musicians and the music for someone else is entitled to some recompense, we cannot for one moment agree that Messrs. Black or anyone else are entitled to anything like 50 per cent of the fee allowed them for each bandsman . . . The bandsmen should sign the ship's articles, be paid their wages direct by the company and not through any agent, and sign off at the termination of any engagement.

The ship's articles were terms and conditions that gave the bandsmen all the privileges of a crew member. It cost one shilling a month to sign on. Ismay's response to the AMU appeared spiteful. Instead of restoring the previous arrangements, he cut all direct employment ties between White Star and the musicians by removing them from the ship's articles and requiring the

Black agency to pay for their tickets as second-class passengers. They were now employees of C. W. & F. N. Black. Like any other White Star passenger, they would go through immigration controls at Ellis Island and be required to produce $50 to prove they were not destitute. Ismay appeared to be saying, "Look. It's nothing to do with me. If you have problems with the wages, go and talk to the agency. We don't set the pay thresholds."

Ships' musicians were now not only poorer but also lower in status. "A musician on board a ship is still but a queer creature," complained the Orchestral Association in its journal. "He is a square peg in a round hole. There is really no place for him on board unless he does a bit of waiting at table. He is not a seaman, fireman, steward, or any article mentioned in the regulations of the mercantile marine. Not even a chattel!" The *New York Times* ran a story on March 24, 1912, headlined "Bandsmen Now Passengers" that ended with the observation "This method takes them out of the jurisdiction of the Captain, as they are not members of the crew." The archives of the White Star Line are incomplete, making it impossible to know the exact terms of the contract with C. W. & F. N. Black.

There's no extant correspondence to reveal how the brothers managed their coup. They may have known J. Bruce Ismay through Liverpool business connections or through social circles on the Wirral peninsula. They lived in a seven-room house on Heron Road. Ismay's inherited family mansion, Dawpool (designed by Richard Norman Shaw, architect of New Scotland Yard, the Savoy Theatre, Bedford Park, and the Piccadilly Hotel among other London buildings and Albion House in Liverpool), was only six miles away, overlooking the River Dee at Thurstaston.

The Blacks would have followed the progress of the building of the *Titanic* and the battle between Cunard and White Star for supremacy on the transatlantic route. The two shipping lines had a lot in common. Thomas Henry Ismay, the founder of White Star, was born in 1837, Samuel Cunard in 1839. Ismay's Oceanic Steamship Company was formed in 1869, the Cunard Steamship Company in 1879. Both lines were built out of the remnants of previous companies.

The formative years of Cunard and White Star witnessed the transition from sail to steam and from wood to iron. It also saw a rapid increase in emigration from Europe to America. The question both lines faced was how to best capitalize on the lucrative North Atlantic route. Cunard opted to sell speed. It reasoned that most of the passengers were one-way ticket holders who weren't sailing in order to pamper themselves but to get to their destinations in the shortest time. White Star instead chose to highlight luxury, reasoning that it was possible to transform the journey from an ordeal into a memorable experience by the addition of comfort, splendor, and style.

The innovations on White Star liners were impressive. First-class accommodation was shifted from the back of the ship to the middle where there was less noise from the engines. Spacious promenade decks, more portholes, and grand dining saloons were introduced. The capacity for third-class passengers was doubled and they were given their own dining room with linen napkins, silverware, and printed menus.

Thomas Ismay died in 1899 and J. Bruce Ismay, his son, inherited his company and his position. In 1902 the line was acquired by John Pierpont Morgan (J. P. Morgan), whose International Mercantile Marine Company was slowly swallowing up British shipping. Along with White Star, it would acquire Dominion, Red Star, Leyton, and Atlantic Transport. To avoid high U.S. port taxes and potential violation of the 1890 Sherman Antitrust Act, however, Morgan ensured that the ships remained registered in Britain and had British captains, crews—and orchestras.

The British government saw White Star's access to American money as a threat to the supremacy of its country's shipping, and so it bolstered Cunard with a £150,000 annual subsidy plus a low-interest loan of £2.5 million. As a direct result, Cunard began an ambitious building program for two of the fastest liners ever constructed—the *Lusitania* and the *Mauretania*. The *Lusitania* made its maiden voyage in September 1907 and the next month made history by slashing more than eleven hours from the existing record for a westbound crossing and ending German dominance of the Blue Riband, an unofficial accolade given to the ship with the fastest transatlantic crossing.[3] It was the first time a ship had made the crossing in less than five days.

For years White Star had worked exclusively with the Belfast ship-builders Harland & Wolff. Thomas Ismay had met a Liverpool merchant, Gustavus Schwabe, who offered financing if Ismay had his ships built by his nephew Gustav Wolff, who was in partnership with Edward Harland. Ismay accepted the deal. Harland died in 1895, but the arrangement continued under his successor, William James Pirrie, later Lord Pirrie.

The legend is that the *Titanic* was conceived in the spring of 1907 during an after-dinner conversation between Pirrie and Ismay at Downshire House, Pirrie's London home in Belgrave Square (now the Spanish Embassy). Sometimes the tale is rounded off with Ismay making provisional sketches of the great ship on his table napkin. Several aspects of the story don't ring true. The most obvious is that the *Lusitania* had already been launched by then, and so it was a bit late for a White Star response. Also, Ismay was a ship owner, not a ship designer. What details could he have communicated in a crude sketch that he couldn't explain in words?

Swiss *Titanic* scholar Gunter Babler has picked up on several other inconsistencies in this story based on the preparations made at Harland & Wolff for the construction of a bigger class of ship. The earliest of these was the building of the large Thomson dock in 1904. Babler believes that the *Olympic*-class liners were decided on in 1903, although the specifics were kept under wraps for obvious reasons. The earlier date makes sense in light of the purchase of White Star by J. P. Morgan in 1902, which made the larger ships possible, and the response to this by Cunard.

Babler traced the dinner story back to a single source: the 1961 book *The Ismay Line* by William J. Oldham. No previous account had mentioned it. As Oldham had access to Ismay's widow before she died in 1937, it's likely that she told him the story. It may be that the dinner happened but in another year or that the talk of the *Titanic* at a 1907 meal was merely the culmination of a four-year planning process. Possibly Mrs. Ismay didn't know the year of the dinner, and Oldham guessed based on the fact that the orders for ships 400 and 401, as the *Olympic* and the *Titanic* were initially known, were registered in Harland & Wolff's books on April 30, 1907.

The plan was for three ships: first the *Olympic*, then the *Titanic*, and finally the *Gigantic*.[4] Responsibility for their design was given to Thomas Andrews, Pirrie's nephew and newly promoted head of Harland and Wolff's design department. Ismay and the other White Star directors approved his drawings in July 1908. The *Titanic* would accommodate up to 2,599 passengers and 903 officers and crew. It would have twenty-eight first-class suites, four electric elevators (three of them in first class), a heated swimming pool, a squash court, a fully equipped gymnasium, two libraries, four restaurants, a medical bay, and an operating theater. In first class it would have all the luxuries of an English country house, a gentleman's club in London, or a town house in New York, and rich passengers would pay as much as one hundred times more than those in steerage for the privilege.

All the latest advances in marine construction would accompany these embellishments. There would be sixteen watertight compartments with electronically operated doors and sensors to detect water levels. This was believed to virtually guarantee that the ship could deal with any puncture. It had three propellers, twenty-four double-ended boilers, and five single-ended boilers. Although the advance publicity did not specifically boast that the ship was unsinkable, it did state that it was "designed to be unsinkable," and *Shipbuilder* magazine in 1911 declared it to be "practically unsinkable."

Because the proposed liners were so much bigger than anything built before—50 percent larger than the *Lusitania* or *Mauretania*—the Belfast shipyards of Harland & Wolff had to be reconfigured to make room for them. Two new slipways were created from three old ones, and new gantries over 200 feet tall with electric lifts had to be built above the hulls. It would take an unprecedented three thousand men to work on the *Titanic*, and everyone concerned was aware that this was the largest man-made transportable structure ever built.

Charlie and Frederick Black would have known of the *Titanic*'s advancement not only through their connections in Liverpool but also because there was national interest in this feat of British engineering and example of twentieth-century progress. Ships were an indication of a nation's wealth, power, and technological advancement. They were the most powerful form of transport then known, and the shrinking of the distance between Britain and America gained the sort of attention that the Space Race would get in the 1950s and 1960s.

News coverage of the ship's building expressed awe and wonder. It was an age of record breaking, invention, and mankind's seemingly limitless

White Star booklet featuring the *Olympic* and *Titanic*.

ability to master nature. Reports were full of dizzying statistics about the weight of iron plates, the numbers of rivets, and the measurements of decks. It was hard to know what to do with such facts as "the stern frame weighs 70 tons," or "it would take 20 horses to haul one rudder." The accumulative effect was to impress the average reader with the ingenuity of designers and the capacity of humans to construct on such a large scale.

The first report on the ships in the *Times* came on September 1, 1908, in a page-ten story headlined "The New White Star Liners." It mentioned that all the preliminaries had been settled and that construction had been started.

> They will be longer, broader, and deeper than the *Lusitania* and the *Mauretania*. The exact dimensions are not yet obtainable but the gross tonnage will be about 8000 tons more than that of the two Cunarders. It is reckoned that the vessels will take three years to build. One is to be called the *Olympic*; the name of the other is not yet decided upon, but it will probably be the *Titanic*. The question of speed, which will not be high in a record-breaking sense, is being left in abeyance, doubtless pending the result of an experiment which is now being made by Messrs. Harland & Wolff with a combination of reciprocating and turbine engines, in which exhaust steam from the first engine is utilized in the second.

In November 1909 the paper reported that Trafalgar Dock in Southampton would have to be rebuilt to take these huge ships. (Ismay had decided to switch his transatlantic operation to Southampton rather than compete directly with Cunard from Liverpool.) The new dock would be 1700 feet long and 400 feet wide, and would require four new cargo sheds to be built.

In April 1910 there was news that the channel leading to Southampton docks would need to be deepened. It had already been dredged to 30 feet for the American Line and then to 32 feet for the *Adriatic* and *Oceanic*. Now the bed beneath the shipping lanes would need to be lowered an additional 3 feet. The International Mercantile Marine Company then had to petition the federal government in America to allow the city of New York to lengthen its piers by 100 feet. The New York Dock Commission was happy to do it, but the government was concerned that the additional length would constrict the river.

News interest turned to insurance in January 1911. This was no small matter because sea travel still had a high element of risk. In its Mail and Shipping Intelligence column, the *Times* had a regular list of the latest wrecks and casualties, and in the January 6 edition that carried news of the *Titanic* and *Olympic* insurance, it mentioned fourteen calamities during the past two days, mostly involving collisions resulting in damage. The report claimed that the *Titanic* and *Olympic* had been insured for between £700,000 and £800,000 although the actual cost of each ship was £1,500,000.

The *Titanic* was launched on May 31, 1911, "in brilliant weather, and in the presence of thousands of spectators," according to the *Times*, the same day that the *Olympic*, which had been launched in October, left Belfast for England to commence her maiden voyage. For the first and only time the ships that had grown up alongside each other were briefly seen together on the water. Despite the *Titanic*'s size it apparently slid with ease down an incline greased with twenty-four tons of tallow, soap, and oil, once the shores had been removed. With an eye on detail, the *Times* recorded that it took sixty-two seconds to move from land to river, that her maximum speed as she did so was twelve knots, and that "the wave produced as her stem dropped into the water was much smaller than might have been expected considering the mass of the structure."

Although thousands of paying spectators and many dignitaries—including Lord Pirrie, J. Bruce Ismay, and J. P. Morgan—were present, there was no traditional naming ceremony, and tugs quickly towed her to a berth where she would spend the next eight months being fitted out. Flags hung on the side of the ship spelled out the word *success*. On February 3, 1912, she left the wharf and was taken to her dry dock for the final preparations.

The Black brothers knew that they were to supply the musicians for this much-talked-about ship. They would also have known that besides the traditional five-piece band for the main first-class restaurant, there was to be a trio for the ship's nearby Café Parisien which, as the name suggested, would have a Continental flavor and would appeal to those who looked to Paris as the arbiter of taste in food, fashion, and art. It was a knowing touch of sophistication that allowed passengers to move from Pall Mall to Montmartre in a few easy steps.

Everything on the *Titanic* had to be the best that money could buy, and the onus on the Blacks was to look through the lists of musicians they knew or had worked with and find the best quintet and trio it was possible to come up with. The men needed to be experienced, versatile, smart, and able to converse easily with the wealthy and powerful.

Key to building a successful band was an inspirational bandleader. The ideal person would be someone who commanded respect among musicians, had an outstanding moral character, and was used to playing for a well-traveled, sophisticated, and international clientele. It also helped if this leader could recommend players, because a good band worked when the musicians gelled both personally and musically. They found their man in Wallace Hartley, a thirty-three-year old Lancastrian who was currently bandmaster on the *Mauretania*, the ship that had taken the Blue Riband from the *Lusitania*.

3

"A Man with the Highest Sense of Duty."

Wallace Hartley was an obvious choice as bandleader. Five feet ten inches tall with dark hair, blue eyes, and a winning smile, he'd had extensive experience as a musician both on land and on sea and had worked with many of the best players in the business. He was also a man of fine moral standing. Raised as a Methodist, he exhibited the diligence, honesty, and sobriety characteristic of a Christian denomination that had transformed working-class life in Britain. His first employers at a local bank found him "steady, attentive and capable." John Carr, a cellist on the White Star liner *Celtic*, said that he was "a man with the highest sense of duty." Another fellow musician spoke of his "commanding stature." A Colne friend called him "one of the nicest and most gentlemanly lads I ever knew."

Wallace Hartley.

Other than the few photographs that we have of Hartley, the best physical description of him comes from an interview given to the *Dewsbury District News* by his friend John Wood. "I seem to see him now in a characteristic attitude when seated—half reclining in an easy fashion in the armchair. Two long, white fingers of his left hand held along his chin, and two supporting his head—a long, lean face, dark-brown eyes, long hair, blackish, with a rich brown lustre—not overlong, but I never saw it short."

By the time Charlie Black invited him to lead the band on the *Titanic,* he had been at sea for almost three years working his way up from second violin on the *Lucania* to bandmaster of the *Mauretania.* Each Atlantic crossing at this time took between five and six days. There would then be four days at the port for refueling, maintenance, replenishment of essential goods, and the taking on of cargo and passengers. It was during these times that Hartley came to know and love New York with its vibrancy, optimism, and range of new entertainment.

When Katherine Hurd arrived there with her husband, Carlos, in April 1912 to board the *Carpathia,* these were her initial impressions as conveyed in a letter to her mother: "New York is tremendous—something like I expected it to be only a thousand times more so. And with all its size it is so beautifully clean." Although New York was large and bustling, it was still far from the densely packed city bristling with skyscrapers that we bring to mind today.

Often described as a Yorkshireman because his last address was in Dewsbury, Yorkshire, Hartley was born and spent his formative years in Colne, Lancashire, five and a half miles north of Burnley. It was close to the Yorkshire border but the historic rivalry between the two counties, which had started on battlefields and continued on cricket pitches, meant that you belonged to one county or the other regardless of geographical proximity.

Hartley's roots on both sides of the family were deep in the Lancashire soil. His father, Albion Hartley, was born in Colne, as were Albion's parents, Henry and Mary. Albion married Elizabeth Foulds, also from Colne, whose parents had grown up in the area. All of them worked with cotton, the town's primary industry. Henry Hartley had been a cotton weaver and Mary a dressmaker. Elizabeth was a worsted weaver (a person who worked with worsted wool), and Albion started as a cotton-sizer (a worker who applied a gluelike substance to prepared cotton to make it easier to work with) and eventually became a mill manager.

Cotton and the industrial revolution had turned Colne from a small hilltop village into a typical mill town of industrial buildings and back-to-back workers' houses. An 1872 gazetteer summed the town up in numbers: three churches, five dissenting chapels, a mechanic's institute, two endowed schools, a post office, a bank, and two inns. There were 1,357 houses and a population of 6,315. Twenty years later the population had tripled.

John Wesley, the great British preacher, visited Colne several times in the latter half of the eighteenth century and knew of its tough and violent reputation. Although still a minister of the Church of England, Wesley believed in evangelizing in the open air and he relentlessly traveled across Britain on horseback, preaching the gospel to those who would never enter a place of worship. His approach outraged traditional churchmen who believed it degraded preaching and removed the mystery and splendor from religion. George White, the vicar of Colne, was a vociferous opponent of Wesley and would organize drunken mobs to attack him when he visited the area. One of Wesley's helpers was even thrown to his death off a bridge.

Wesley never left the Church of England, but his followers did. The breakaway denomination became known as Methodism and had a particular appeal to ordinary working people who found the established church out of touch with their needs—too much a church for the well-off and powerful. When Methodism gripped a community it had observable social effects because Wesley taught that followers of Christ should be thrifty, charitable, sober, honest, and concerned with developing their minds and bodies as well as their souls. The result was an increase in schools, music groups, orchestras, and benevolent societies, and a decrease in wasteful drunkenness, violence, poverty, and ignorance. Methodists believed not only in personal salvation but also in holiness, self-improvement, and charity. Communities became more law abiding and better educated. Husbands became more responsible. Workers became more eager to learn.

In this way the Colne that had once spurned Wesley became a beneficiary of his ministry. The first Methodist chapel was built in 1722 and by the time Wallace was born in 1878, there were eight chapels catering to different areas of the town and different stripes of Methodism (Free, Primitive, Independent, and Wesleyan). All of the buildings were funded by donations from benefactors (as Methodists improved their lives some became leaders in industry) and public subscriptions. Then the chapels built schools in the same way and the schools used their premises to found Reading Associations and Friendly Sick Societies, (groups who helped financially when someone was out of work due to ill health). Methodism affected Colne life at every level and produced many citizens who were the first in their families to make the transition from laboring to clerical work and eventually to management.

The remains of Bethel Chapel. The main building was on the right.

Albion Hartley was a prominent member of the Bethel Independent Methodist Chapel on Burnley Road. Since it was built in 1871 he had been its choirmaster and was also the superintendent of the Sunday school. When Wallace Hartley was born on Sunday, June 2, 1878, at the family home, 92 Greenfield Hill, the visiting doctor joked with Albion that he'd give him five shillings for the collection plate if the chapel choir would sing "Unto Us a Child Is Given" at the Sunday school anniversary later that day. Unbeknown to the doctor, the song was already in the repertoire and Albion replied: "Let me have your five shillings. We have been rehearsing it and will sing it today!" That day the collection reached £100 for the first time.

Birthplace of Wallace Hartley at 92 Greenfield Road, Colne.

Wallace was the second Hartley child but the first son. His older sister, Mary, had been born the year before and Elizabeth and Hilda would soon expand the family to five, but two more sons born to Elizabeth wouldn't make it to their second birthdays. Hartley was seven when Ughtred Harold Hartley died and nine when Conrad Robert Hartley suffered the same fate. Both children were buried in Colne Cemetery.

In 1885 the mill where Albion worked burned down and many of the workers lost their jobs. Albion took the opportunity not just to get a new job but also to move and start a new career. At the age of thirty-four he left the cotton industry, became an insurance agent in the nearby town of Nelson, and moved the family from Greenfield Hill, which was an isolated row of cottages on the outskirts of the town, to a larger property at 1 Burnley Road, close to Bethel Chapel and not far from Wallace's school.

Hartley had begun his education at George Street Wesleyan School. The building had been built as a Methodist Sunday school in 1869 but eighteen months later had become a day school capable of accommodating more than six hundred children. Emphasis was put on teaching the children to read, write, and do basic math.

The former George Street Wesleyan School, Colne, where Hartley was educated.

Musically Hartley learned from his father, who had him join the choir at the Bethel Chapel, and from one of the congregation, Pickles Riley, who taught him violin. One of his school friends, Thomas Hyde, recalled music lessons at school around 1890. "We all started learning music and the violin together in the bottom classroom at George Street," he remembered. "There would be about 20 of us and we were all about eleven or twelve years old. I don't remember that Wallace was any different from any of us in his violin playing but he seemed to come on remarkably afterwards." Writing to the *Huddersfield Examiner* in 1958, the old headmaster's son, J. M. Baldwin, had a slightly different recollection of Hartley's reputation from the same period. "He was one of my heroes," he said, "for I knew from the talk of my elders that he was already a musician of repute, but more definitely because he possessed a bicycle, one of the earliest 'safeties' to be seen in Colne."

Just as his schooling came to an end, his father was promoted to assistant superintendent at the Refuge Assurance Company in Colne. Possibly because of the increased wage, he moved to 90 Albert Road, a terraced

Wallace Hartley at eighteen, with his music teacher Pickles Riley, after receiving an award at a Methodist music festival.

house close to the railway station and on Colne's main street. Albion wasn't keen for his Wallace to become a professional musician. He wanted him to pursue something more secure. An obedient son, Wallace took his first job as a clerk at the Craven Bank that stood on a corner five minutes up the road from the Hartley home.

90 Albert Road, Colne. Hartley's early teenage home.

Hartley didn't like office work. He said he found it "irksome." His joy in life was to be playing music and he sought every opportunity to do so. He accompanied his sister Mary on the violin when she sang at local concerts. And when the manager of the bank, James Lascelles Wildman, who was a Methodist circuit preacher and the son of a Sunday school superintendent, formed the Colne Orchestral Society, he joined.

It's not easy to build up a picture of Hartley's character at this time because all the comments made by those who knew him were collected after he'd become a national hero. Albion thought he was "an ideal son" who "never caused his father or mother a single moment's trouble." A Methodist preacher, Thomas Worthington, confirmed that he was a "strong Christian"; Thomas Hyde found him "smart looking," "fun," and a "very nice lad"; an anonymous friend described him as "a noble manly fellow,

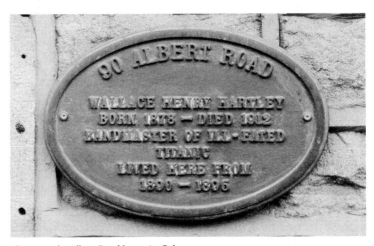

Plaque on the Albert Road house in Colne.

incapable of anything mean." The only note of discord came when Hyde added that he was "a bit what you might call 'roughish,' " a description that seems at odds with all the talk of delicate fingers, artistic sensitivity, and filial obedience.

Hartley left Colne with his family in 1895 when he was seventeen. Albion's career was still progressing and he would soon become a superintendent. They moved over the border to Yorkshire and a home at 35 Somerset Street in Huddersfield. It's unclear where Hartley worked during his early years in the new county, but we

The former bank building where Hartley worked in Colne.

know that he played with the Huddersfield Philharmonic Orchestra and that in the 1901 census he was able to describe his occupation as "professional musician." Two years later he was first violinist with the Municipal Orchestra of Bridlington, a resort on the Yorkshire coast.

It was in vogue at this time in Britain to employ Austrian and German conductors because of their connection to the lands that produced Bach, Beethoven, and Mozart. The Bridlington Orchestra was no different. It had engaged the services of Sigmund Winternitz, a thirty-three-year-old musician from Vienna with a waxed mustache, whose influence on the orchestra was such that it became known as the Royal Viennese Band. The members were kitted out in dark trousers, military-style jackets, and stiff felt hats and were expected to give two daily performances at the bandstand during the week and a concert of sacred music on Sundays. In 1904 they moved indoors to the Floral Pavilion, which could hold seventeen hundred.

In 1905 Hartley's parents moved to 48 Hillcrest Avenue in Leeds. This is likely to have been when he joined the Municipal Orchestra in Harrogate, which performed at the newly built Kursaal at least twice a day, excluding Sundays, alternating performances with a military band. Leeds became his new base. He apparently joined a local bohemian arts group called the Savage Club that met in an artist's workshop, and certainly led the orchestra at Collinson's Café in King Edward Street in the heart of a newly developed shopping area.

Wallace Hartley with the Bridlington Municipal Orchestra aka Royal Viennese Band (front row fourth from left). Orchestra director Sigmund Winternitz stands next to him.

The recording industry was in its infancy in the early 1900s and music was still synonymous with live performance. Children learned to play instruments not with the hope of becoming a "star" but because playing and singing were regarded as social assets. (James McCartney, born in Lancashire in 1902, told future Beatle Paul: "Learn to play the piano, son, and you'll always get invited to parties.") It was the age of sheet music and the pianoforte, when families would gather in living rooms to sing the latest popular songs. Collieries, mills, and factories, particularly in the north of England, formed bands and the Victorian emphasis on temperance and clean living resulted in parks, "recreation grounds," and "pleasure gardens" furnished with often-ornate bandstands.

Teahouses and coffeehouses began as genteel rest spots where people could take light refreshments in a nonalcoholic environment. They were safe alternatives to public houses, and women, in particular, were drawn to them. During the first decade of the century, they began to offer afternoon "tea dances" and fashionable restaurants introduced dance floors. Prestigious hotels such as the Ritz and Savoy in London already had their own orchestras that would play during afternoon tea and evening drinks.

Collinson's Café, Leeds, now a Jigsaw fashion store but with many origianl features retained.

Roof at the site of Collinson's Café, Leeds, where Hartley played in the orchestra.

Collinson's Café was a stylish property that opened in 1903 and would become a Leeds institution. A long narrow entrance area opened up into a large semicircle where the orchestra would have played. Above them was a balcony and above the balcony a tall glass dome. Staircases swept upward from the ground-floor level and all the windows were leaded with stained glass designs. The streaming light, colored glass, and music combined to produce an atmosphere of elegance and beauty.

Towns and cities considered their musical calendars to be indicators of sophistication, and seaside resorts used music to pull in visitors. Visitors might choose Eastbourne over Bournemouth or Southport over Blackpool simply because of the quality of music available in the hotels, bandstands, pavilions, and concert halls. Local councils would subsidize orchestras because of the value they added to their towns.

This all helped make music a viable profession. There was an increasing demand for players, teachers, conductors, and directors. A good versatile musician could move from opera house to tearoom and from concert hall to bandstand. Many of the great classical composers—including Mahler, Delius, Elgar, Ravel, Holst, and Debussy—were still writing, their latest works being premiered around the country and appreciated by the same people who liked Gilbert and Sullivan or the latest hits from the music hall.

It must have been while working at Collinson's that Hartley met Maria Robinson, a tall dark-haired girl who lived with her family twelve miles away in Boston Spa. She was the eldest of four children, her father, Benjamin, being a woollen manufacturer in the Leeds suburb of Wortley. He'd become prosperous enough to buy St. Ives, a huge detached villa in Boston Spa that had once been an inn. Hartley became a regular visitor and he and Maria, along with her sister Margaret and Margaret's boyfriend John Wood, would go for long walks in the surrounding countryside or take a rowing boat out on the River Wharfe.

By the time of his thirtieth birthday in 1908, Hartley didn't yet feel ready to settle down with his twenty-seven-year-old girlfriend. There was a world to see, more money to save, and more musical avenues to explore. His parents moved to Dewsbury, where the Refuge Assurance Company had relocated Albion, and the traveling distance between Wallace and Maria doubled. He was also now touring with opera companies, first with the Carla Rosa Opera Company and then the Moody-Manners Company. Although Dewsbury was now home, he was rarely ever there.

It's not known why, but in 1909 Hartley decided to go to sea. Charles Black, who had just started booking for Cunard, could have spotted him, or maybe a musician he met in the opera companies had suggested it. It's not hard to see the appeal. He not only would have consistent and varied work, but also would get to see places that few of his British contemporaries could ever hope to see.

This was an age of emigration to America and yet there were few young people who traveled there with a return ticket other than the wealthy or employees of shipping lines. Many of his contemporaries in Colne, Dewsbury, or Leeds wouldn't have traveled more than a few miles from their birthplaces. America was a country they only read about in newspapers and books and most of them would have never met an American.

Hartley's first ship was the 12,950-ton *Lucania*, a Cunard liner that had once held the record for the fastest crossing of the Atlantic. He boarded her in Liverpool bound for New York on June 6, 1909, and arrived back on July 3. It was to be a short-lived association because on returning the *Lucania*, which had been in service since 1893, was taken into dry dock for repair and there it caught fire. It was then sold for scrap. Hartley was transferred to another Cunard liner, the great *Lusitania*.

Life on board the *Lusitania* was unlike anything he had experienced before. When he boarded her on July 16, 1909, for a nineteen-day round trip to New York, she was, along with the *Mauretania*, the last word in luxury travel. It was said that the second-class accommodation was equivalent to first class in any other ship and that first class was comparable to the glory of King Solomon's palace.

The first-class dining saloon, where Hartley played, was spread over two stories, the centerpiece of which was an open circular well capped with an elaborate dome that must have reminded him of the glass roof of Collinson's Café. The style was sixteenth-century French. One of Cunard's innovations was to have the band playing on the balcony while passengers were eating, as well as on the saloon floor later in the evening when tables and chairs were removed to allow passengers to dance. The *New York Times* found the idea of music at mealtimes so amusing that it published a cartoon portraying the musicians trying to play during a storm while plates, glasses, cutlery, and bottles of wine flew off the nearby tables.

When Hartley joined the *Lusitania*, the Blue Riband for the fastest westbound crossing of the Atlantic was held by its sister ship the *Mauretania*, but on its fifty-ninth westbound crossing, the *Lusitania* beat this record by arriving in New York four days, eleven hours, and forty-two minutes after leaving Liverpool. The passengers were drawn into the spirit of competition, counting the miles covered each day and calculating the ship's chances of entering the history books. During a concert mounted on the last evening at sea, a resolution was announced congratulating the captain, the chief engineer, and the ship's crew for the speed of the journey and the privilege of crossing "in the steamship when it breaks the transatlantic record between Europe and the United States."

It must have been a heady time for Hartley and the band, knowing that they'd been a part of a record-breaking trip, but the victory was to be short-lived. Only a week later the *Mauretania* won the Riband back after clipping just seven minutes off the *Lusitania*'s time. The *Lusitania* would never regain it . This meant that the *Mauretania* was regarded as the supreme ocean liner. In October 1910 the Black brothers approached Hartley with an offer to work on the *Mauretania*, not just as a member of the band, but as its leader. On October 28 Hartley signed the deal and the next day was on board sailing for New York yet again.

He brought with him three members of the *Lusitania* band—Pat O'Day, Henry Taylor, and Albert Felgate—and sailed to New York the next day. It was to be the first of twenty-six round trips he would make on the *Mauretania* between England and America. With the addition of Fred Stent, the five-piece band would remain unchanged until May 1911 when Clarence Kershaw replaced O'Day and Ellwand Moody of Leeds replaced Taylor. Then, in November 1911, Ernest Drakeford took over from Kershaw.

Moody later described the band on the *Mauretania* as a very happy group. So why did Hartley leave? Some contemporary newspaper accounts suggested that Charlie Black approached him with the offer to become bandleader on the *Titanic* when he arrived back in Liverpool on the *Mauretania* on April 8, 1912, with the *Titanic* about to leave from Southampton on April 10. Hartley's letter of that day to his parents ("I've missed coming home very much & it would have been nice to have seen you all if only for an hour or two, but I couldn't manage it . . .") implies a hurried change of plan, but it's implausible that the Blacks would leave such an important appointment to the last minute.

By 1912 he had become engaged to Maria and a wedding was planned for the summer. Since going to sea their meetings had been snatched between trips. Sometimes she would visit him in Liverpool and at other times they would meet at the Hartley family home in Dewsbury and go to a Sunday service at St. Mark's Church in Halifax Road. His intention was to give up the sea and return to concert work.

The evidence is that Hartley had been offered the *Titanic* job long before April 1912. Ellwand Moody later told the *Leeds Mercury* that he spoke about it while on the *Mauretania* and tried to persuade Moody to join him. Moody's twelve-month contract expired on April 9, 1912, but he was determined to stay on land. "I should not have gone on any other boat in any case," he said, "but I didn't fancy the *Titanic* at all. The *Mauretania* was plenty big enough for me."

Moody was one of a handful of musicians who later claimed to have turned down the *Titanic*'s maiden voyage. Another was Seth Lancaster, a cellist from Colne, who said that he'd been approached as far back as December 1911. It wasn't until early April 1912 that he was told he wasn't needed. If this story is true, the Black brothers had been planning and sounding people out for at least four months. The trip that Lancaster was given in its place was on the *Mauretania*, in the band that Ellwand Moody and Hartley had just left. The ship sailed from Liverpool on April 13, three days behind the *Titanic*.

Violinist Ernest Drakeford rejected the *Titanic* offer because he'd recently settled in Liverpool and didn't want to move to Southampton. He was married and his wife, Priscilla, was expecting their first child. Ironically he went on to join the band of the *Lusitania*, which was sunk by a German U-boat in May 1915. He was only saved after clinging to a wooden barrel for two hours.

For Hartley's final journey on the *Mauretania* he had taken on two extra musicians while in New York—Frenchman Roger Bricoux and Londoner William Theodore Brailey. They'd arrived together in America after a two-month Mediterranean cruise on the *Carpathia*. The Blacks had definitely chosen them by mid-March because on March 17 Bricoux wrote to his parents to say: "As for sending letters, I can no longer do this because we are going to New York where I will board the *Mauretania*, the biggest ship in the world at 32,000 tonnes, and once we have arrived in Liverpool I leave for Southampton where I will board the *Titanic* which will be launched on April 10th and will be the biggest ship in the world at 50,000 tonnes."

Bricoux was a very conscientious correspondent and therefore it's reasonable to assume that the transfer news from C. W. & F. N. Black was recent. The Blacks clearly wanted him and Brailey badly enough to get them back to England as soon as they'd arrived in New York. A scribbled note in the margin of the ship's register indicated the speed of the transfer. Against the names of Brailey and Bricoux is the remark: "Owing to being transferred to *Mauretania* on the point of sailing, this seaman was unable to appear before consul."

Had Hartley requested them or were they chosen by the Blacks? There's no evidence that Hartley had ever played with them. Roger Bricoux had been part of the orchestra at the Grand Central Hotel in Leeds from the spring of 1910 to early June 1911, but this was at a time when Hartley was regularly crossing the Atlantic. He wouldn't have had time to play with the orchestra, but Charlie Black, who was the hotel's music agent, could have recommended that he check him out. It's less likely that he had met Theo Brailey. By the end of the month the names of these three musicians returning on the *Mauretania* would be inextricably tied together.

4

"I WILL WRITE TO YOU ON BOARD THE *TITANIC*."

At twenty years of age, Roger Bricoux was the youngest of the *Titanic's* musicians, yet he'd also had the most thorough formal training. The son of a talented horn player, he had studied music in conservatories in Italy and France (1906–1910) before joining an English orchestra as a cellist. The *Leeds Mercury* remembered him as "a very handsome young fellow, although his gait was somewhat marred by a limp, the result of an injury due to a motor bicycle accident. When he first came to Leeds he could speak scarcely a word of English, but he quickly picked up the language."

Roger Bricoux.

He was chosen for the *Titanic* voyage to be part of the trio in the Café Parisien, adding an authenticity to the Continental ambience. It would be his third voyage on a ship and it was something he was looking forward to. When he was on board the *Carpathia*, he told a steward named Robert

Vaughan: "Soon I'll be on a real steamer—with real food!" To his parents he wrote excitedly about the prospect of Turkish baths, bicycles that could be used on deck, a gymnasium, and a one-hundred-meter swimming pool.

Bricoux was born Roger Marie Leon Joseph Bricoux on June 1, 1891, 168 miles south of Paris in the Burgundy (Bourgogne) town of Cosne-sur-Loire. This was the home region of his mother, Marie-Rose, and the place where she had met his father, Leon, during his service in the army with the 85th Infantry Regiment, but it wasn't where the couple were currently living. The house on la rue de Donzy most likely belonged to Marie-Rose's parents, because after marrying in 1883, Leon had taken a job playing first horn in the resident band at the famed Casino de Monte Carlo and Monaco had become their principal home.

In the 1850s Monaco's ruling Grimaldi family was on the verge of bankruptcy, but the arrival of the first casino and the development of the seafront transformed the fortunes of both the Grimaldis and Monaco. It rapidly became the stylish place to go, attracting the affluent, foreign royalty, writers, artists, actors, dancers, and musicians. The landmark Casino with its commanding pinnacles and cupola in the Beaux Arts style was designed by Charles Garnier, architect of the Paris Opera, and opened in January 1879 with a performance by the French actress Sarah Bernhardt, who read a poem and waved a palm branch.

Because Monte Carlo attracted some of the most urbane people in the world, it found itself in the advance of many new developments. Car races were organized between Marseilles and Monte Carlo; movie competitions were held starting in 1897; the Palais des Beaux Arts presented lectures on exciting new scientific discoveries, such as the X-ray; renowned architects and designers such as Gabriel Ferrier and Gustave Eiffel worked on new hotels; and the streets of the principality were the first to be covered in tar.

It was in this vibrant place that the first two sons of Leon and Marie-Rose had been born, but both died in infancy. Marius, the eldest, was a victim of diphtheria and then, six months before Roger's birth, her second-born son, Marcel, died unexpectedly. These tragedies could have been what sent Marie-Rose back to her mother for comfort and help. With Leon at work in the Casino she would have had a lot of free time and yet would have been apprehensive about the possibility of losing a third child. Two years later there was another son who lived, Gaston Leon Carolus Bricoux, nicknamed Lolo by the family.

It seems to have been from his father, Leon, that Roger inherited his love of the arts. Leon had grown up in Paris during the 1860s and 1870s when bohemianism was flourishing and the world was looking to the city as a capital of culture. It was the era of authors Flaubert and Hugo; of artists Gauguin, Renoir, Courbet, and Manet; of the poets Baudelaire and Rimbaud; of the first exhibition of impressionism and the founding of the Folies Bergere; of Haussmann's creation of modern-day Paris with its wide boulevards, radiating circuses, and public parks. Leon's

Roger Bricoux (left) with mother Marie-Rose, father Leon, and brother Gaston.

father was a painter and his brother, Charles, a teacher of drawing. He was given music lessons from an early age.

In Monaco Leon earned enough money to buy a grand home at 37 rue Grimaldi and also to finance regular visits back to Cosne where they would stay in a house they owned in Bannay. The fact that Leon knew the royal family of Monaco and drove his own car impressed the locals. With his neatly trimmed hair, flourishing mustache, and air of dignified success, Leon Bricoux cut a dash in rural France.

Roger was given a Catholic education in Monaco, first under the Christian Brothers at College St-Charles and then under the Jesuits at the College de la Visitation. When Prince Albert I separated church and state, Leon decided that Roger would continue his Catholic education over the border in Italy at the French speaking College St-Charles in the village of Bordighera, and later la Coeur Immacule de Marie in Taggia. He was confirmed at l'Eglise Sainte-Devote in Monaco in 1903, the same church where he and Lolo would later take first communion.

On graduation Roger was accepted by the Accademia Filarmonica di Bologna, Italy, Mozart's alma mater, which had a great reputation for teaching cello. He studied there for three years, winning first prize for his cello playing, and then moved to France, where he spent an additional year studying at the Conservatoire de Paris. While in the city he was able to work to pay his tuition fees. One short-term contract was with the orchestra of the spa town of Uriage-les-Bains. After this he returned to Monaco.

Roger Bricoux with cello.

In 1910, at the same time that Wallace Hartley was on the *Lusitania*, Bricoux accepted a twelve-month contract with the Grand Central Hotel orchestra in Leeds. Somehow he must have come to the attention of the Black brothers. The Grand Central Hotel, which had opened in 1903, was on Briggate, not far from the Grand Theatre (1878), which presented serious drama and opera, and the Grande Arcade (1897), and around the corner from Collinson's Café (1903). Bricoux traveled to England by train and ferry and took lodgings on Melbourne Street, a ten- to fifteen-minute walk away from the hotel.

It was a stirring prospect for a twenty-year-old boy, especially for one who barely spoke English. Leeds had only recently become a city (1893) and its center was being modernized with a series of elegant shopping arcades with high glass roofs and ornate moldings. Its university had opened in 1903 and its first cinema in 1905. The prosperous local engineering and tailoring businesses had produced a wealthy class of people who wanted cultural attractions.

We don't know much about Bricoux's time in the city except that he apparently "possessed many friends among the musicians of Leeds" according to the *Leeds Mercury* and was known for his "joviality and friendliness." As with most hotel musicians he would have had to work for at least two sessions each day and be available for concerts, dances, and special events.

It's very likely that he would have made use of the time to travel in England, make new friends, and learn about British culture. In April 1911, as his contract drew to a close, he wrote to his brother who was planning a trip to London, possibly as an eighteenth birthday present:

Dear Lolo,

Father wrote to tell me that you're coming to London. I'd like to take the opportunity to tell you that if you want to come to see me that would give me such pleasure that I will put you up, feed you and pay for your journey to London and back so it would cost you nothing apart from the effort but I think you know you'll have some fun too.

It would take you two or three days with an excursion ticket from Cook's agency. That means you get your ticket from Monaco direct to Leeds and the return from here to London I will get for you. But secure your ticket from Cooks' otherwise you get taken on a more round about journey and it will also be more expensive. Give my love to father and mother and love to you too.

Roger.

Bring my contract with you. I'm counting on you to come.

The letter, and others like it, reveals Bricoux as a sensitive boy from a close family. He wrote home regularly, was always concerned for the health and happiness of his parents, and was unafraid to discuss his emotions. His father understood the precariousness of the freelance life and Bricoux seemed keen to show that he was becoming self-sufficient. His greatest pride was making a living from music without having to give lessons. Yet it was tough. Work hours were inevitably late and interfered with normal socializing. Wages weren't huge, so accommodation had to be cheap and was often cramped. He dreamed of a time when he could afford a wife and start his own family

When his contract with the Grand Central Hotel expired, he left Leeds for Lille where he found lodging with a Monsieur and Madame Caron-Guidez at 5 place du Lion d'Or, the address published in the wake of the

Titanic disaster. When settled in, he played at various Lille establishments, including le Cecil Bar and le Kursaal on rue du Vieux Marche aux Poulets. The Cecil consciously imitated the bars of New York and Chicago, but its music was European and bohemian. In an advertisement it described itself as "an American bar, the most luxurious in Lille, with a gypsy orchestra of the first order, authentic American drinks, warm suppers and diverse attractions."

The revival of interest in "gypsy music" was part of a movement that prized intuition over formal study, passion over reason. It was a reaction to the dominance of science, engineering, and the doctrine of progress. What was thought of as gypsy music varied from country to country, but there was a shared emphasis on stringed instruments, Oriental ornamentation, and harmonic transitions.

He may also have played at the Café Jean because it was on its headed notepaper that he wrote to his parents on December 30, 1911, when his time in Lille was drawing to a close.

> My Dear Parents,
>
> As it is New Year I am writing to you as I have done in previous years to wish you a good and happy year, good health and as few cares as possible because I know you have some but believe me when I say that I do not have any. You would be right to say, "You'll see when you earn your living" and I do see and it's hard. But it seems to me that I am unburdening myself of a huge weight because I love you very much. I have many faults perhaps but don't think that I do not think about you often. I also believe that you are in good health and that consoles me for all the worry I've put you through, which I wholeheartedly regret. If the cello from the Sun Palace is no good, tell Morlais to send it to Eldorado in Nice as that's where I had to go and it's Morlais who has the business.
>
> All my love,
> Roger

The business of the cello and Morlais is unclear and unexplained. He may have been contemplating work in Monaco or Nice but in the end decided to return to England. Madame Caron-Guidez later spoke to *L'Echo du Nord* about the day of his departure from his lodgings in Lille: "All he had was a little trunk and it was my husband who took him to the station when he went. He left us with a wonderful memory." If this description is accurate, he must have sent his cello ahead of him.

His departure appears to have been sudden and uncharacteristically he didn't keep his parents informed of his arrangements. He'd been back in touch with the Black brothers who'd offered to give him work as a ship's musician for a trial period. It was only when already at sea that he let his parents know his plans:

Dear Parents,

At last I can write to you. After receiving my letters you must have been surprised to discover that I was making such a strange and unexpected journey. This is what happened: after finishing at Lille I left for England and got this contract. I think that I'm going to take up my position there as I had such a good time that I haven't been able to prevent myself from returning and am getting ready to go. It is a trial voyage I am making. That is to say, they are trying me out for two months (paid, of course) to see if I'm up to scratch and afterward I would have a good position. I hope that despite my negligence you are not angry.

I am very well and I hope you are too. Write to me on board the *Carpathia*—in Trieste (Italy) or Naples if you reply later. Naples would be best. The voyage is marvelous. We left Liverpool on February 10th and passed through Gibraltar, Tangier, Algeria, Malta, Alexandria and Constantinople, then (we will call at) Trieste, Fiume, Naples and finally New York. I assure you that it is splendid. We had a storm but I wasn't at all sea sick. I was amazed. I have very little time as the post is about to leave. I send you all my love.

Roger

I will write at greater length at Trieste.

The *Carpathia*, soon to play such a great role in the *Titanic* story, had been launched in 1902 and regularly cruised from New York to the Mediterranean. In tonnage it was less than a third of the size of the *Titanic* and only carried one hundred passengers in first class. The two-month

cruises would call in at up to fifteen ports and typically the outward journeys were populated with wealthy Americans while poorer emigrants were
picked up in Naples, Fiume, and Liverpool on the way back. The bandmaster in 1912 was twenty-two-year-old Edgar Heap and on piano was
William Theodore Brailey, the London musician who would transfer with
Bricoux to the *Titanic*.

The *Carpathia* arrived in Trieste, where Bricoux would post his letter on March 4, and docked there for two nights, setting sail for Fiume
(now Rijeka in Croatia) on the sixth. Bricoux omitted to mention the next
ports of call—Messina and Palermo in Italy. There was an overnight stay in
Naples on March 14, but he used the opportunity to take a one-day excursion (perhaps to Pompeii) leaving no time to write the promised letter to
his parents.

On March 5, in Hanley, Staffordshire, an eighteen-year-old domestic
servant named Adelaide Kelsall gave birth to a daughter whom she named
Laura. Adelaide told her family that the father was a cellist about to join the

The likely daughter of Roger Bricoux,
Laura Kelsall, in the 1920s.

Titanic. The father's name was left off the
birth certificate and the only clues as to any
possible connection with Bricoux are this
story passed down in the family and the
fact that when Laura Kelsall was a young
girl she bore a strong resemblance to him.[1]

Is there a possibility that he stayed on
in England after his stint at the Grand in
Leeds and had a dalliance with Adelaide,
who lived with her two brothers and her
widowed mother? He did make some
oblique comments about his bad behavior
and how much strain he put on his parents,
but nothing in the letters that have survived
makes any mention of getting a girl pregnant. It may be significant that although
the birth took place in early March, it was
not registered until April 11, the day after
the *Titanic* sailed. Did Adelaide take the

child to Liverpool or even to Southampton to meet the child's father before getting the official documentation?

Bricoux's final chance to communicate with his family before arriving in New York came on March 18 as the ship approached Gibraltar for the second time on the trip. His parents didn't yet know about the *Titanic* job and he excitedly explained the size and luxury of the much-talked-about vessel. He concluded:

> I love this life but I would happily be with you. As for getting married, I will never marry unless it's to a girl with money because with my tastes . . . I only want "love in silk"[2] or at least "a comfortable home," not living in attics with the fear of not eating the next day. Ambition? Perhaps. And why not? Something tells me that it is necessary if one is to succeed. Finally, I send all my love. Roger. Write to me on board the *Carpathia*, New York (America).

The *Carpathia* arrived back in New York on Friday, March 29. Bricoux was able to enjoy a weekend in the city before boarding the *Mauretania* on Tuesday April 2 with Theo Brailey and meeting Wallace Hartley for the first time. While sailing to Liverpool he wrote what would be his final letter to his father.

> Dear Papa,
>
> You may find that my letter is delayed but that won't be my fault because I have been on board the Mauretania for ten days [*sic*] and haven't had a chance to post it. At last I come to the point which is to wish you a happy anniversary [April 9 was their wedding anniversary] and good health. Nissotti wrote and told me that you were suffering a bit but I hope it's nothing serious and that my letter will find you well. If not, let it bring you health. The boat's vibration is so annoying that I can't write. Just think, we are doing 400 nautical miles in 24 hours, a world record! [A mile is 1,837 meters.] Five days from New York to Liverpool. I will write more on board the Titanic. Love to Maman and you. Best wishes, Roger, on board the *Titanic*, Southampton, England. I am counting on a letter from you in New York.

"An Exceptionally
Good Performer
on the Piano."

Family legend says that William "Theo" Brailey had been told by his father, Ronald Brailey, not to sail on the *Titanic*, but he was determined to go anyway. Like Wallace Hartley, Theo was recently engaged and planning to give up the sea, but until then he wanted to take advantage of every opportunity to travel. He would have known that shipwreck was always a danger, but the *Titanic* was supposed to be the last word in safety.

Normally such parental warnings could be dismissed as signs of overprotectiveness but Mr. Brailey wasn't like that. He'd let his son join the army at fifteen and Theo had hardly been back home since. His fears were probably connected with his profession because he was an established clairvoyant who was well known in spiritualist circles and had even been featured in the national press.

Spiritualism had grown in popularity during the late nineteenth century, just as traditional religion was being questioned by modern science. Spiritualists believed in an afterlife not merely as an article of faith, but through experiences with what they believed to be the spirits of the dead. Thus spiritualism appeared to satisfy the demand of modern science for proof and the requirement of religion for comfort. Spiritualists offered reassurance of reunions with departed loved ones, while at the same time claiming that their encounters could be verified by impartial observers.

The Christian church opposed spiritualism, pointing out Bible verses that forbade contact with the spirits of the dead.[1] Spiritualists were therefore keen to demonstrate the compatibility of Christianity and spiritualism. It was possible, they argued, to be a faithful church member yet to attend séances. Spiritualism, they said, was not an alternative to religion but a companion. Their best-loved example of this harmony was the newspaper editor, social campaigner, and Nobel Peace Prize nominee W. T. Stead, who was a spiritualist but also a faithful member of his local Congregational church. Ironically, he would be a passenger on the *Titanic*.

Spiritualism naturally attracted charlatans and fraudsters. The hunger to witness the miraculous frequently clouded the judgments of people anxious to hear good news from "the other side." In 1906 a supposed psychic named Charles Eldred, who claimed to be able to conjure up visible spirits and produced photographs of himself with various emanations, was exposed as a fraud who used theatrical props concealed in his specially made chair. The person brought in to reveal his chicanery was not a skeptic, however, but Ronald Brailey. Inside the arm of Eldred's chair, he found a head made

Ronald Brailey.

of marl (a claylike substance), a flesh-colored mask, six fragments of silk, three beards, two wigs, and a metal frame. An account of the exposé was run in the *Daily Mirror*.

The same year the *Daily Express* engaged Ronald after a girl's skeleton was found during an archaeological dig at Avebury near Marlborough. The paper figured that his fabled gifts could be used to tell who the girl was and how she died. Ronald gripped onto a bone and claimed that images of her past life appeared to him. He could see tented structures near Stonehenge and five or six white-bearded druids surrounding the girl. Then one of them lifted a dagger and plunged it into her body in a ritual sacrifice. The *Daily Express* thought it had got its money's worth out of the "Bayswater seer" and the story was run on the front page.

Two years later Ronald Brailey appeared in the *Daily Mail* after a skeptical reporter watched him in performance at the sixth annual Spiritualists' Convention held in Finsbury, North London. "Mr Ronald Brailey gave a touch of novelty to his clairvoyance. With a blackboard and a piece of chalk he produced portraits of the spirits he said he saw," the journalist wrote. He explained further:

> As works of art Mr Brailey's drawings had the superlative merit of leaving much to the imagination. They were outline drawings, dimly but distinctly suggestive of the human profile. They were frequently recognised as indeed seaside silhouettes are by the expectant eye that knows beforehand whom to look for. But to the general view they conveyed less a suggestion of portraiture than an idea that spiritualism has receded into kindergarten stage.

The headline was "Is Spiritualism Declining?"

Within the world of psychics, however, Ronald Brailey enjoyed good standing. In March 1909 he was, for instance, invited to the Dublin home of the writer James Cousins and his pioneering feminist wife, Margaret, who, like their poet friend William Butler Yeats, were curious about psychic phenomena.[2] They wanted to test the clairvoyant's powers, especially his automatic writing that he claimed to act as a conduit for the messages of the dead. James Cousins remembered:

> Brailey sat quietly in a chair looking over Dublin Bay from the windows of our drawing room. When the writing ceased, the clairvoyant said he had not the slightest impression of what was behind it, probably because his attention had been caught by what appeared to be a special event taking place over the hill [Howth] across the water. A procession in archaic costumes circled in the air just above the hill. It was not a joyous procession, but sorrowful. We could throw no light on the phenomenon. Next

day's newspaper announced the death of the aged Earl of Howth, the last of an ancient line of Irish nobility.[3]

18 Clarendon Road, Walthamstow, birthplace of William Theodore Brailey.

Theo (back row, center) celebrating Queen Victoria's diamond jubilee in 1897.

William Theodore Brailey was born at 18 Clarendon Road in Walthamstow, Essex, on October 25, 1887. He was the first child for William Richard Brailey (who only started calling himself Ronald in 1902) and his wife, Amy. There was a piano in the home and Theo, as the family called him, and his sisters, Mabel and Lily, were encouraged to play. When they were of school age they were sent to Miriam Geary, a lady who ran a private school with her daughter Elizabeth at their large rambling home on the corner of Clarendon Road and Copeland Road.

Brailey family with Ronald standing second from left and Theo seated (center).

Miriam Geary was a teacher with a special interest in music. She had married a man almost thirty years older. When he died, she turned her house into a school especially for children who'd shown musical ability. A boot repairer named Clifford Buttle, who knew the Brailey family at this time, spoke about Theo's talent in a 1955 interview. "From the commencement of his education the boy displayed a marked talent for music," he said. "So much so that he soon outpaced his teacher and as there was no further advancement to be made in Walthamstow, Mr. and Mrs. Brailey, with their family of three, moved to Lancaster Road, Ladbroke Grove, West London."

Buttle may have been accurate about the musical aptitude, but he was wrong about the reasons for the move to Ladbroke Grove. The Brailey family was living at 36 Merton Road, Walthamstow, in 1902 when Theo left home. They didn't leave there until 1903, going first to Charlotte Street in London's West End and then, four months later, to Elgin Crescent in Notting Hill. The move to Lancaster Road wasn't until 1906, first to 142 and then, in 1910, to a larger three-story house at 71.

Theo Brailey's family home when he left on the Titanic. 71 Lancaster Road, London.

Did the moves have anything to do with Brailey's musical progress? Following school he'd become an office clerk, but by 1902 he was part of the orchestra at the Kensington Palace Hotel in West London under newly arrived Dutch conductor Simon Von Lier who would go on to work at the Grand Hotel in Eastbourne. Von Lier was impressed with Brailey's musicianship, later describing him as "a highly efficient pianist." His work in

London may have prompted Ronald to consider leaving Essex where there were fewer opportunities for musicians.

Leaving Walthamstow might also have had something to do with Ronald's aspirations as a clairvoyant. His employment record indicates a knack for reinvention. In 1887, at the time of Theo's birth, he was a commission agent. By 1891 he was working in insurance but somehow managed to combine that job with being a Baptist minister. Ten years later he was a traveling salesman selling watches. Then, in 1902, he began advertising himself as a "trance clairvoyant, medical and general psychometrist" able to give private readings at his Walthamstow home. Psychometrics was the ability to make predictions from handling something that the subject had worn, touched, or owned.

This latter change coincided with Theo's departure from the Kensington Palace Hotel orchestra to join the army, signing up as a boy soldier with the Royal Lancashire Fusiliers (motto *Omnia Audax*—"Daring in all things"), whose regimental headquarters was in Bury, Lancashire. It seems unusual that a boy who'd grown up in Essex and was currently living in London would join a regiment based two hundred miles away with no obvious emotional ties. A possible motivation is that in February 1901 soldiers from the Lancashire Fusiliers lined Piccadilly for the funeral procession of Queen Victoria and then on August 3, 1902, a composite battalion was sent to do the same job for the coronation of King Edward VII. While in London they camped in Kensington Gardens, just across the road from the Kensington Palace Hotel, which was in De Vere Gardens.

It's easy to imagine the teenage Brailey seeing these soldiers and being impressed by their red tunics with white facing and

Theo in the uniform of the Royal Lancashire Fusiliers.

black trousers with red side stripes. Possibly he heard the regimental band practicing in the park or soldiers came to see Van Lier's orchestra play and spoke to him enthusiastically about military life. Coincidentally, the Lancashire Fusiliers originated as the East Devonshire Regiment of Foot and Brailey was a Devonshire name. Ronald Brailey had been born near Exeter and his father, William Brailey, was in the Royal Marines based near Plymouth in the mid-nineteenth century.

He signed up on October 9, 1902, at the age of fourteen years and eleven months at the regimental headquarters in Bury. He was five feet four and a half inches tall, weighed 106 pounds, and had a thirty-inch chest. He contracted to serve for twelve years. After just six weeks of basic training, he was dispatched to Barbados in the Caribbean. To modern ears it sounds an exotic posting, but in the early years of the twentieth century, Barbados was an impoverished West Indian island that had recently suffered riots and assassinations and needed a massive bailout from Britain to avoid total economic collapse.

Brailey left England on RMS *Tagus* on November 26 with ninety-nine other privates, one sergeant, and two corporals from the 4th Battalion. When they arrived in Barbados on December 9 they were absorbed into the 3rd Battalion, bringing its strength up to 1,003. The battalion diary shows that other than quelling riots in Trinidad in March 1903, they had no incidents to deal with during their tour, which allowed for a lot of practice (marches, maneuvers, field training, shooting, bayonet drills), sports (athletics, polo, football, horse racing), and entertainment (meals, concerts, dances).

Music threaded its way through many of the activities: a string band at a moonlight picnic in honor of the birthday of the lieutenant-colonel's wife, "minstrel" entertainment to raise money for a memorial fund, the Trooping of the Colour on August 1, smoking concerts, playing off senior personnel who were returning to Britain.

It was never Brailey's intention to be an ordinary private. The British army was one of the biggest employers of musicians and he had his eyes set on being part of the regimental band. On October 26, 1903, just over a year after signing up, he was appointed as a bandsman. He would then have taken part in the torchlight tattoo on November 5, a dance later that night in the officer's mess, and a ball on December 14 at Government House.

On December 4 a telegram was received from the War Office ordering the 3rd Battalion to South Africa via St. Helena. When Brailey boarded HMT *Dunera* on December 17, it already contained three companies of Lancashire Fusiliers from Jamaica and would later pick up two more companies from Trinidad. Two companies disembarked on January 4, 1904, at St. Helena to take over from the 3rd Manchester Regiment, then the *Dunera* proceeded to South Africa, arriving in Cape Town on January 13.

Brailey and the rest of the bandsmen took a train the same day from Cape Town to Naauwpoort along with the drummers, six boys, and the staff needed to set up their HQ. It was a three-day journey at the hottest time of the year that involved traveling almost nine hundred miles in a north-westerly direction toward Johannesburg and Pretoria. A writer, who had made the same journey four years previously with troops from New Zealand, commented: "The place [Naauwpoort] is nothing but a huge desert. In fact, ever since we left Cape Town, we have seen nothing but sand and rocks, except at the townships, where little patches are irrigated."

Naauwpoort was a strategic railway junction and had become a garrison town subject to frequent attacks during both Boer wars. Now that the fighting was over, there wasn't a lot to do other than to ensure there were no additional uprisings. The men of the Lancashire Fusiliers were housed in tin huts and their main activities were reconnaissance and mapmaking. When they had time off they played football.

Brailey didn't stay long because to progress as a bandsman he had to study for two years at the Royal Military School of Music back in England. The school then, as now, was at Kneller Hall in Twickenham, on the outskirts of London, and his accommodation was on site. Although the 1912 annual for the Lancashire Fusiliers praised him as "a talented musician, and an exceptionally good performer on the piano," his chosen instruments when he enrolled on March 12, 1904, were cello and flute. He would have been taught performance, harmony, and instrumentation, with the rest of the time being taken up with individual and band practice, general education, and some sport. In January 1906 he was awarded two certificates—one to say that he had attained a "good degree of proficiency" on the cello and the other that he had attained a "very good degree of proficiency" on the flute.

He was promoted to lance corporal on leaving Kneller Hall on January

1906, and posted to the 4th Battalion of the Lancashire Fusiliers at their headquarters in Tipperary, Ireland. In April and May his band competed with other military bands based in Ireland and was awarded third place. When reporting the achievement, the regimental annual commented on the youthfulness of the band. Brailey, still only eighteen, was clearly a typical member. "It may be truthfully stated that it would be impossible to collect sufficient hairs from the faces of the reed players to make up one respectable moustache."

On November 15, 1906, the 4th Battalion was disbanded and Brailey was transferred to the 2nd Battalion stationed in Fermoy, forty-six miles northwest of Cork. The move may have been a catalyst because three months later he left the army. The full term he had signed up for committed him until October 1914, so he took the only option available and bought himself out. On February 22, 1907, he left the Royal Lancashire Fusiliers, the entry on his army record noting: "At his own request, on payment of £18."

His family was now living at 142 Lancaster Road in Ladbroke Grove, close to Notting Hill, where Ronald the psychometrist offered private consultations, advice by mail for five shillings, and five séances a week. Brailey came home for a while but soon found work with the Pier Pavilion orchestra in Southport, Lancashire, on the coast south of Blackpool. This seaside resort was among the most prestigious and popular of the era and had the latest in entertainment technology. Close to the seafront there were two large artificial lakes and, at the southern end, the Pleasureland Amusement Park with its Toboggan Railway, Flying Machine, Aerial Glide, and Helter Skelter Lighthouse. It was the ideal place for factory workers from such nearby northern towns as Liverpool, Bolton, Blackburn, Manchester, and Preston to let off steam.

The Pier Pavilion, at the entrance to the renowned pier, was a twelve-hundred-seat theater that put on variety shows. The orchestra's job was to welcome the audience, support the performers, and play the national anthem. In January 1909 the nightly show featured ventriloquists, jugglers, wire walkers, dancers, vocal comedians, roller skaters, acrobats, equilibrists, a tambourine player, and someone who could whistle (a siffleur). Then there was Miss Vera Gaine, "the champion ball puncher"; Mr. Paul Lemaire, "the whimsical wizard" and a singing group known as the Nonentities.

During his time off he met a local girl, Teresa Steinhilber, who lived on a street close to the seafront. Known as Terry to her friends, she was two years younger than Brailey and working as a milliner. They began dating and Brailey was a welcome guest at the family home where she lived with her Irish mother, Kate; her German father, August; three brothers; and a sister. August, who'd arrived in Britain in the 1870s, was a watchmaker with two shops in Southport.

By 1910 Brailey and Teresa were sufficiently recognized as a couple for her to be invited to the London wedding of Brailey's oldest sister, Mabel. In the wedding photographs, taken in the garden of the new Brailey home at 71 Lancaster Road, she stands at Theo's right side, directly behind Mabel, wearing a wide-brimmed black hat and a light light-colored suit. It was a photo of Brailey taken at this wedding on September 10, 1910, with a carnation in the left lapel of his dress jacket, that would be circulated around the world in the immediate aftermath of the *Titanic*'s sinking.

Wedding of Mabel Brailey to Percy Hanson, Sept. 10, 1910. Teresa Steinhilber is in the black hat behind the bride. Theo stands to her left.

His main interest outside of music and his relationship with Teresa was aviation. Like many boys of his age, he was captivated by the exploits of the first generation of pilots and the great advances being made in aircraft

Ronald and Theo Brailey standing. Amy Brailey, Percy Hanson, Mabel (Brailey) Hanson, Lily Brailey seated.

technology. Yet his interest went beyond merely reading about the latest records to be broken. According to the *Liverpool Echo*, "Mr. Brailey was at one time associated with Mr. Compton Paterson at the Freshfield aerodrome and Mr. J. Gaunt at the Southport hanger." *Associated* is a strangely imprecise word to have used. Was he merely a friend or was he involved in some way with their flights? Or did he have a financial stake in their experiments?

Freshfield was eight miles south of Southport, close to the town of Formby, and the "aerodrome" at the time was no more than an expanse of heather- and sedge-covered dunes where aviators could fly and land their planes without fear of crashing into houses. The hangar in Southport was built by the Southport Corporation in 1910 and then rented out to John Gaunt who designed, built, and successfully flew a plane from there in 1911.

If Brailey's connection with these two men was notable enough to warrant a mention in the *Liverpool Echo*, he may well have flown with them because they often took paying passengers for a spin. Paterson once took two schoolboys who'd won the opportunity through a local lottery. These people would be among the first in the world to experience flight, although the altitudes were ridiculously low and the length of the journeys quite short.

Orville Wright had made the first "manned, powered, sustained and controlled flight by a heavier-than-air aircraft" in 1903—duration, twelve seconds. He and his brother, Wilbur, regularly broke records. In 1907 the first "aerodrome" with hangars was built in France and in July 1909 French aviator Louis Blériot became the first person to fly across the English Channel. Transport and warfare would never be the same again. The U.S. Army quickly signed up the Wright brothers and commissioned them to develop a biplane for use in combat.

The 1911 census records Cecil Compton Paterson as a twenty-six-year-old "aviator" living in Freshfield. John Gaunt, from Southport, was a thirty-five-old "aero plane builder." During Brailey's time at the Pier Pavilion they were both at elementary stages in getting their homemade contraptions off the ground. It was a time when a one-hundred-yard advance at ten feet off the ground was still considered a successful flight and would duly be reported in newspapers and magazines.

Brailey spent two years in Southport, apparently building up a wide circle of friends. Then, according to the *Southport Guardian*, he left the town "to go to a musical college to complete his education," although there are no records of him attending any of the major colleges of the day. By 1911 he was composing instrumental music and two manuscripts of his work survive—"Ballet of the Roses" (February 1911) and "A Little Scherzo" (November 1911).

He must already have gone to sea by this time. His first ship was the *Saxonia*, a 14,281-ton Cunard vessel built in 1900 that boasted one distinct 106-foot-tall black funnel. Originally it sailed constantly between Liverpool and Boston but in 1911 began the New York to Mediterranean route, and then Liverpool to New York calling in at Queenstown, Ireland. One of these trips got him back to Liverpool late in January 1912 and on February 10 he joined the *Carpathia*.

On the *Carpathia*, playing alongside Roger Bricoux, he heard of the *Titanic* work for the first time. It was a spectacular offer for someone so young. His only apprehension at first was that he'd recently become engaged to Teresa and had promised to bring his seagoing days to an end. Then, when he got back to England, there was the warning of his clairvoyant father who felt that the *Titanic* would come to no good . . .

6

"A Thorough and Conscientious Musician."

On May 1, 1911, the *Oruba*, a 5,850-ton steamship, arrived back in Southampton after a twenty-four-day trip from the British colony of Jamaica via Trinidad, Barbados, the Azores, and Cherbourg. On board, traveling as class passengers, alongside some members of the MCC cricket team who'd recently played thirteen matches on the island, were a group of five musicians who had just spent the past three and a half months as the orchestra of the Constant Spring Hotel at the foot of the Blue Mountains, six miles outside the capital of Kingston. This establishment had a checkered past. Built as a luxury hotel for the 1891 Jamaica International Exhibition, it had never made money for its owners. Despite its desirable location, 165 acres of grounds, one hundred rooms, a swimming pool, tennis courts, a croquet lawn, and a nine-hole golf course, it had suffered from bad management and incompetent staff. Guests repeatedly complained about everything from the irregularly manned reception desk to the length of time the kitchen took to boil an egg.

Things became so bad that the government took it over. Then in 1908, Sir Alfred Jones, of the British shipping line Elder, Dempster & Co, bought it and attempted to turn around its fortunes by marketing Jamaica as a holiday destination for wealthy Britons.[1] He died the following year and Elder Dempster was taken over by Sir Owen Phillips, later Lord Kylsant, who was described by the *New York Times* as "the Napoleon of British shipping." Phillips was based in Liverpool and one of the lines he owned was the Royal Mail Steam Packet Company, a client of C. W. & F. N. Black. The *Oruba* was a Royal Mail ship.

Through this connection the Black brothers became musical agents for the hotel, responsible for providing a top-notch orchestra the equal of anything to be found in Paris, London, or New York. By December 1910 the hotel that called itself "the finest in the West Indies" was able to advertise in the local newspaper that it was offering "two music concerts a day and a Saturday Cinderella Ball" for the winter season ending April 1911. "A first class orchestra consisting of five professionals has been engaged in England who will play at all our dances. Select concerts will be given daily from 1–3 pm and every evening from 7:30 to 11 o clock. The orchestra is bringing a full programme of classical and all the latest dance music." In the *Times* of London, Elder Dempster had a series of advertisements promoting Jamaica as "The New Riviera" and offering an inclusive deal that included transport to Kingston on one of their ships and six days at the Constant Spring.

A correspondent for the *Times* captured the experience of staying at the Constant Spring Hotel in a story titled "An Impression of Jamaica," which opened:

A large proportion of tourists get their first view of the West Indies from Kingston Harbour in the early morning, and there are not many things in the world to be seen more beautiful than the sunrise on the Blue Mountains. But most vividly is likely to live in the memory the delight of waking on the following morning at, for choice, the Constant Spring Hotel, when, having but a few days before left behind a land grey and locked in ice, one wakes to brilliant sunshine with the air full of the music of the "Jamaican Nightingale" or mockingbird; and one goes out on the balcony to look down on a sea of bougainvillea, where great butterflies flutter, with, beyond, a tangle of tropical shrubbery in which humming-birds hang poised at the white trumpets of the Beaumontia.

Whites were in a minority in Jamaica—only around 15,000 out of a population of 830,000—but they were the governing elite who owned and ran the valuable sugar plantations that provided the island with its most valuable export. They lived in the best houses, didn't mix socially with the descendants of slaves, and, as in India and Africa, created a parallel society where British customs, values, and prejudices prevailed. The world that the *Daily Gleaner* of Kingston reported on at this time could have been in Tunbridge Wells or Brighton, as could the goods the paper advertised. It was for these people that the orchestra from England played.

Edgar Heap was one of the musicians returning to England that May. He was soon to be bandmaster on the *Carpathia* with Roger Bricoux and Theo Brailey under his direction, and immediately after that voyage, part of the *Mauretania* band with Wallace Hartley. Although it's not on record that Heap was ever approached for a job on the *Titanic*, he's the one person who unites all five *Titanic* musicians with previous experience of playing on ships, because in the Constant Spring orchestra were violinist John Law Hume and cellist John Wesley

Portrait of John Wesley Woodward.

Woodward. It's possible that he could have recommended the two players to Hartley when sailing back to Liverpool on the *Mauretania*.

Like Wallace Hartley, "Wes" Woodward, as he was known, had been raised in a Methodist family and his father, Joseph, had been as conscientious as Albion Hartley, working his way up from a maker of molds for holloware (pots, pitchers, bowls, teapots, trays, pans, scoops) at Hill Top Iron Works, West Bromwich, to become manager. Wes, the youngest son of Joseph and his wife, Martha, was born on September 11, 1879, at 24 Hawkes Lane in Hill Top, just over five miles northwest of Birmingham. When Hill Top

Methodist Chapel was demolished in 1962, four large sealed jars were discovered in the foundations with newspapers from 1874 and the names of the chapel's officers. Prominent among them was Joseph Woodward, who was also a trustee of the Methodist school.

West Bromwich lay in what was known as the "Black Country"—one of the most heavily industrialized areas of Britain during the late nineteenth century. The locally mined coal was used to fire the furnaces of the foundries that produced pistols, guns, locks, screws, nails, springs, and kitchen utensils. They also produced the soot and fog that gave the region its bleak nickname. Queen Victoria is said to have pulled down the shutters of her train carriage window when she passed through the region.

Woodward had six brothers and two sisters, but by the time he reached his midteens he had lost two of his brothers as well as his father. Martha was left to raise the large family on her own with the older boys having to leave school early and work in the foundry to bring in an income. An opportunity for a better life came in 1894 when Thomas, the oldest son, who had left home the year before to become a chorister at Gloucester Cathedral, auditioned to become a tenor lay clerk in the Chapel Choir of Magdalen College, Oxford. According to the college records, he was one of sixty applicants but the only one to be offered a job.

The choir was made up of what they termed "academical clerks" (undergraduates at the college who sang until they graduated) and "lay clerks" (professional musicians who might have other work to top up their income). Because of the post the whole Woodward family left West Bromwich and moved to a house in Cowley Road, Oxford. After the industrial midlands, life in the university town offered a literal breath of fresh air along with inspiring architecture and a fascinating sense of history.

It's likely that Woodward left school at around the time of the move and may have done some casual work, but, like his brother Tom, he wanted to make music his career. The Woodwards were a musical family. Relatives on his father's side had been church organists, choirmasters, and players in professional orchestras. In 1900 Woodward took exams set by the Royal College of Music in London that would qualify him to teach music. With a pass mark set at 75 percent, he passed and was awarded a licentiate as a performer of the cello. In the next year's census he described himself as "a musician," meaning that at the age of twenty-one this was how he earned his living.

His years in Oxford are not documented beyond a passing comment by the *Oxford Times* that "he appeared in several solos and string quartets, notably with the Misses Price and Mr H. M. Dowson." The Misses Price, who were violinists, have been lost to history, but Henry Martin Dowson is remembered because he was married to Rosina Filippi, one of the best-known stage actresses of the time. He lived in Iffley, a village outside of Oxford, played the viola, and was a brewer.

Rosina Filippi came from Venice, where her father, Filippo Filippi, was a celebrated writer and music critic. Her mother, Vaneri Filippi, was a French singer and professor of singing at the Milan Conservatoire. Rosina had wanted to be an opera singer, but her voice didn't develop sufficiently and she turned to acting. She became a popular figure in the London theater, involved herself in tutoring younger actors, and was an author. One of her greatest achievements was adapting Jane Austen for the stage for the first time. Her book *Duologues and Scenes from the Novels of Jane Austen Arranged and Adapted for Drawing-Room Performance* was published in 1895, and in March 1901 her production *The Bennets* ("A Play without a Plot adopted from Jane Austen's Novel 'Pride and Prejudice'") was premiered at London's Royal Court Theatre. The critic from the *Times* wasn't impressed: "Is there not something of a profanation in throwing the glare of the footlights upon the art of Miss Austen, so dainty, so demure, so private and confidential?" he asked. "Is there not something of callousness in abandoning to the noisy traffic of the stage those exquisitely discreet duologues which are properly to be enjoyed at leisure, word by word, in little sips?"

Dowson certainly performed around Oxford and was known by the musicians who belonged to the Oxford University Music Club (later to become the Oxford University Music Society). Woodward was becoming familiar with a more cultured world than he would have been exposed to if he had stayed in West Bromwich. Rosina Filippi was a well-connected woman who played opposite many of the giants of British theater and by playing with her husband Woodward would have been introduced to that layer of society.

In photographs John Wesley Woodward looks neat, solid, and

dependable. He's broad shouldered and well groomed with a carefully waxed mustache. His spectacles are wire rimmed and in some photos he instead wears a monocle in his right eye. His friends and acquaintances remembered him as being easygoing and having a positive attitude. He was "amiable," "good natured," and "modest," and had "an easy, equable temper." Outside of music he had an interest in photography and building primitive internal combustion engines, a technology still in its infancy.

His career accelerated in 1907 when he was invited to join the newly formed Duke of Devonshire's Band, sometimes known as the Duke of Devonshire's Private Orchestra, based on the south coast of England at Eastbourne.[2] The 8th Duke of Devonshire, Spencer Compton Cavendish, was an aristocrat and statesman who had entered parliament in 1857 and had at one time been leader of the Liberal Party. His family was one of the wealthiest and most powerful in Britain, its ancestral base being Chatsworth House in Derbyshire, one of Britain's most impressive stately homes.

Duke of Devonshire's Orchestra (Woodward is to the immediate lower right of the conductor).

No one is sure why the Cavendish family took the title Devonshire. Some suggest it was a misreading of Derbyshire made back in the sixteenth century. They went on to acquire land in other parts of the country, most notably in Eastbourne, where the Cavendishes and another family carved up the territory between them. The railway arrived in 1849 and ten years later the 7th Duke of Devonshire planned a new-look town that would be "built by gentlemen for gentlemen." By 1891 the town's population had gone from four thousand to thirty-five thousand and it had become a resort with a promenade, hotels, and a one-thousand-foot-long pier crowned with a four-hundred-seater pavilion.

Eastbourne attracted a distinguished and prosperous clientele who were able to spend much of their time in leisure pursuits. It was imperative for them to let everyone know that they were "in residence" and the *Eastbourne and Sussex Society and Fashionable Visitor's List* announced their comings and goings. Typical of the paper's entries was the news that "the Duchess of Norfolk has been in very delicate health" and that "Lord Wimbourne's condition has undergone no appreciable change." The following advice was given for those contemplating driving in a newfangled motor car: "To make winter driving really enjoyable great care must be bestowed upon the choice of proper garment, for if one gets cold whilst driving, especially in ones hands or feet, all enjoyment is gone at once."

The Duke of Devonshire took a particular pride in Eastbourne and was careful that no other British resort would outclass it. He was alarmed that nearby Bournemouth, which had its own symphony orchestra, might outstrip it. For this reason the 8th Duke created his own orchestra. With forty-two musicians (fifty-four in the summer) and an average wage bill of £150 a week, it was an expensive project but one that produced the necessary effect. The *Eastbourne Chronicle* wrote in April 1907 that the Duke's Orchestra was "an orchestra of such commanding size and proficiency as will serve the double object of making a powerful addition to the list of high class attractions and of assisting to advertise the town."

The Duke hired Dutch conductor Pieter Tas at the end of January 1907, so we can assume that the hiring of musicians took place in February and March. The conditions were that they could be required to play in any property owned by the Devonshire Parks & Baths Company, giving up to a maximum of twelve performances per week. They had to provide their own evening dress for the later performances but could have to "wear such uniform or costume as the company shall at its own expense provide." Woodward was paid £2 15s. 0d. per week and lodged at "Leathorpe" on Upper Avenue with George Stevens, a fifty-five-year-old retired builder, and his wife, Mary.

Grand Hotel, Eastbourne, as it looks today.

Winter Garden, Eastbourne, venue of many concerts by the Duke of Devonshire's Orchestra.

Most of the orchestra's concerts were given at the Winter Garden on the edge of Devonshire Park. In April 1908, for example, it gave a symphony concert on a Thursday afternoon, orchestral concerts on Tuesday afternoon and Thursday evening, a grand chamber concert on Friday afternoon, a Sullivan Night on Friday, a popular concert featuring a vocalist on Saturday night, a Grand Concert on Sunday at 8:00 p.m. (for which the audience chose the program), and a concert of songs by Madame Liza Lehmann on Tuesday evening.

Devonshire Park Theatre, another Eastbourne venue well known to Wes Woodward.

The music it played was varied. In a symphony concert in March 1909, it played Dvorak's *New World Symphony* and Liszt's Second Rhapsody, and worked with a visiting composer, Dr. J. W. G. Hathaway. The Sunday evening program, which featured vocalist Edith Clegg, included *Marche Solennelle* by Alexandre Luigini; the overture from *Fingal's Cave* by Mendelssohn; Ernest Guiraud's violin and orchestra piece "Caprice"; extracts from André Messager's ballet *Les Deux Pigeons*, Wagner's opera *Lohengrin*, and Charles Gounod's opera *Faust*; and "The Bees Wedding" by Mendelssohn.

They also did concerts of what were called Popular music, which were light orchestral numbers: Julius Fucik's "Entry of the Gladiators," Jules Massenet's "Scenes Napolitaines," Schubert's "Marche Militaire," and a selection from

Arthur Sullivan. The local paper commented: "Nobody nowadays associates the term popularity in music with anything that is cheap or tawdry, least of all may they do so in connections with Mr Tas' programmes which are culled from the most fascinating works, and are so well compiled as to echo the last note of variety."

The audiences had high expectations for the music, as did the critics on the local papers. If it fell below the expected standard, they would make their objections known. In February 1908, Tas briefly handed his baton over to Dan Godfrey from Bournemouth and apparently the standard slipped. "A world of difference is interposed between the Duke's Orchestra at their best and at their ordinary level," wrote a critic from the *Eastbourne & Sussex Society*. "It was regrettable that under the direction of so eminent a conductor, they should have fallen somewhat beyond the high water mark on Friday last. Their achievements could not, for instance, in any way be compared to those chronicled at the Edward German concert of a fortnight ago, and their want of enthusiasm naturally spread to the audience, who received some of the works tamely."

Very occasionally Woodward would perform a solo. On February 15, 1908, for example, he played "Cavatina" by Joachim Raff (originally written for piano and violin but often adapted for cello) and "Danse Rustique" by British composer William Henry Squire. On January 9, 1909, he again played the piece by Raff along with "Mazurka" by David Popper. A local novelist and music lover, Emeric Hulme Beaman,[3] said of Wes:

> On several occasions he exhibited brilliant qualities as a solo executant but he excelled rather as an orchestral player than a soloist. His orchestral playing was uniformly sound, steady and reliable; while these same invaluable qualities, conjoined with much natural taste and a cultured style, enabled him to appear to utmost advantage in chamber music. He was a thorough and conscientious musician, whose playing, whether in solos or concerted work, was always interesting and always enjoyable.

Many of the orchestra's musicians did extra work, such as playing at the roller rink in Devonshire Park, but, according to the Duke's wages books,

Woodward restricted himself to the main orchestra work. This may have been because he wanted to play music with other ensembles in his free time. In 1908 *Strad* magazine reviewed him in concert at the Town Hall in a fund-raising event for St. Peter's Church. Apparently "his violoncello solos formed quite a feature." The *Brighton Advertiser* reported that he also performed with the orchestra in the Lounge Hall of the Grand Hotel under Simon Von Lier, the conductor who had been with the Kensington Palace Hotel Orchestra when Theo Brailey played there.[4]

The hiring of Von Lier in 1903 was indicative of the importance that orchestral music played in the marketing of middle-class resorts and hotels at the turn of the twentieth century. It was the sign of culture and sophistication. The chairman at the time wrote:

> I believe you will agree with us that music (especially that of a high class) is now considered almost an essential requirement for hotels of the character of the Grand. If so, I am sure you will approve of the engagement of this orchestra which plays daily in the Hall, afternoon and evening. It is admitted by all who have heard it to be one of great merit and considerable note and has, so far, proved an attraction and has given great pleasure to the visitors, as is evidenced by the applause with which their music is greeted.

The composer Claude Debussy came to stay at the Grand in 1905 with his pregnant mistress, Emma Bardac, and while there completed his best-known composition, *La Mer*.

The Hall in the Grand Hotel, Eastbourne, where the orchestra would have played.

The Hall at the Grand was reputed to have extraordinary acoustics and for this reason would later become a key venue for live radio broadcasts of orchestral music. A guest named George Bagshaw, who spent time at the hotel while Woodward was in Eastbourne, said it truly was a "grand" hotel in that era. "In the evening the hotel porters were dressed in livery with white wigs, knee breeches and silk stockings. The Palm Court had a famous quartet orchestra conducted by a German [sic] Von Leer who played the violin and other players on piano, double bass and cello."

If Woodward did play at the Grand, it's not certain whether he fitted it in with his work with the Duke's orchestra or whether he did a short stint there in 1910 when the orchestra was winding down. The 8th Duke of Devonshire died at the Hotel Metropole in Cannes in March 1908 and was immediately succeeded by his nephew, Victor Cavendish, who became the 9th Duke. The new Duke continued the sponsorship of the orchestra but by 1910 had second thoughts because the box office revenue fell below expectations. The total wage bill between January 1908 and January 1910 was £17,000. He decided that the town itself would need to at least offer partial finance if the orchestra was to continue, and so it was that it played its final symphony concert on October 27 and disbanded four days later.

It could have been during November that Woodward filled in at the Grand before setting sail on the Elder-Dempster-owned RMS *Port Royal* from Bristol to Kingston on December 10, 1910, to work at the Constant Spring Hotel. The ship didn't arrive until early on Christmas morning because it was dogged by storms all the way. There was a strong southerly wind as soon as it left port and then for the next four days it had to contend with a westerly gale before being lashed by a variety of bad weather for the rest of the crossing.

He told friends in Eastbourne that the Caribbean sojourn had greatly improved his health. The main Jamaican daily newspaper, the *Daily Gleaner*, would say that he made many friends during the visit and had time to give lessons at the hotel. The orchestra, the paper added, was "the best of its kind that has ever visited Jamaica." The *Brighton Advertiser* wrote of his Jamaica trip that he had "won much appreciation as a soloist. Like other artists who visit the island, he experienced great hospitality and kindness his sunny disposition rendering him a favourite wherever he went."

His connection with C. W. & F. N. Black and his newly awakened appetite for travel attracted him to the life of a ship's musician. Back in Southampton on May 1, 1911, he and John Law Hume signed on for the maiden voyage of the *Titanic*'s sister ship the *Olympic*, which was to leave Southampton on June 14 bound for New York. It was the largest and most luxurious ship ever to sail and its maiden voyage completely sold out.

The best of White Star's crew were selected for the trip. As with the *Titanic*'s maiden voyage ten months later, the captain was the white-bearded Edward Smith, a favorite with wealthy customers, and White Star chairman J. Bruce Ismay and Harland & Wolff designer Thomas Andrew were VIP passengers. The eight musicians were mostly from the bands of the *Majestic* and the *Arabic*, the oldest of them only thirty years old. Violet Jessop, a first-class steward on both the *Olympic* and the *Titanic*, later remembered the excitement among the crew: "The great day came when the *Olympic* finally became a fact, the 'largest and finest' to fly the British flag. A crew, handpicked from every ship in the line, was assembled for muster on sailing day, feeling proud of the honour of being chosen but trying to hide it under the nonchalance that was only too obvious."

The ship sailed first to Cherbourg in France, then to Queenstown in Ireland, before heading across the Atlantic to New York. A writer for the *New York Times* was on board and could hardly conceal his excitement at the opulence, size, and range of activities available. He heard the band play. "The dining room lounge, an experiment on the part of the builders, the great success of which was hardly anticipated, proved to be the most popular resting place on the ship. Here a very good orchestra plays before and after meals, and tables and chairs were always at a premium for the demitasse."

The unnamed writer also speculated on the safety of the ship in an unusually prescient way. He suggested that part of the adventure of sailing was the outside chance that something could go wrong.

> To begin with, there is always to the imaginative person the joy of speculation, the mystery of untried things, perhaps the lingering uncertainty as to actual accomplishment. You know, for instance, that the

ship-building and navigation are scientifically accomplished, that the least possible element of chance enters in, that the departure and arrival of the ocean steamers is almost as definitely fixed, under normal conditions, as the rising or the setting of the sun. And yet in the case of an untried vessel there is always that feeling of an added element of chance. What if this man or that has erred in his estimate, what if the unexpected should happen for just once, what if a dozen different ifs should develop to upset the calculations and bring you face to face with the hitherto unencountered?

The *Olympic*'s arrival in America on June 21 was hotly anticipated and Violet Jessop described it as a mass welcome that seemed to involve the whole city. Large and small boats were snapping at its heels as soon as it entered the Hudson and the edge of the river was thronged with cheering crowds. "Not a window, however small, but had a little flag or handkerchief waving from it, as we slowly passed on to the accompaniment of shrill tooting of greetings from everything afloat that had a whistle to blow."

Woodward had a week to spend in New York because the *Olympic* wasn't due to depart until June 28. He threw himself into discovering the best music he could find and told friends back in England that he learned a lot from his exposure to music in America. "He thoroughly enjoyed the opportunities he had of visiting New York where he made many friends," reported the *Brighton Advertiser*. "He had a very high opinion of the Americans as lovers of music."

He made three more trips to America on the *Olympic*, with a band reduced to five from the eight on the maiden voyage. Then, on September 20, 1911, just as he was about to leave on his fifth *Olympic* crossing, the unexpected happened. Shortly before 1:00 p.m., as the ship headed down the dredged channel in the Solent, the Royal Navy cruiser HMS *Hawke* appeared on its starboard side making toward the same narrow exit between shoals marked on the navigational maps. According to the "Rules of the Road" the *Olympic* should have slowed down and given way, but it didn't. The *Hawke* vainly tried to turn at the last moment but its helm jammed and the seven-ton warship ploughed straight into the side of the Cunard steamer.

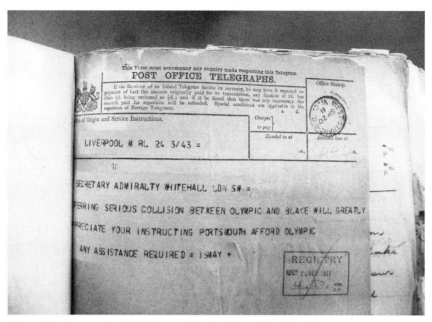

Telgram from Ismay to the Admiralty regarding the *Olympic/Hawke* incident.

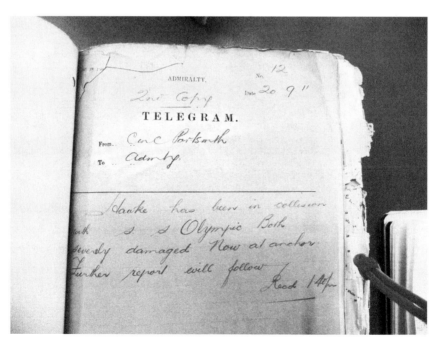

Notification from Portsmouth's Commander-in-chief.

Woodward was playing checkers in a cabin with members of the band during a break from a lunchtime performance when the collision took place, the main point of contact with the bow of the *Hawke* being only feet away. The impact on the big ship was felt so slightly by the players, however, that they carried on with their game. This was to be an eerie portent of the initial response to the *Titanic's* encounter with an iceberg. It was only on closer inspection that it was realized that the *Olympic* had been badly damaged: Three blades of the starboard propeller ended up looking as though they'd been chewed by rats, a large triangular hole about twelve feet in length had been torn in the side just above the waterline, cabin bulkheads and fittings had been broken, and the dynamo room had been flooded. It wasn't until divers looked under the ship that they realized there was another pear-shaped hole in the plating below the waterline.

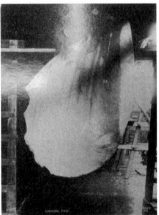

Damage to the side of the *Olympic*.   Damaged propeller of *Olympic*.

This was to say nothing of the damage caused to the *Hawke*, whose bow was so twisted and bent that it looked like a boxer with a crumpled nose. It was clear within a short time that the *Olympic* would not be going to New York. It would, first of all, have to remain anchored in the Solent, and then it would return to Southampton before heading back to Harland & Wolff's dockyards in Belfast for emergency repairs. It was not only a disappointment for almost twenty-five hundred passengers, but also a humiliation for the White Star Line. Its greatest ship, so far, was out of action after only three months of active service. There was the obvious loss of revenue and prestige along with the additional prospect of having to pay damages to the Royal Navy if found guilty of negligence.

The collision with the *Hawke* affected the *Titanic*. Not only was a diversion of effort required, but the only speedy way of repairing the damaged propeller was to replace it with one destined for the *Titanic*. It forced White Star to shift the date of the *Titanic*'s maiden voyage—as announced in September 1911—from March 20, 1912, to April 10, 1912. If the *Hawke* and the *Olympic* had never met, then neither would the iceberg and the *Titanic*.

HMS *Hawke*'s broken bow after her collision with the *Olympic*.

One of the findings of the court of inquiry into the incident was the likelihood that the displacement of water caused by a ship as huge as the *Olympic* set up a suction that dragged the smaller ship into its wake once it was so close. However, this did not excuse the *Olympic*. If it had adhered to Article 19 of the Regulations for the Prevention of Collisions at Sea it would have given way. "The *Olympic*, though perhaps not the overtaking ship according to the definition laid down, had excess of speed over the *Hawke* and could have reduced speed to keep astern of her in the narrow channel, seeing that she was obliged by the Rule of the Road to keep out of the way. Instead of which she attempted to pass the *Hawke*." The summary was: "We are of the opinion that from the evidence heard that the *Olympic* alone is to blame."

Woodward was transferred to the band of the much smaller Cunard steamer *Caronia*, which was doing regular summer crossings from Liverpool to New York, calling in at Queenstown on the outward journey. He left Liverpool on November 4, arriving in New York on November 12, where he spent almost a week before the *Caronia* embarked on the first of its winter cruises for the 1911/1912 season, going directly to Gibraltar on the way out and returning via Liverpool.

The *Caronia* arrived back in New York on Christmas Eve and sailed again on January 6, 1912, for a similar Mediterranean cruise. On February 20 it left New York for Alexandria, Egypt, calling in at Madeira, Monaco, and Naples. Visiting so many countries in such a short time, Woodward put his camera to good use, taking photographs of scenes that seemed exotic to British eyes. "When he was at one of the Mediterranean ports he snapped an Arab in the act of shaving a boy's head outside a mosque," reported the *Brighton Advertiser*. "The Mussulman manifested the indignation prompted by the well-known scruples of his co-religionists."

He told his friends that he enjoyed the "change and variety" that came with life at sea. Along with his friend Jock Hume, however, he planned to leave ship life at the end of the summer of 1912. He had his eye on a position with the Devonshire Park Orchestra in Eastbourne. "He was full of hope and life and spirits," summarized Emeric Holmes Beaman. "He was looking forward confidently to the future, and yet quite content with the present."

7

"THE LIFE OF EVERY SHIP HE EVER PLAYED ON."

John Law Hume, known to his fellow musicians as Jock and to school friends as Johnny, had separated from Wes Woodward after the *Olympic*'s collision with the *Hawke*, but their paths remained remarkably similar. Hume was assigned to the *Caronia*'s sister ship, the *Carmania*, and like Woodward sailed to New York and cruised the Mediterranean. He arrived back in Liverpool three days later than Woodward on April 2, 1912.

Born in Dumfries, Scotland, on August 9, 1890, Jock Hume appears to have been the liveliest, cheekiest member of the band. Few people could speak of him without mentioning his huge grin, his appetite for life, his professional ambition, and his love of practical jokes. A tall, slim boy with fair curling hair, he left home at sixteen and despite his age had been on more ships than any of the other musicians on the *Titanic*. This was not unusual for the time. Boys growing up in towns with limited opportunities to work in industry joined the merchant navy straight from school for the security of employment as well as the promise of adventure.

John Law Hume.

The photograph of him released after the sinking didn't do his personality justice. It was of a smartly dressed, tight-lipped young man in a high collar trying to give an impression of respectability. In contrast, a photo given to fund-raisers in New York and published in the *New York Times* revealed his true character. Dressed in high waist trousers, a white shirt, white shoes, and a kipper tie, he had an insouciant look on his face. The thumb of his left hand was tucked into his belt and his right elbow rested on a post. He looked a snappy dresser, and proud of it. In an age characterized by formality, particularly when being photographed, Hume was casual. In the middistance, to his right, a young woman reclined on a lawn looking toward the camera. She wasn't identified but seemed to be an admirer. One friend said of Jock Hume, "A cooler young fellow I never knew."

He was from a musical family, although not as musical as he would sometimes suggest. His father, Andrew, was a music teacher and accomplished violin and bow maker who had studied under Prosper Sainton, a French violinist and professor at London's Royal Academy of Music. By 1894 Andrew was sufficiently well thought of to be given a small entry in David Baptie's encyclopedic work *Musical Scotland*. In 1915 he told a reporter from *Strad* magazine that he'd started making violins thirty years ago and that he'd learned the craft by visiting the workshops of Erlbach, Schönbach, and Markneukirtchen in the Saxony region of Germany, visits that he was still making each year.

Andrew liked to tell the story that his great-grandfather was a well-known composer and poet—the author of "The Scottish Emigrant's Farewell" and the Popular music to Robert Burns's poem "Flow Gently, Sweet Afton." Jock Hume must have believed this story because Louis Cross, a musician who had worked with him on the *Celtic*, told a journalist in 1912 that Hume "came of a musical family" and that "his father and his grandfather before him had been violinists and makers of musical instruments. The name is well known in Scotland because of it." Another version reported that Cross said Hume told him that his ancestors "were minstrels in the olden days."

"The Scottish Emigrant's Farewell" was written by a Mr. Hume—Alexander Hume (1811–1859)—but this Hume was not directly related to

Andrew or Jock. He was from Edinburgh and only had one son, William Hume, who was born in 1831. Andrew's father, John, was born the following year to a laborer named Robert Hume and also spent his early life laboring before becoming an attendant in a lunatic asylum in his late thirties. He could also have played the violin, of course, but he wasn't a household name or a minstrel. The Humes of Dumfries were of more modest stock and, as we shall see, given at times to fantasizing and conveniently forgetting the particulars of stories.

Dumfries is a small town in southwest Scotland close to the border with England, nearer to Carlisle than Glasgow or Edinburgh. Bordered on three sides by mountains and straddling the smooth flowing River Nith, which empties into the Solway Firth, it feels relatively isolated from both countries. In the early years of the twentieth century, it had a population of around fourteen thousand and was best known as the place where Robbie Burns, Scotland's greatest and best-loved poet, was living when he died at the age of thirty-seven in 1796.

7 & 9 Nith Place, Dumfries, where Jock Hume spent part of his childhood.

Jock Hume was a first son, born on August 9, 1890. He was later joined by three sisters—Nellie, Grace, and Catherine (Kate)—and one brother, Andrew. He started school in 1895 at St. Michael Street School, a few minutes away from the family home, which was over a shop on Nith Place. The head teacher, John Hendrie, encouraged the teaching of music. He arranged for the purchase of a school piano in 1894, hired a teacher named Miss Nellie Lockerbie "to undertake to provide musical training for the children" in 1896, and later established his own violin classes in the school hall. Hendrie would remember the schoolboy Hume as "a merry, bright, laughing boy."

St. Michael Street School, Dumfries, where Jock Hume enrolled in 1895.

His religious education came from the Congregational Chapel at Waterloo Place where he became a member of the Sabbath School and later signed up with the temperance group the Band of Hope. Every meeting began with a group recital of "The Pledge" that they would eventually sign up to:

I promise hereby grace divine
To drink no spirits, ale, or wine,
Nor will I buy or sell or give
Strong drink to others while I live.
For my own good this pledge I take
But also for my neighbour's sake
And this my strong resolve shall be
No drink, no drink, no drink for me.

Andrew Hume also tutored Jock on the violin and in his early teens Jock was competent enough to play both at church and at the Theatre Royal on Shakespeare Street, Scotland's oldest playhouse. He also liked playing football. An anonymous school friend later tried to capture his dynamism: "No one was a greater favourite at school than 'Johnny,' as he was always called." He remembered him as "the happy-faced lad" who was in love with his violin. "In the old days we have heard him, in the old Shakespeare Street Theatre, playing till the curtain should rise on many a mimic tragedy. We thought he would fiddle himself into fame . . ."

The Theatre Royal, Shakespeare Street, Dumfries, where Hume would play at as a teenager.

When school finished, probably in the summer of 1905, he worked as a clerk for James Geddes, a local solicitor, at 8 English Street in the heart of Dumfries. The job didn't suit his artistic temperament or his wander-lust, just as banking hadn't suited Wallace Hartley. Like Hartley, he was a conscientious worker but couldn't stand the incarceration he felt in a small office space. He wanted to be out and about, with his violin if at all possible.

"He was an intelligent, assiduous and courteous lad and was reliable and painstaking in all of his work," Geddes remembered. "He was of a character that would enable him to carve out a career for himself in any walk of life he was likely to follow. Like many great men, he found that his bent was not for being confined within the four walls of an office, and it was a good thing for him that his father decided that he should devote his talents to music."

His home life had been unsettled for some time and this may have provided an additional spur for his musical career. His mother, Grace Law Hume, had suffered from depression since the birth of her daughter Kate in 1897, and had become a virtual invalid. In 1906 she died of cancer of the esophagus and Andrew quickly married Alice Mary Alston who found it hard to slip overnight into the motherly role. When speaking about Hume in 1912, his minister Rev. James Strachan implied that he left both the church and home in his midteens.

Unfortunately crew lists from this period are incomplete and those that have survived are split between some British repositories and the Maritime History Archive in Canada. We know the ships on which Hume played, from comments made by colleagues and family after his death, but have to make an educated guess at the order in which he served on them.

It's likely that his first ship was the Anchor Line ship *Columbia* because it sailed to New York from Glasgow, which was only eighty miles from Dumfries. The Anchor Line had three ships continuously on the trans-atlantic run—the *Caledonia, California,* and *Columbia*—to ensure an outward and an inward sailing every Saturday. The outgoing ships called in at Moville in County Donegal on the northern tip of Ireland to pick up passengers and mail. The brochure advertised "all the accommodations to appeal to people of refinement" and promised "plenty of space for prom-enading." The special music saloon, with its molded ceilings, cylindrical wooden pillars, and comfortable armchairs, looked like the smoking room in a gentlemen's club.

Once familiar with the life of a ship's bandsman, he moved to the larger ships sailing out of Liverpool. The first of these was most likely the White Star Line's *Celtic*, which crossed to New York. More than twice as big as the *Columbia*, it had been the first passenger ship to exceed twenty thousand tons. Two of the *Celtic*'s musicians, viola player Louis Cross and cellist John Carr, later spoke about Hume. Cross, who referred to him as "Happy Jock Hume," remembered him as "the life of every ship he ever played on and beloved of every one from cabin boys to captains." Cross considered Hume's musical ability to be "exceptional" and added: "He studied a great deal, although he could pick up without trouble difficult compositions that would have taken others long to learn."

Hume loved to combine the folk elements of Scottish music with American and European tunes, moving from table to table in a saloon, playing his favorite reels and jigs. He also showed a good sense of humor. Cross remembered him playing a joke on a woman passenger: "She'd given us a lot of trouble, pretending that she knew a great deal about music. Once she asked us to play a particularly intricate classical piece. Jock whispered instructions, and at the close the woman came up and thanked him. But the piece we'd played was American ragtime played slowly—and the woman didn't know the difference!"

Cross mentioned that Hume played on the *Majestic*, a White Star liner that sailed from Liverpool to New York until 1907, when J. Bruce Ismay moved the White Star operations to Southampton. He also was part of the orchestra on the *Megantic* and as that made its first voyage on June 17, 1909, he could only have been on it for its earliest sailings, possibly on the maiden voyage. The *Megantic*, also owned by White Star, sailed to Montreal, Canada.

When Hume signed up for the *Olympic*'s maiden voyage in June 1911, he said that his last ship had been the *California*, an Anchor Line vessel working the Glasgow to New York route. This wasn't strictly true, because the last ship he'd played on was the *Port Royal* sailing out of Bristol for Kingston on December 10, 1910, with Wes Woodward, headed for the Constant Spring Hotel. The orchestra appears to have gone out as a ship's band but returned as passengers. His work on the *California* must have taken place before this.

Although from time to time he returned to smaller ships, his overall progression was toward the larger, more prestigious steamers. When he was at the Constant Spring Hotel he met Americans who promised to look after him when Stateside, and this must have been an added incentive to keep returning to New York. When the *Hawke* collided with the *Olympic*, he thought nothing of it, but allegedly it worried his stepmother, who thought he should call a halt to his seagoing. According to friends, "he just laughed at her fears and took the chance" and signed up for more transatlantic crossings on the *Carmania*, where he was made bandmaster.

For some time he'd had a steady girlfriend in Dumfries who was two years younger than him. Mary Costin lived with her widowed mother, Susan, and two brothers over a solicitor's office in Buccleuch Street, less than two hundred yards from the Humes' new home in George Street. Just as Hume had lost his mother, she'd already lost her father and a sister and would soon lose her oldest brother, William, who died at the age of twenty-four in 1911.

Former Costin home on Buccleuch Street, Dumfries.

It's very likely that the teenage Mary Costin was the girl in the background of the *New York Times* photograph. They'd become inseparable and were planning to marry once Jock had saved up enough money from his work on the ships. His plan was to then concentrate on concert work in Scotland.

During the second week of January 1912, Hume came back to Dumfries while the *Carmania* was docked at Liverpool and he and Mary spent a lot of time together. In March the *Carmania* sailed from New York to the Mediterranean, a monthlong trip that would take him to Gibraltar, Villefranche, Algiers, Monaco, Naples, and Alexandria. This was the first time he'd been beyond North America and the Caribbean, and his longest sea journey.

He must have been in New York preparing for the Mediterranean trip when Mary discovered that she was pregnant. Presumably she would have sent him a telegram with the news, knowing she wouldn't see him again until early April. Later, when things became difficult for Andrew Hume, he would deny that his son was responsible for the pregnancy and even refused to confirm they were engaged. Yet Hume had clearly told his friends of his intentions. In April 1912 Louis Cross told the *New York Times* that he knew of a "sweet young girl" who had been anxiously awaiting Hume's return on the *Titanic*. "Jock, " he said, " was to have been married the next time he made the trip across the ocean."

8

"AN INTELLECTUAL TURN OF MIND."

Three of the musicians on the *Titanic* had never played on ships before. Violinist Georges Krins was in the orchestra at the Ritz Hotel in London's Piccadilly and there's a chance that Percy Cornelius Taylor may have played there too. They could have been spotted by Black on a London visit or by his southern agent, Enos Green. Bass player John Frederick Preston Clarke, who was from Liverpool, had an uncle who had played alongside Charlie Black in the Liverpool Philharmonic Orchestra. He also apparently played at the Kardomah Café at 37 Castle Street, which was across the road from the Blacks' office and was a venue they used for auditions.

Percy Cornelius Taylor is the least known of the musicians, as well as the oldest and the only one who was married. There were no obituaries or personal appreciations in Britain's newspapers for him when he died, and although his name is included on all band memorials, he was never individually honored. This may simply be because he was from London rather than a small, close-knit community where his loss would have been felt more personally or it may be that he didn't become a professional musician until late in his life and therefore had no longstanding reputation.

When Louis Cross described him in 1912, he even got his name wrong.

"Herbert Taylor, the pianist, was considered a master of his instrument," he was quoted as saying. "He was a man of an intellectual turn of mind, with a thin studious face." As Taylor hadn't sailed before, it's difficult to believe that Cross knew anything about him. The observation could have been something the journalist discovered from another source and then attributed to Cross. Or maybe the journalist made a guess based on his photograph, although it's difficult to tell from the head shot released after his death whether he was studious, imperious, or just an ordinary Edwardian trying to look appropriately respectable.

He was born at 144 Queens Road in Hackney, East London, on March 20, 1872, the third son of Martin Taylor, a printer's compositor and bookbinder, and his wife, Emily. The Taylors shared their house with Emily's widowed mother, Caroline Wheeler. Martin's father, William, had run a business in Yorkshire employing five people and Emily's father, Cornelius (the source of Percy's middle name), was an auctioneer in the city of London. Cornelius Wheeler became a representative of the ward of Aldgate, which meant wielding some political power in the administration of the city. In 1837 he and Caroline were invited by the Lord Mayor to a banquet at the Guildhall "on the occasion of Her Majesty Queen Victoria honouring the Corporation with her presence." They were seated on a table next to that of the royal household and Caroline would never tire of telling how she sat so close to the teenage Queen Victoria. Sixty years later, in November 1897, Victoria had an anniversary banquet to which Caroline was invited as one of only three of the original invitees still living. This resulted in a flurry of publicity where the elderly Caroline was interviewed and photographed. Taylor, then twenty-five, must have felt proud of his grandmother and her connection with the great queen who ruled over the most populous empire the world had ever known.

Although Taylor is usually associated with his birthplace of Hackney, East London, or his final residence of Clapham, South West London, the largest part of his life was spent in Peckham, South East London. In 1876, when Taylor was four, he lived with his family in a three-bedroom terraced house on Lausanne Road and the next year moved around the corner to Selsdon Road. He started school at Hollydale Road Infants School, a ten-minute walk away.

In February 1880 he graduated to the school for older boys, Hollydale Road School, by which time the family was living in an end of terrace house close to the railway line in Brabourn Grove. He left the school in 1886, the year his only sister, Emily, was born, and four years later his father, Martin, died of cirrhosis of the liver at the age of fifty-two. According to the census of 1891, the remaining family had moved to a bigger house on the corner of Brabourn Grove and Hollydale Road where part of the ground floor was used as a grocery store run by Emily. At nineteen Taylor was working as a clerk.

His life becomes difficult to track from this point. Somehow he evaded the 1901 census and so the next official record comes from 1906 when he married at the age of thirty-four. On his wedding certificate he described himself as an accountant. The only clue to any musical prowess was the fact that he was a choir member of St. Antholin, a Peckham church where his brother Frederick was the organist. Another brother, George, apparently played in local dance bands.

By the time Taylor got married, he had left Peckham and was living in a second-floor flat at the recently completed Glenshaw Mansions on Brixton Road in Brixton. He lived at flat 13, two doors away from Sydney Chaplin and his soon-to-be-famous brother, Charlie, who were then performing in local venues such as the Canterbury Music Hall and the South London Palace of Varieties. At flat 37 was music hall entertainer Jock Lorimer, whose son Maxwell, born there in March 1908, would become the great

British comedian Max Wall. Percy's bride, Clara Alice Davis, the daughter of a gas superintendent from Dulwich, had her own stage aspirations.

Taylor could have met Clara through his brother George who married her sister, Minnie, in September 1901. Clara was still single then, but two years later married an auctioneer from Somerset named Ralph Davis. He was only twenty-one and she was thirty-one, although when it came to filling in the wedding certificate she knocked four years off her age.

Poor Ralph didn't last long. In 1905 he died while being operated on. The cause of death was given as "cardiac failure when under the influence of chloroform for operation and suffering from fatty disease of the heart." The verdict at the inquest was "misadventure." He and Clara had been married for less than two years, leaving her a widow at thirty-three.

It was fourteen months later, on May 25, 1906, that Percy Taylor and the newly widowed Clara made their vows at Christ Church, North Brixton, in the presence of his brother Frederick, his sister Emily, and Clara's parents. On August 10 he composed his will, bequeathing all his possessions including loose cash, credit in the London and County Bank, and two insurance policies to his "dear wife Clara Alice Taylor."

Clara had made no entry in the "profession" box on either of her wedding certificates so far, suggesting that her father supported her before marriage and her husbands afterward. The story passed down the family is that it was an unhappy marriage and Taylor took the *Titanic* job in the hopes of picking up work in New York and leaving his past behind.

If this were true, it would make sense of the only facts available. Taylor doesn't appear in the 1911 census, even at the address in Vauxhall (9 Fentiman Road) that he gave to the White Star Line. Neither was Clara at this address. She was back at home in Dulwich living with her parents. In the box for "profession" she put "actress." An album of family photographs left behind by Taylor's mother, Emily, when she died in 1927, has photos of Percy and even of Clara's sister Minnie but none of Clara or Clara and Percy together. The *Daily Telegraph*, which played a leading role in raising money for the dependents of those who died on the *Titanic*, later made the cryptic comment: "It may take the public by surprise to know that there was only one actual bandsman's widow, a lady who, no doubt, has benefited beyond her expectations." This was possibly written in the knowledge that they were living apart at the time of his death.

John Frederick Preston Clarke, bass player on the *Titanic*, was born at 2 Churchill Terrace in the Manchester suburb of Chorlton-cum-Hardy on July 28, 1883, the son of a seventeen-year-old solicitor's clerk named John Robert Clarke and his twenty-two-year-old wife, Ellen Preston. The story is told in the ages and dates. Their wedding date—January 21, 1883—must have been set when Ellen knew she was pregnant. During the next four years they had two daughters, Ellen and Emily, and then between Emily's birth in 1887 and the census of 1891, John Robert apparently had deserted the family. Emily told her daughter Freda that he fled to America with his brother Edward, where they both started new lives.

John Frederick, known to everyone as Fred, was sent to live with his paternal grandparents in Croydon while Ellen Clarke and her girls settled with her spinster sister Mary in the Toxteth Park area of Liverpool. In the census of 1891, she described her marital state as "married" and her occupation as "dressmaker." Robert Clarke, the grandfather with whom Fred went to live, was a solicitor's clerk and his wife, Mary Ann, a schoolmistress. By 1901 Robert was on his own in Eastbourne and Clarke had returned to his mother at 174 Tunstall Street and was working as an insurance clerk. Aunt Mary, a music teacher, was still with the family.

The Liverpool street, about to be demolished, where Fred Clarke lived with his family.

In 1884, the year after Clarke was born, another of his mother's sisters, Elizabeth, married an up-and-coming violinist from Bradford named Vasco Akeroyd. By the turn of the century, Vasco was in Liverpool playing violin for the Liverpool Philharmonic and giving lessons from his home at 35 Falkner Square. Clarke became one of his pupils and during the coming years Vasco would use his influence to get him work.

In 1909 the Vasco Akeroyd Symphony Orchestra was founded and Clarke became one of its six bass players. The orchestra would play eight concerts each season at the Philharmonic Hall, almost always to rapturous reviews from the Liverpool press who admired Vasco's choice of music, the quality of his leadership, and the high standards of the musicians. Early in the second season, the *Liverpool Post* commented that the local public had been "quick to appreciate the excellencies of the orchestral and other fare that Mr Akeroyd is seeking to provide," and in January 1911 the *Liverpool Evening Express* said: "Excellent as these concerts invariably are, their promoters surpassed all previous efforts with the programme submitted last night. It is doubtful if a more attractive and interesting concert has been given in Liverpool for some time past, and a packed and warmly appreciative audience testified their approbation in unmistakable fashion."

As part of this orchestra, Clarke performed everything from Bach concertos and Tchaikovsky symphonies to contemporary works by Szigeti, Saint-Saens, and Dvorak. There were guest vocalists, guest conductors, and the occasional child prodigy visiting from America. One of the most popular concerts in each series featured a program chosen entirely by the audience.

At the same time Clarke was in the orchestra at the Argyle Theatre of Varieties in Birkenhead, which was over the Mersey on the Wirral Peninsula, where the Black brothers had their home. The theater, built as a music hall in 1868 and able to seat an audience of eight hundred, was one of Britain's best-known entertainment venues. Artists of the era who appeared there include, Charlie Chaplin, Stan Laurel (of Laurel and Hardy), W. C. Fields, Dan Leno, and Harry Lauder.

Clarke would have worked in the orchestra pit providing backing to vocalists and incidental music for sketches. There were two shows a night for six days of the week and a matinee at 2:30 p.m. every Thursday. During the same period he also appeared with the Philharmonic Orchestra of Port Sunlight and at the Kardomah Café. Port Sunlight was a model village built by William Lever for employees of his soap factory on the Wirral. It had almost thirty societies ranging from an Anti-Cigarette League to a Scientific and Literary Society. On June 22, 1911, Clarke played with the orchestra to celebrate the coronation of King George V.

Clarke's connection with Charlie Black could have come through his Uncle Vasco, who for several years played violin alongside him in the Liverpool Philharmonic Orchestra. According to family legend originating with Emily Clarke, Clarke's reason for taking work on the *Titanic* was to make it to New York because he had heard that his father, John Robert Clarke, had lately been killed there in a house fire. He wanted to work his passage to America and, once there, sort out his father's estate.

John Robert appears to have eluded the record books after he left his family. He doesn't show up in British censuses after 1881 and there is no record in the UK of his death. His common name makes him hard to track in American records. The rumor about his brother leaving his family in Croydon and moving to New York, however, is confirmed by living relatives in Canada. Edward Fulcher Clarke went to America ahead of his wife and four children ostensibly to settle in before they joined him, but instead had affairs with several other women. When his wife eventually showed up, he was caught and they separated.

Georges Alexandre Krins was born in Paris on March 18, 1889, but moved with his family to the town of Spa in Belgium in 1895, where his parents opened a haberdashery store. His father, Auguste, was part Russian, part Belgian. His mother, Louise, was French. He had two sisters, Madeleine and Anne, and a brother, Marcel.

Spa was a very musical city with a number of orchestras, including la Grande Symphonie of seventy musicians. He developed an early love for the violin but there were no music schools in Spa, so at the age of thirteen he enrolled at the Conservatoire Royal de Musique in Liege where he would study for the next six years. Early on he was recognized as a brilliant and hardworking student. In the academic year 1904–1905, he won second prize in musical theory and also in violin. The next year he won first prize for violin and in 1906–1907 he again won second prize. His professor considered him a "model pupil" who exhibited a solid grasp of technique. "Georges Krins has made enormous progress in one year." The Spa newspaper *Saison de Spa* marked his achievement in its issue of July 24, 1907: "We note with pleasure that Mr Georges Krins, who has played in the Grande Symphonie, won the second prize for violin at the Conservatoire Royal de Liege. We give him our congratulations."

He left the Conservatoire in 1908 after again winning first prize in violin and returned to Spa where he joined La Grande Symphonie for the 1908 and 1909 seasons. Then, early in 1910, he was engaged as first violin at the Trianon Lyrique

Georges Krins with two friends in London, 1911.

in Paris, a theater at the foot of Montmartre that at the time was specializing in comic opera. It was from Paris that he left for London to join the orchestra at the recently opened (1906) Ritz Hotel on Piccadilly. Here he played in the elegant Palm Court where the celebrated "tea at the Ritz" was served.

Georges Krins with his father and sister at the Promenade des Artistes, Spa, Belgium.

While in London, Krins took a flat at 10 Villa Road, a short walk from Percy Taylor's home in Fentiman Road. For a while he contemplated joining the army, mainly because he had a deep fascination with the Napoleonic Wars, but his father managed to talk him out of it by telling him how dangerous it was. He should stick to music. It was far safer.

9

"The *Titanic* Is Now About Complete."

It would have been with a sense of excitement and relief that cellist Wes Woodward sailed into Liverpool on the *Caronia* on March 30, 1912—relief that such a long journey was finally over and excitement at seeing his family and being able to share his adventures with them. We know that he was in Headington before leaving to meet the *Titanic*, so we can assume that he took a train down to Oxford, possibly after visiting Charlie Black in Castle Street to sort out his contract.

It could be that Woodward was a last-minute replacement for Seth Lancaster, the musician who was first offered the job. Lancaster apparently at this point still thought he was set to sail with the *Titanic*. Maybe Hume or Edgar Heap had pushed Woodward's name. He was certainly older than Lancaster and had a more impressive track record.

Woodward's mother was living at the Firs, Windmill Road, with his unmarried brother, Herbert, who was working as a gardener. He would probably have visited his brother Thomas, who was still singing at Magdalen College, and it was maybe through this meeting that the plan was hatched for him to come and play at the college's May Ball on the night of April 30, when he arrived back on the *Titanic*. He may also have gone down to Eastbourne to meet up with old friends, such as the newspaper advertising executive Syd Wardingly and local musicians Bill Read and Edward Peilgen.

The house (center) in Headington from which Wes Woodward left to join the *Titanic*.

The Britain he came back to was enduring a miners' strike that was threatening to disrupt everything from train services to shipping, so dependent was the country on coal. The *Daily Mirror* was mounting a self-congratulatory campaign to provide milk for children whose fathers had lost employment because of the strike. "Child victim of the coal strike fed with milk by generous readers of the *Daily Mirror*" ran one of its headlines on the day that Woodward got back.

Suffragettes (or "suffragists" as the *Mirror* referred to them), who were upset by the progress of the Women's Bill, were planning to exert their economic power to show that they were a force to be reckoned with. "The time has now arrived," said a Mrs. Despard of the Women's Freedom League, "for us to take deeper and more general militant action. I do not believe in injuring private property, but the commerce of this country depends a great deal for its success on the women of the country. I want all of our women to become a hatless brigade and boycott the male makers of hats. In fact, not to buy anything that is not absolutely necessary. That would more seriously affect tradesmen than the breaking of their windows."

In Hertfordshire hundreds of women were taking part in mock military maneuvers in readiness for the possibility that a European nation might try to invade. They were marching, camping, digging trenches, and performing rescue operations on "wounded" comrades. A photo of them wearing long dresses and tin helmets appeared in the newspapers along with the observation that women troops were far more cost-effective because they ate less than men.

If there was a fear that women were challenging male domination, there was an equal concern that men were becoming too feminine. The annual Oxford and Cambridge boat race taking place that day would be distinguished by the fact that "for the first time in the annals of the historic contest a long-haired crew will appear on the Thames." The Oxford crew had apparently gone all tousled and had become the subject of mockery. The *Mirror* caught the mood: "In the dim past, when the boat race was young and innocent, be-whiskered and bearded young gentlemen may have rowed for their respective Varsities, but never, never did they appear with their locks blowing blithely in the breeze."

But there were still real men around. Men like Captain Robert Falcon Scott who had set off in June 1910 to be the first person to reach the South Pole only to find, when he arrived on January 17, 1912, that he had been beaten by the Norwegian explorer Captain Roald Amundsen, who had arrived a month earlier using a different route. It was a harrowing journey of exploration in the most inhumane of climates without any of the benefits of modern communications. Messages back to civilization took months. One such message appeared in the British newspapers on April 1, 1912. When the British Antarctic Expedition ship arrived in New Zealand, there was an expectation that Scott would be on board, but instead all the commander had was a note from the explorer that read: "I am remaining in the Antarctic for another winter in order to continue and complete my work."

This stoicism and determination to finish the job in hand turned Scott into a hero. He was a man willing to put his country and the progress of science ahead of his own personal comfort and well-being. His story was also an illustration of humanity's increasing ability to use nature rather than be used by it. Few places on earth now seemed to be out of bounds and the earth itself was giving up its secrets to determined scientists. "Motor-Cars and telephones at work on Antarctic Ice," crowed a *Mirror* headline. "Astounding narrative of Man's triumph over nature."

What the world didn't know at the time was that Scott and his comrades were already dead. They had perished through exhaustion, hunger, and extreme cold. Scott made his last diary entry on March 29, the day he is presumed to have died, and left calmly composed letters to his family, the families of his fellow explorers, and a nation he hoped would understand his sacrifice. "Had we lived," he wrote, "I should have had a tale to tell of the hardihood, endurance, and courage of my companions which would have stirred the heart of every Englishman. These rough notes and our dead bodies must tell the tale, but surely, surely, a great rich country like ours will see that those who are dependent on us are properly provided for." Their bodies weren't found for another eight months.

At 6:00 a.m. on Tuesday April 2, the *Titanic* began moving slowly down the Belfast Lough, pulled by the tugs *Hercules, Huskisson, Herculaneum, Hornby,* and *Herald.* Despite the early hour the banks of the river were lined with cheering crowds. This was a big day for the city, especially if you were one of the people who had directly or indirectly helped to bring the great ship into being. As the largest man-made movable object slid down toward the sea, there was the sure knowledge that history was being made.

Two miles off Carrickfergus the tugs withdrew their support and the giant liner had to turn its propeller in the sea for the first time. On board was a skeleton crew of seventy-eight needed to feed the boilers, stoke them, and keep all the wheels greased. There were also forty-one officers, cooks, and storekeepers. Chief radio engineer Jack Phillips was fine-tuning the new Marconi equipment, assisted by Harold Bride. Thomas Andrews, the designer from Harland & Wolff, monitored every movement of the ship he had nurtured all the way from the drawing board to launch and fitting. Most importantly there was Mr. Carruthers, the surveyor from the

Olympic (left) and *Titanic* in the Thompson Graving Dock, Belfast, 1911.

Board of Trade, whose job it was to decide whether the vessel was seaworthy and could be given an Agreement on Account of Voyage and Crew, which would be valid for the next twelve months.

Once the *Titanic* began churning up the sea and it was taken up to a speed of twenty knots, it was time to test its ability to stop, to turn using only the rudder, to turn using only propellers, and then to alter its direction. At 2:00 p.m. it took a straight course out into the Irish Sea for its first uninterrupted journey; at 4:00 p.m. it made its way back to Belfast, where it let off anyone not staying for the transatlantic voyage and checked its anchors; and at 8:00 p.m. it began the six-hundred-mile journey to Southampton, where it would arrive on the morning of April 3 ready to stock up with fuel and provisions.

Jock Hume had arrived back in Liverpool on the *Carmania* the same day that the *Titanic* was undergoing its sea trials. Although he must have been desperate to get back to Dumfries to see his family and his expectant girl-friend, Mary, we know he stayed around in Liverpool for at least two days, because on Thursday, April 4, he paid a visit to the naval outfitter J. J. Rayner at their shop on Lord Street to collect his bandsman's uniform. Actually, according to the receipt, it wasn't so much a new uniform as whatever he had been wearing but cleaned up, mended, pressed, and with White Star buttons and a new collar sewn on. The uniforms recovered after the sinking were described as having "green facing," which most likely referred to the collar, and Hume's receipt refers to his "tunic" having a "new collar" (cost: two shillings and sixpence). He was also charged two shillings for a small lyre, the White Star emblem, to be worn on the lapel. It's likely that he had handed in his uniform for alteration the day before, which would explain why he hadn't been able to proceed to Dumfries immediately.

Fred Clarke played his last concert with the Vasco Akeroyd Symphony Orchestra at the Philharmonic Hall on February 27. On the night of April 6, knowing that he was about to leave Liverpool, he took the ferry over to Birkenhead to meet up with some of his old colleagues still working at the Argyle Theatre. He struck his friends as being a little "morose." They couldn't tell whether he was feeling ill or whether he was just apprehensive about his first sea voyage. Rather than about the excitement of the journey, his talk was more about his hopes of making good tips from what would be a very rich collection of travelers. Maybe inspired by being back at the Argyle, he spoke of his desire to get back into the theater. "You know, it would be just my luck to go down with the ship," he apparently said to his drinking companions. "I've kept away from it so long it might finish me on this trip."

He went to the second performance of that Saturday night, which was a typical variety show of the period headlined by magician Gus Fowler ("the latest London novelty") and comic singer Cissie Curlette and included some moving film images by Brooke and Brown's Royal Bioscope. Fowler's act was based around watches and clocks, which he could seemingly make appear and disappear at will, ending with the sound of thirty bells coming from his hat. Cissie Curlette, a British singer who'd made her American debut in 1910, was, according to the *New York Dramatic Mirror*, "a talented and quite good-looking English singer [with] songs which relied for their success solely upon the double entendre of their lyrics and theme, rather than any tunefulness or brightness of lines." Among her songs were "Toodle-I-Oddle-I-Oo," "Yea Verily Yea," "I'd Rather Lather Father," and "What You've Never Had You Never Miss."

He probably stayed at Birkenhead overnight because the newspaper reports claimed that he left for Southampton on the Sunday morning

best. It is good also to prepare for the worst. Both happiness and ill fortune shall be the reward of the man who considers each step before he takes it."

Finally Hartley, maybe in the company of Bricoux and Brailey, made his way by rail from Liverpool to Birmingham and then from Birmingham directly to Southampton via the Midlands towns of Coventry, Leamington, and Banbury. Seated in a carriage with the smoke of the engine billowing past the window, he wrote a letter to his parents that he was able to pop into a post box on the platform at Reading before the train set off for Basingstoke and Winchester. In London, Georges Krins and Percy Taylor must have made plans to catch the boat train from Waterloo to Southampton Docks, a train that would arrive at 9:30 a.m. on the day of departure. Wes Woodward left from Oxford with his "best cello" and possibly caught the same train that Hartley was already on. Jock Hume, with two expensive rented violins that he planned to try out, took the train down to London from Dumfries.

The *Titanic* continued to fill its holds. Its eventual load would total almost 560 tons of cargo (including 11,524 individual pieces) and 5,800 tons of coal, 4,427 tons of which had to be taken from other ships. By Monday it was time to load the more perishable goods, such as 75,000 pounds of meat, 11,000 pounds of fish, and 7,000 heads of lettuce. Another Board of Trade surveyor, Captain Clark, inspected the ship, as did the captain appointed for the job, Edward Smith, who was photographed on the bridge for the one and only time. Thomas Andrews wrote home to his wife: "The *Titanic* is now about complete and will, I think, do the old Firm credit tomorrow when we sail."

10

"WE HAVE A FINE BAND."

Whether or not they had traveled down to Southampton on the boat train that arrived early in the morning of April 10, the musicians would have joined the crowd of second- and third-class passengers streaming toward berths 43/44 of the White Star's dock, where the majestic *Titanic* lay with its bow pointed at the Solent. They would have boarded by the second-class entrance on C Deck, toward the back of the ship, and taken the elevator or staircase two flights down to E Deck, where there was a designated musicians' room on the starboard side with three sets of bunk beds, drawers, a wardrobe, a basin, and a separate cabin in which to store their instruments. A second room, again for 5 musicians was on the port side, squeezed between a room for washing potatoes, and accomodation for its workers. It's likely that the 'saloon orchestra' took the better cabin.[1]

While the attention of the world was on the glamour and high living of the top decks, the musicians, along with stewards, nurses, clerks, cooks, waiters, and other second- and third-class passengers were down below, not far from the casings of the ship's engines, in what the crew jokingly referred to as "the glory hole." They would have perhaps been on board by 10:00 or 10:30 a.m., preparing for the arrival of the first-class passengers who were traditionally played on to the ship and offered a glass of champagne from a silver tray.

For Jock Hume and Wes Woodward it would have been a reunion after not having seen each other since the *Hawke* had rammed the *Olympic* six months previously. There was time to share their experiences of the Mediterranean—they were in Alexandria, Egypt, within days of each other—and discuss the highs and lows of life on the sister ships the *Carmania* and *Caronia*. They must have both felt a certain sense of *déjà vu* on entering the *Titanic* at Southampton, having gone through exactly the same process on the *Olympic* on her maiden voyage. Even though they'd only yet taken a short walk on this ship, they must have started making comparisons. Stewardess Violet Jessop, who'd also served on the *Olympic*, thought the crew accommodation was a vast improvement and was pleased that architect Thomas Andrews, who had canvassed her and her colleagues about how things could be made better, had implemented many of their suggestions. She thought the *Titanic* was "decidedly grander and improved in every way."

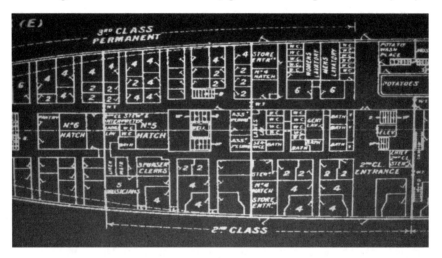

For Wallace Hartley, Roger Bricoux, and Theo Brailey, there were only a few days of catching up to do. There would have been light conversation about how they'd spent their time and perhaps about their regrets at not being able to see their families and girlfriends during their time off. Hartley, Brailey, and Hume were all planning weddings by the year's end and Woodward was said to have a girlfriend in London.

If Hartley hadn't already met Woodward and Hume, now was the time to introduce himself as bandleader. He'd no doubt heard good things about them from their mutual friend Edgar Heap and it was Hartley's job now to exert his authority and explain what was expected. Perhaps Hartley had been given an advance passenger list in order to impress on his musicians the gravity of their task on this voyage. There was John Jacob Astor, one of the richest men in America; the steel tycoon Benjamin Guggenheim; historian Archibald Gracie; French aviator Pierre Maréchal; the American president's chief military advisor, Archibald Butt; English fashion designer Lady Lucille Duff-Gordon; British journalist and author W. T. Stead; young film actress Dorothy Gibson; novelist Jacques Futrelle; Broadway producer Henry B. Harris; and the painter Francis Davis Millet. Then there was J. Bruce Ismay, chairman of the White Star Line, and Harland & Wolff designer Thomas Andrews.

Theo Brailey would certainly have known who W. T. Stead was and may even have met him through his father because he was the best-known and most respected advocate of spiritualism in Britain. He was certainly the highest-profile Briton on the ship. He was on his way to New York to address a peace conference at Carnegie Hall for the Great Men and Religions Congress where he would share a stage with the black political leader Booker T. Washington, the great orator and politician William Jennings Bryan, and the president of the United States, William Howard Taft.

Fred Clarke, Georges Krins, and Percy Taylor must have felt like outsiders at this early stage. They knew how to play their instruments, but they had no experience working on a liner. They may have wondered how the rolling of the ship might affect their ability to play. The names and places that the others spoke about so knowingly wouldn't have meant anything to them. There's a chance that Taylor and Krins were already acquainted through musical circles in London. If they weren't already familiar with each other, they would have found common ground in their knowledge of Vauxhall and Brixton. Of course, Krins and Bricoux would have been able to talk to each other in their native French tongue. Clarke may have still been feeling a little unwell or a little apprehensive, not knowing what life would be like on the ship plus wondering what he would discover when he arrived in New York to settle his father's estate.

But the fellowship of music would soon have overridden the initial atmosphere of caution. Once they got their instruments out of their cases, the only thing that mattered was how well they played and how sensitive they were to each other's moves. They would have already been given

White Star music book listing 352 tunes.

copies of the White Star Line's current music book—actually a small booklet produced by the Black agency—that listed the titles of the 352 tunes the musicians needed to know. Each first-class passenger would have a copy and could call out the number of the tune, knowing the band could play it.

Hartley would then have talked them through their duties. Three of the musicians would mainly be on B Deck playing in the reception room immediately outside the first-class à la carte restaurant or at the Café Parisien, which was on the starboard side of the ship. Their job was to create an ambience of the city that the *Daily Mirror* thought had become the contemporary equivalent of Athens—the city of philosophy, poetry, art, gastronomy, cabaret, dancing girls, pavement cafés, and love. They would have their own library of tunes that would differ from the library of the quintet.

The Prince of Wales was in Paris on a royal visit and the *Daily Mirror* had compared the delight of a Briton visiting Paris with that of a Roman youth making his way to Athens in a bygone age. Paris, it observed, was where the daughters of the rich went for a year to improve themselves. "It is a wise choice, and an example bound to be followed by innumerable youths of humbler birth in England. The Americans, more generally than ourselves, have realized how much Paris can contribute to education." Paris was a "civilising city" and a "studious city" that made London seem crude and frivolous by comparison.

The Parisien was an innovation introduced on the *Titanic*—a French café with wicker chairs and large picture windows that could be rolled up when the weather was good, that served coffee and pastries. The à la carte restaurant differed from the main saloon in providing a choice of as many as ten courses and allowing passengers to eat at a time of their choice. The cost of meals here was not included in the fare. All bills had to be settled at the tables by cash or check. It had the effect of creating a class division even among first-class passengers—the division between the rich and the really rich.

The other five musicians would play in a variety of places, mainly in the first-class lounge during afternoon tea and the dining saloon on D Deck for luncheon and dinner. Passengers reported hearing them in the second-class reading room, the first-class reception area, the companion-way, and the Palm Room. In addition they could be asked to play at the Anglican church service conducted by the captain on Sunday morning in the dining saloon, and on special occasions such as galas, concerts, and receptions.

By 11:30 a number of the musicians were assembled in the first-class reception area playing music to welcome the ship's most wealthy and glamorous passengers on board. That job done, they would have had to hurry back downstairs to be in place as a quintet and a trio in the dining saloon and outside the à la carte restaurant, respectively, for the first luncheons to be served on the ship.

The Southampton dock from which the *Titanic* sailed as it looks today.

The *Titanic* left its moorings at midday pulled by its tugs and was still in Southampton Water when it narrowly avoided a collision with the American steamer *New York*. The suction caused by the displacement of the *Titanic*'s bulk was so strong that it snapped the *New York*'s mooring ropes, causing the ship to swing toward her. Only quick action by the *Vulcan*, one of the *Titanic*'s tugs, prevented a minor disaster. Passengers and crew were aware of what was happening, as it delayed the exit from Southampton by an hour.

Without doubt Brailey and Woodward would have had flashbacks of their previous experience of being rammed by another vessel in the same waters. Passenger Lawrence Beesley wrote:

> As we steamed down the river, the scene we had just witnessed was the topic of every conversation. The comparison with the *Olympic-Hawke* collision was drawn in every little group of passengers, and it seemed to be generally agreed that this would confirm the suction theory which was so successfully advanced by the cruiser *Hawke* in the law courts, but which many people scoffed at when the British Admiralty first suggested it as the explanation of the cruiser ramming the *Olympic*.

This was not a minor near miss that we only know about now because it could seem to be an omen; it was reported and commented on at the time. The *Daily Telegraph* of April 11 headlined the story "An Alarming Incident":

> A sensational incident attended the sailing of the *Titanic* yesterday, from Southampton, on her maiden voyage. Having to pass at the Test Quay the liners *Oceanic* and *New York*, the latter seems to have been so seriously affected by the suction of the *Titanic*'s screws that her stern ropes, seven in number, parted, and her stern swung into midstream. The *Titanic*'s engines were stopped and the *New York* was towed to another berth.

The *Titanic*'s first stop was in Cherbourg, France, which it reached at 5:30, anchoring outside the port and taking on passengers and mail from

Daily Telegraph report on *Titanic*'s near collision on leaving Southampton.

two tenders. The musicians were already playing for diners taking tea or for the early evening meal, delayed because of the late start. The placid mood was captured in a recently discovered letter written by perfumer Adolph Saalfeld to his wife in the late hours of that first day:

> The weather is calm and fine, the sky overcast . . . I have quite an appetite for luncheon. Soup, fillet of plaice, a loin chop with cauliflower and fried potatoes, Apple Manhattan and Roquefort cheese, washed down with a large Spaten beer iced, so you can see I am not faring badly. I had a long promenade and a doze for an hour up to 5 'o' clock. The band played in the afternoon for tea but I savour a coffee in the Veranda café with bread and butter and quite thought I should have to pay but everything in the eating line is *gratis*.

By 11:30 the musicians would have completed their duties and have been making their way back down to E Deck. Either then or early the next morning, Wallace Hartley wrote what would be his last letter home, a letter to be taken ashore by tender at Queenstown when the *Titanic* put down anchor and took on its final passengers. "Just a line to say we have got away all right. It has been a bit of a rush but I am just getting a little settled," he wrote. "This is a fine ship and there ought to be plenty of money around. We have a fine band and the boys seem very nice. I missed coming home very much and it would have been nice to have seen you all, if only for an hour or two, but I could not manage it. Shall probably arrive home on the Sunday morning. All love, Wallace."

It's hard to imagine that he didn't also write to Maria Robinson, expressing the same regret at not meeting and the desire to see her as soon as possible after his intended arrival back in Southampton on Saturday, April 27. His sight of the Irish coastline as it slipped by the starboard side of the *Titanic* was the last he'd ever see of dry land. The observation made by almost everyone who survived is the contrast between the smoothness and uneventfulness of the ship's progress across the Atlantic and the enormity of the tragedy they were about to take part in.

Shipwreck was an ever-present possibility in 1912. Radio communication was in its infancy, radar had not been invented, and safety measures were not highly evolved. Ships sinking in storms, or through collisions with rocks or other vessels, were commonplace events. That year *Chambers' Journal* reported that 1,453 ships had been lost since 1841 and on the transatlantic route 24 steamers had been lost without trace. The fact that such attention was focused on the *Titanic's* safety features—such as the watertight compartments sealed off by double-cylinder doors—was an indication that White Star saw value in allaying fears of vulnerability. As the *New York Times* reporter said of his experience on the *Olympic*, the thought that disaster could strike is something that heightens the senses. Everyone was conscious that transporting the luxuries of the French court or the English country home to the middle of the icy Atlantic was cheating nature and that nature could try to reclaim its supremacy.

Our knowledge of the band's movements during the next four days can be assumed by what is known of the normal routine on transatlantic liners and supplemented by the few firsthand observations of passengers who survived. Although the musicians were to become eight of the most celebrated men to sail on the *Titanic*, they maintained a low profile. They were to be listened to, not watched, and were as anonymous to those they entertained as waiters were to those they served. If they played badly, it would be noted, but if they played well, it would be accepted as something that first-class passengers deserved.

The musicians were playing to a sophisticated audience, men and women who were used to buying the best of everything. There were, after all, a leading novelist, painter, journalist, actress, and Broadway producer on board. These socialites consumed culture in the same way they consumed champagne and caviar. Jean Hippach of Chicago, after noting that the band played three "programmes" each day—before luncheon, in the afternoon, and after dinner—went on to say: "They were all real musicians and were appreciated by the people on board who were the finest lot of people I ever crossed with—people of leisure and good breeding, all of them." Jean Hippach was only sixteen at the time.

The quintet also played in the second-class saloon and may have played some lighter fare there. Mme Juliette Laroche wrote to her father after leaving Cherbourg: "I am writing you from the reading room ['*salon de lecture*'] and there is a concert next to me: a violin, two cellos [and] a piano." This is not only interesting in that it places the musicians in second class for a session, but also mentions them as a quartet. Since she was looking at the musicians as she wrote, it's unlikely she was mistaken.

Another second-class passenger who recorded seeing the band was Kate Buss, a thirty-six-year-old English woman from Sittingbourne, Kent, on her way to meet her American fiancé in San Diego, California. She kept a journal in which she referred to some of the people she encountered by her own invented names. Dr. Ernest Moraweck, of Frankfort, Kentucky, became "Doctor Man"; an unidentified passenger became "Mr Sad Man"; and Wes Woodward became "Cello Man."

On April 11, as the ship sailed away from Ireland, she had written: "We have three promenade decks, one above the other. Each one has a sort of hall lounge, and on the one above my cabin the band plays every afternoon and evening. The Cello Man is a favourite of mine. Every time he finishes a piece he looks at me and we smile."

On April 12, she was again listening to the orchestra: "Saw Doctor just after dinner and reminded him of his promise to ask our Cello Man to play a solo. Says he would if I'd go to Kentucky. He waited for us and we took our seats on the stairs. Too late to arrange, so going to ask for it tomorrow. Cello Man quite nice. Very superior bandsman, and he always smiles his parting to us."

The next day she persisted, arranging to meet the doctor and go together to listen to the orchestra. "I couldn't get near to ask our Cello Man for a solo. Went up and had a walk with Doctor; then down on deck . . . After luncheon we went with a French lady to hear her sing. We had previously met the Cello Man and asked if he would play a solo. He is quite gentlemanly. He agreed and we chatted, amongst other things, about the *Olympic*. He was on her when the accident happened."

Violet Jessop, the first-class stewardess who knew Woodward and Hume from the *Olympic*, claimed to have recalled the group's final performance on the fateful night. "On that Sunday evening," she wrote, "the music was at its gayest, led by young Jock, the first violin. When I ran into him during the interval he laughingly called out to me in his rich Scotch accent that he was about to give them 'a real tune, a Scotch tune to finish up with.' Always so eager and full of life was Jock."

Some have questioned the accuracy of this memory and think she may have confused it with another night because of the mention of an interval and the implication that Hume was the bandleader. Could he have led the four-piece band in the second-class saloon that Juliette Laroche noticed? Could the interval have been some downtime between two performances in different areas of the ship? Her description of Hume's personality seems spot on, as does her memory of his keenness to slip some Scottish music into the repertoire, but as the final piece of music on the night of April 14, it contradicts the memory of the Countess of Rothes that they played something by Offenbach.

Kate Buss didn't identify the final tune but claimed in her diary that her friend "Mr N" (twenty-eight-year-old Robert Douglas Norman from Glasgow) had told her that it had been played at his request and that they had also played "Nearer, My God, to Thee." "That night," she wrote, "the pianist had asked me if I would mind taking round the subscription [collecting tips] as I had appreciated the music. At supper I talked Mr N and Doctor P into promising to do it for me and as a joke the former rehearsed a possible speech, and then said: 'Meet me on the upper deck at six in the morning. I will talk it over.' I saw the pianist as I was going to bed, and promised. That was the last I saw of them."

Colonel Archibald Gracie mentioned the musicians in passing when describing his after-dinner socializing on the night of April 14 with "playboy" James Clinch Smith and architect Edward Kent. "According to usual custom we adjourned to the Palm Room, with many others, for the usual coffee at individual tables where we listened to the always delightful music of the *Titanic*'s band. On these occasions, full dress was always *en règle*; and it was a subject both of observation and admiration, that there were so many beautiful women—then especially in evidence—aboard the ship."

Earlier that day Gracie had been at the church service in the dining room. Although he didn't mention the band, it would have been one of their duties to provide music for the hymns. He particularly remembered singing "Oh God Our Help in Ages Past" both because of the poignancy of the words in retrospect and the fact that the next time he sang it was at a memorial service for his friend, Clinch, for whom the hymn was a favorite.

O God our help in ages past,
Our hope for years to come,
Our shelter from the stormy blast
And our eternal home.

One of Gracie's ship companions was Helen Churchill Candee, a spirited American who was to become a role model for later generations of feminists. Divorced from an abusive husband, she'd developed her own career as a novelist, journalist, and interior designer, going on to become a traveler and explorer as well. In 1900 she had written an influential book *How Women May Earn a Living* and had served as a consultant when the West Wing of President Roosevelt's White House was remodeled in 1906. She had been traveling in Europe to research *The Tapestry Book* when she was given the news that her son had been badly injured in a car crash in America. For her the *Titanic* was the fastest and most convenient way of getting to his bedside.

Her impressions of life on the *Titanic* were published on May 4, 1912, in *Collier's Weekly* and were among the most evocative descriptions of life in first class with its indiscretions, love of luxury, and mild flirtations. She described the same dinner and after-dinner drinks referred to by Gracie, but with a designer's eye for detail, a novelist's sense of atmosphere, and a journalist's ear for conversation. She also took more note of the band than most.

"At dinner, two hours later, the scene might have been in London, or New York, with the men in evening jackets, the women shining in pale satins and clinging gauze," she wrote.

> The prettiest girl even wore a glittering frock of dancing length, with silver fringe around her dainty satin feet. And after dinner there was coffee served to all at little tables around the great general lounging place, for here the orchestra played.
>
> Some said it was poor on its Wagner work, others said the violin was weak. But that was for conversation's sake, for nothing on board was more popular than the orchestra. You could see that by the way everyone refused to leave it. And everyone asked of it some favourite hit. The prettiest girl asked for dance music, and clocked her satin heels and swayed her adolescent arms to the rhythm. He of the Two who had walked the deck [her reference to the British businessman Hugh Woolner] asked for Dvorak, while she asked for Puccini, and both got their liking, for the orchestra was adroit and willing.

The Puccini was probably from *Madame Butterfly*, the Dvorak could have been "Humoresque," a piece in the White Star music book. Mahala Douglas specifically remembered Puccini and Tchaikovsky being played. Lucy Noel Martha, Countess of Rothes, remembered that the last piece they had played that night was from Jacques Offenbach's 1881 opera *The Tales of Hoffman*. This was possibly "The Barcarolle." When she heard it being played in a restaurant in the spring of 1913, she felt "a cold and intense horror" but didn't immediately know why. Then she remembered the last time she'd heard it.

Although we know the type of music the band played and what may have been in the White Star music book, there are very few tunes that we can be absolutely certain the band played. Chief Steward Edward Wheeler said the pieces were "selections from the opera and the latest popular melodies from England and America." Amelie Icard recalled Gounod's "Ave Maria," based on a melody by J. S. Bach, and something from Lehár's operetta *La Veuve Joyeuse* being played after lunch. Others mentioned ragtime, waltzes, fox-trots, show songs, and, as already mentioned, classical. There has been speculation that they played "Oh, You Beautiful Doll" and "Pleasant Memories," but these claims aren't sourced.

Although recordings were available in 1912, they hadn't become the primary vehicle for making a hit song. Sheet music still ruled and power resided with songwriters and their publishers. The new wonder child of songwriting was twenty-two-year-old Irving Berlin, whose breakthrough song in 1911 was "Alexander's Ragtime Band." By the end of that year he'd had more than a dozen hits including, "Everybody's Doing It Now," "I Want to Be in Dixie," "You've Got Me Hypnotized," and "When You Kiss an Italian Girl."

Ragtime, popularized by Scott Joplin more than a decade before, would go on to start a dance craze that would make some observers think America was having a collective breakdown. Berlin's songs, with their simple catchy melodies and straightforward conversational lyrics, were indications of a new, more relaxed era. Said Berlin: "My ambition is to reach the heart of the average American, not the highbrow nor the lowbrow, but that vast intermediate crew which is the real soul of the country. The highbrow is likely to be superficial, over trained, and supersensitive. The lowbrow is warped, subnormal. My public is the real people."

In 1912 ragtime was as controversial as rock and roll would become in 1957. The syncopated beat was initially disturbing and commentators were divided as to whether it was merely a reflection of the increased pace of life or whether the music itself made people behave more frenetically. "A man playing ragtime can't keep still," said the conductor of New York's Trocadero Orchestra. "The music grips player and audience alike and sets everybody on the jump." An English music publisher explained: "We live in an age of rush. Ragtime music suits the period. The old song or smoking concert, with its slow, gentle boys' chorus, is finished. Life is too short for it . . . The whole busy world is now humming to the new music which rushes just as fast as modern, hustling life." The *Music Trade Review* thought ragtime might simply be a protest against monotony. Something different yet crude is often preferable to something familiar yet perfect. "This rage for change is a law of life, and is illustrated in architecture and literature as well as in music. It is illustrated even in the fashions governing dress."

Whatever the band played, it agreed with Helen Churchill Candee. It was music to relax to, music to oil the flow of conversation. One of her group told stories, one of them told jokes, and the normally restrained ones began to lose their inhibitions. "The lady felt divinely flattered to be in such company," she remarked of herself. The music stopped at eleven. "Folk drifted off to their big cabins, with happy 'see-you-in-the-mornings,' until a group formed itself alone, and the only sounds the musicians made were those of instruments being shut in their velvet beds."

11

"A Solemnity
Too Deep for Words."

It was 11:45 at night according to ship's time when the *Titanic* grazed along the iceberg that would send it to the ocean bed. The musicians would have been in their cabins probably having a smoke before retiring. They would have felt the collision more sharply than those higher up because E Deck on the starboard side was close to the point of impact. Lawrence Beesley, above on D Deck, only sensed an increased vibration: "Nothing more than that. No sound of a crash or anything else. No sense of shock, no jar that felt like one heavy body meeting another." Lady Duff-Gordon's maid, Laura Francatelli, who was on E Deck, felt a distinct shudder and when she left her cabin twenty minutes later noticed that the corridors were flooding. E Deck was already below the waterline.

Ice fields were an ever-present threat to transatlantic ships at this time of year and after only two days at sea the *Titanic* had begun to receive warnings from eastbound ships. On April 14 alone, it had heard from the *Caronia, Noordam, Baltic, Amerika, Californian,* and *Mesaba.* One message wasn't passed to the bridge, one was passed on but ended up in J. Bruce Ismay's pocket, and yet another was ignored as the *Titanic's* wireless operators struggled with the volume of messages needing to be sent on behalf of passengers. When the iceberg that would do the damage was first spotted, it was only around five hundred yards away. The engines were consequently cut and the ship turned toward port by the helmsman, but there wasn't enough time to sufficiently navigate so large a vessel and therefore, although the bow avoided the ice, the starboard side rubbed along it in what at the time seemed like a glancing blow.

Passengers out on the open decks initially thought the worst that could have taken place was damage to the paintwork. Ice fragments from the towering block had tumbled onto the decks and some people were picking them up in handfuls and starting snowball fights. But, in fact, the damage had been more wounding than if the ship had rammed the berg head on, crumpled the bow, and been spun around. Projections from the wall of ice had acted like tin openers, slicing into the steel plates and allowing water to seep into the much-vaunted bulkhead compartments. These had been designed on the premise that only one or two of the compartments were ever likely to be penetrated. If more than two were allowed to flood, of course, the weight of water taken on would eventually drag the ship down.

According to passenger Laura Francatelli, the potential gravity of the situation was recognised earlier on E Deck than on the upper decks where men continued to drink, read books in the library, and play cards. Shortly after the impact she was informed that the ship had hit an iceberg but was told that it was nothing to worry about. By 12:05 the situation was tangibly worse, as she described in a letter to a friend: "Then the water was on my deck, coming along the corridor and I found all the people, running up and down the stairs. Oh Marion, that was a sickening moment. I felt myself go like marble."

There is only one account of the musicians making their way to their position. It comes from stewardess Violet Jessop, who knew Woodward and Hume from their time on the *Olympic*. She was in her bunk on either E or F Deck and heard a "low, rending, crunching, ripping sound" on impact but didn't leave her cabin until the call to lifeboats came. On the way up the stairs she passed Captain Smith, J. Bruce Ismay, Chief Purser Herbert McElroy, and the ship's surgeon, Dr. O'Laughlin, none of whom seemed overly concerned. She wrote that as she turned at the top of the staircase, "I ran into Jock, the bandleader and his crowd with their instruments. 'Funny, they must be going to play,' thought I, and at this late hour! Jock smiled in passing, looking rather pale for him, remarking, 'Just going to give them a tune to cheer things up a bit,' and passed on."

By 12:15 a.m. the musicians had set up on the Promenade Deck and played for around twenty-five minutes in the entrance as the passengers awaited instructions. Jack Thayer, only seventeen at the time, recalled them playing there as crowds milled around. Then they moved upstairs to the Boat Deck level of the grand staircase, where there was a piano, before eventually moving out onto the Boat Deck itself. This fits with Lawrence Beesley's account of seeing a cellist walking down the deck at 12:40 a.m. "Soon after the men had left the starboard side, I saw a bandsman—the 'cellist—come round the vestibule corner from the staircase entrance and run down the now deserted starboard deck, his 'cello trailing behind him, the spike dragging along the floor." This was probably Woodward.

According to an unidentified third-class steward, who spoke to the *Western Daily Mercury*: "As the musicians ran after their instruments they were laughed at by several members of the crew who did not realize how serious matters were." According to a separate account in the *Sphere*, this was because they thought the band members were anxious to save their instruments. The crew didn't realize they were about to play.

What has never been absolutely certain is how many of the eight musicians were involved in this exercise, as they'd previously worked as two separate groups with different repertoires. If they combined, what did the two pianists, Percy Taylor and Theo Brailey, play after they were out on the Boat Deck itself? It seems unlikely that they would have hauled a piano onto the deck of a sinking ship. Others have questioned the ability of the cellists to remain in place once the ship listed beyond a certain degree because cellists need to be firmly seated. The survivors mostly referred to "the band" or "the ship's orchestra" without enumerating them.

The two sources that did bother to describe the size of the band suggest that all the musicians were present. Within a week of the *Carpathia* arriving in New York, the *Brooklyn Eagle* ran a story that acknowledged the existence of a five-man "saloon orchestra" and a three-man "deck band." The story specifically said that the deck band was "known to have joined Hartley when the call came for music." As the *Brooklyn Eagle* had interviewed survivors, it's reasonable to assume that this is where the information came from. The other source is survivor Elizabeth Nye who, when describing her experience to author Walter Lord in a 1955 letter, said that "the ship's orchestra of ten young men were standing knees deep in water playing." She got the number wrong, but it was clearly a guess at eight rather than five. Lord didn't use her comment when he wrote *A Night to Remember*.

It's possible that Brailey and Taylor could have continued playing on other instruments once they moved away from the upright piano at the top of the staircase. We know, for example, that Hume had two violins with him and that Brailey was a multi-instrumentalist. The fact that the musicians played for the passengers as the lifeboats were lowered can't seriously be questioned. There were a handful of survivors who claimed not to have heard them, but the evidence for the music is far too substantial to ignore.

When Frederick Barrett, a twenty-eight-year-old English crew member, was asked at the *Titanic* inquiry whether he had heard the band playing, he answered: "I had not heard the band; my friends told me they heard it; some of my mates said they heard it. I did not hear it." Yet he was in lifeboat 13 in the company of Hilda Slater, who heard them playing "lively airs," and Lawrence Beesley, who heard them playing the hymn "Nearer, My God, to Thee." Thomas Oxenham oddly enough recalled men singing "Nearer, My God, to Thee" on deck but denied that the musicians were involved. "It was impossible for a band to play," he said, "because all the instruments were below in the quarters and the hatches were battened down."

Why the band came to be playing in these circumstances is a question that will never be satisfactorily answered. Pierre Maréchal, the French aviator, informed the chairman of the Amalgamated Musicians' Union that they'd been told to do it. He was sure that instructions had come down from Captain Smith, possibly via Purser McElroy, saying that they should play in order to prevent panic. The sound of bright music would have suggested that even if all was not well, at least all was under control. He reasoned that in the captain's mind, the eventual deaths of eight men were a reasonable sacrifice for the saving of hundreds of passengers.

If Maréchal had hard evidence, he didn't mention it. He was certainly a figure influential enough to have spoken to J. Bruce Ismay and Captain Smith as the ship went down. A steward who spoke to the *Western Daily Mercury* also claimed that orders had come down from the bridge. Even if

Smith had made this demand, however, the band was under no obligation to obey him. As had been made very clear from the outset, they were not employees of White Star, they had not signed the ship's articles, and they had the same rights as any other passenger to expect their safety to be a prime consideration of the crew.

The other possibility is that the idea came from Hartley and was supported by the bandsmen. By all accounts he was a man of faith, character, and moral strength. At Sunday school and later at church, the importance of sacrifice and putting the needs of others first would have been stressed. We know that he had discussed what he would do in the face of death and so he was more prepared than most.

He apparently believed that music could be more powerful than physical force in bringing order to chaos. John Carr, the *Celtic* bandsman previously quoted, had played on ships with Hartley, and in April 1912 told the *New York Times*: "I don't suppose he waited to be sent for, but after finding how dangerous the situation was he probably called his men together and began playing. I know that he often said that music was a bigger weapon for stopping disorder than anything on earth. He knew the value of the weapon he had, and I think he proved his point."

Why he would have said such a thing is not clear, because preventing disorder would seem to be the last thing on the mind of a bandsman playing in the first-class lounges of transatlantic liners, but his point is valid and has since been supported by research into the psychological and neurological effects of music. It also displays Hartley as someone who took his faith, his position, and his craft seriously. Sarah Stap, who like Violet Jessop, had been a stewardess on the *Olympic*, didn't believe that the band had been coerced. At forty-seven years of age, she had vast experience of ships and the ways of captains. She had served on the *Baltic*, *Adriatic*, and *Celtic* and was the daughter of master mariner Captain Henry Stap of the White Star Line. "We could hear the music of the band all the time," she told the *Birkenhead News*. "They were heroes if you like. I must say that everything that has been said about them is perfectly true. They were not asked to play but did it absolutely on their own initiative."

There were sixteen lifeboats on the *Titanic*, divided between both sides, and they were lowered into the sea over a sixty-five-minute period.

Additionally there were four Englehardt collapsible boats kept in reserve. The passengers were mostly calm as the boats were winched down, although husbands were parted from wives and fathers from children because of the established "women and children first" policy and this led to poignant scenes of farewell. At first many of the passengers were reluctant to leave, feeling safer on the listing liner than in a dark and flimsy lifeboat on the freezing Atlantic with no provisions, no heating, and the vague promise that the *Olympic* was somewhere in the vicinity. Many passengers spoke of the unreality of the situation, as though they were observing something being acted out rather than being participants.

Despite the awfulness of what was happening, the backdrop was a scene of beauty: a clear sky, a bright moon, clearly visible stars, flat undisturbed water, and an immense liner blazing with pinholes of light. The music would have carried farther than usual because for most of the time there were no competing sounds from engines or waves. Passengers who left from both port and starboard told similar stories of being able to hear the band as they were quickly rowed away to avoid the inevitable drag of the suction. Emily Rugg claimed she could hear the band from a mile away.

What the band played has always been more a matter of controversy than whether it played at all. This is sometimes presented as an issue raised by modern historians, but it was there from the very beginning in the divergence of the accounts given by Harold Bride to the *New York Times* and by the survivors on the *Carpathia* to Carlos Hurd for the Pultizer newspapers. Had the musicians gone down playing a tune known as "Autumn" or the music of "Nearer, My God, to Thee"? The public inquiries in America and England raised the additional issue of whether they had played any religious music at all. Some witnesses claimed that they'd stuck to popular tunes and that hymns would have been inappropriate at such a time of despair.

The biggest opponent of the story that they'd played hymns was the wealthy merchant Archibald Gracie. In his account written soon after arriving back in America, he said:

> If, as has been reported, 'Nearer, My God, To Thee' was one of the selections, I assuredly should have noticed it and regarded it as a tactless warning of immediate death to us and one likely to create a panic

that our special efforts were directed towards avoiding, and which we accomplished to the fullest extent. I know of only two survivors whose names are cited by the newspapers as authority for the statement that this hymn was one of those played. On the other hand, all whom I have questioned or corresponded with, including the best qualified, testified emphatically to the contrary.

In November 1912, shortly before his death, Gracie gave a talk at the University Club in Washington DC in which he went further, saying that if they had dared play that hymn they would have been forcibly restrained by the men on board who were trying to calm the women. "If the band had played that familiar hymn, panic would have resulted. Fixing the minds of the passengers on the possibility of their being nearer to God, and I say it seriously, would have been the last thing they wanted."

Most passengers who mentioned the band didn't describe the music in any detail, but of those who did, the bias was toward the "lively airs" that Hilda Slater reported hearing. Jack Thayer said he heard "Star Spangled Banner" and someone else the hit tune "In the Shadows." Algernon Barkworth heard a waltz. Lily May Futrelle, wife of the novelist Jacques Futrelle, heard Irving Berlin's "Alexander's Ragtime Band." Gracie, who watched from A Deck as the lifeboats were being lowered on the port side, wrote: "It was now the band began to play, and continued while the boats were being lowered. We considered this a wise provision tending to allay excitement. I did not recognize any of the tunes, but I know they were cheerful and were not hymns." Second Officer Charles Lightoller, who helped lower lifeboat 6 on the port side at 12:55, said that as he did so, "I could hear the band playing a cheery sort of music. I don't like jazz music as a rule, but I was glad to hear it that night. I think it helped us all."[1]

The most likely explanation for this confusion is that they played both Popular music and hymns. After all, by the time the ship started its final heave, they would have been playing for more than two hours. If each piece took four minutes to play, that would have allowed for thirty tunes. It's also worth considering that not all popular tunes were "lively" and not all hymns were "reminders of death." Dr. Washington Dodge told the *San Francisco Bulletin* that before the lifeboats began to be lowered, the orchestra was "playing a lively tune," but added that when he was out on the water he heard the music of the hymn "Lead, Kindly Light."

It can be difficult for contemporary commentators to appreciate the place that hymns occupied in the lives of typical Edwardians. They were not indicators of doom and gloom but of hope and joy. They were also a register of commonly held assumptions about the most important issues in life. The difference between the early twentieth century and the early twenty-first century can be illustrated by Elizabeth Nye's reminiscence: "On Sunday the 14th it became very cold. We couldn't stay out on deck so we all came together in the dining room for a hymn sing." It's hard to imagine passengers on a twenty-first-century cruise liner opting for such an alternative.

When survivors specifically mentioned that hymns were played, the consensus was that it was toward the end. It would make sense that the band members played the popular tunes as the lifeboats were loaded and the more reflective pieces once they only had themselves and their destinies to contemplate. Survivor Charles William Daniels (aka Robert William Daniel), who was on lifeboat 3 lowered at 1:00, recalled: "All the lifeboats reached the water safely and the ship's band played as the boats were being lowered. The musicians played selections from opera and the latest popular melodies from Europe and America. Only before the final plunge did they change the character of their music. They then played 'Nearer, My God, to Thee.' We had been in the water for two hours at least [sic]."

All of the band members had been raised as churchgoers—Bricoux, Krins, and Clarke as Catholics, Hume as a Congregationalist, Woodward and Hartley as Methodists, Brailey and Taylor as Anglicans. Harley and Taylor had sung in choirs, and Hume played his violin in church. It's impossible to determine the commitment they each had to the religion of their birth, but it's likely that they all had knowledge of and affection for hymns.

The *New York Times* drew the conclusion that "Autumn," the music mentioned by Bride, referred to an Episcopalian hymn tune and claimed to have found a hymnal where this tune was the setting to words that began "God of mercy and compassion" and ended with a verse beginning "Hold me up in mighty waters / Keep my eyes on things above." This reference to "mighty waters" appeared to prove the appropriateness of this hymn to the occasion. The *Times* said that line in particular "may have suggested the hymn to some minister aboard the doomed vessel, who, it has been suggested, thereupon asked the remaining passengers to join in singing the hymn, in a last service upon the sinking ship, soon to be ended by death itself."

What no one pointed out at the time was that Bride wasn't an American Episcopalian and, even if he had been, would have been more likely to refer to a tune by the first line of the hymn's words than by its name. The tune "Autumn" wasn't in the White Star music book. Additionally, although there was a hymn known as "God of Mercy and Compassion," it wasn't in the Church of England or Methodist hymnals, and no version that anyone has been able to find, other than that discovered by a *New York Times* journalist in 1912, includes a verse about being held up in mighty waters.

"God of Mercy and Compassion" was written by Edmund Vaughan (1827–1908) and starts:

> *God of mercy and compassion*
> *Look with pity upon me*
> *Father, let me call you Father,*
> *'Tis thy child returns to thee.*

The version quoted by the *New York Times* on April 21, 1912, already deviated from this by the second line of the first stanza:

> *God of mercy and compassion!*
> *Look with pity on my pain;*
> *Hear a mournful, broken spirit*
> *Prostrate at thy feet complain.*

The only clue the *New York Times* gave about its origin was that it was found in "an Episcopalian hymn book." No doubt there was such a collection, but it couldn't have been widely used.

Walter Lord speculated that Bride may not have been referring to a hymn at all but to a hit tune of 1912 (in London, at least) called "Songe d'Automne," written by popular orchestra leader Archibald "the Waltz King" Joyce. Not only was this music commonly referred to as "Autumn," but it was also in the White Star song book carried on the *Titanic*. Lord's source for this information was Fred Vallance, bandmaster on the *Laconia* in 1912, who said there was general agreement among musicians that Bride must have been referring to the waltz tune that was an often-requested number in 1912 and popular in roller rinks and cafés. In several long, hand-written letters to Lord in 1957 written in response to the speculations about music in *A Night to Remember*, he argued that the mournful opening to Joyce's popular tune could have been mistaken for a hymn and the jerky finish could have been heard as ragtime.[2]

Interestingly enough, Bride made no further comment about "Autumn" and, when he arrived back in England after the sinking, he was the honored guest at a memorial service given by his local church in Shortlands, Kent, on May 19, where his father read the lesson and a solo of "Nearer, My God, to Thee" was performed.

The reports of the band playing "Nearer, My God, to Thee" were enthusiastically received, particularly in England where the "Autumn" story was hardly pursued. The words of the hymn seemed so fitting to a culture where religious sentiment still held sway. The gist of the song is that whatever hardships befall us, they can only serve to bring us closer to God. In terms of the *Titanic* disaster, the image was of people being dragged to the depths of the sea and yet, paradoxically, scaling the heights of heaven. It was based in part on the story of Jacob's dream (Genesis 28:10–22), in which he sees "a ladder set up on the earth, and the top of it reached to heaven; and behold the angels of God ascending and descending on it." It may have been a particular favorite at the Bethel Chapel in Colne because Jacob marked the spot where he had the dream with a stone "and he called the name of that place Bethel."

> *Nearer, my God, to Thee.*
> *Nearer to Thee!*
> *Even though it be a cross*
> *That raiseth me;*
> *Still all my song shall be,*
> *Nearer, my God, to Thee*
> *Nearer to Thee!*

Though, like a wanderer,
The sun gone down,
Darkness comes over me,
My rest a stone;
Yet in my dreams I'd be
Nearer, my God, to thee,
Nearer to thee.

There let my way appear
Steps unto heaven,
All that Thou sendest me
In mercy given;
Angels to beckon me
Nearer, my God, to Thee,
Nearer to Thee!

Then, with my waking thoughts
Bright with Thy praise,
Out of my stony griefs
Bethel I'll raise;
So by my woes to be
Nearer, my God, to Thee,
Nearer to Thee!

And when on joyful wing
Cleaving the sky,
Sun, moon, and stars forgot,
Upwards I fly,
Still all my song shall be,
Nearer, my God, to Thee,
Nearer to Thee.

Although popular among mainstream Protestants, the words were actually written by a Unitarian who was smitten by doubt. Raised in Christian orthodoxy, she was concerned about the faith she had lost. For the poet

Sarah Flower Adams, the words were an expression of her one remaining certainty, which was that whatever spiritual torments she endured, God was always there. When the hymn first appeared in 1841 (with music by her sister Ella), and her Unitarian beliefs were made known, the Baptists and Methodists refused to include it in their collections.[3]

American theologian J. Gresham Machen, writing in the 1920s, thought it was not as theologically sound as it first appeared:

> The thought is not opposed to Christianity. It is found in the New Testament. But many persons have the impression, because the word "cross" is found in the hymn, that there is something specifically Christian about it, and that it has something to do with the gospel. This impression is entirely false. In reality, the cross that is spoken of is not the cross of Christ, but our own cross; the verse simply means that our own crosses or trials may be a means to bring us nearer to God. It is a perfectly good thought, but certainly it is not the gospel.

There were suggestions after the sinking that journalist and spiritualist W. T. Stead, who calmly went down on the ship, may have requested that the band play "Nearer, My God, to Thee." This wasn't because anyone overheard such a conversation, but because he'd recently authored a book called *Hymns That Have Helped Me*, for which he asked well-known people for their recommendations. "In our pilgrimage through life we discover the hymns which help," Stead wrote in the introduction. He continued:

> We come out of trials and temptations with hymns clinging to our memory like burrs. Some of us could almost use the hymnbook as the key to our autobiography. Hymns, like angels and other ministers of grace, often help us and disappear into the void. It is not often that the hymn of our youth is the hymn of our old age. Experience of life is the natural selector of the truly human hymnal.
>
> There is a curious and not a very creditable shrinking on the part of many to testify as to their experience in the deeper matters of the soul. It is an inverted egotism—selfishness masquerading in disguise of reluctance to speak of self. Wanderers across the wilderness of Life ought not to be

chary of telling their fellow travelers where they found a green oasis, the healing spring, or the shadow of a great rock in the desert land. It is not regarded as egotism when the passing steamer signals across the Atlantic wave news of her escape from perils of iceberg or fog, or welcome news of good cheer.

Titanic featuring violinist Jonathan Evans-Jones as bandleader Wallace Hartley (1997).

The Prince of Wales chose "Nearer, My God, to Thee" for Stead's project and it became widely known as the prince's favorite hymn. He thought there was no hymn "more touching nor one that goes more truly to the heart." Stead printed all five verses along with two stories of people who had gained sustenance from the words. The second of these was of a boy soldier in the American Civil War who had lost both arms at Fort Donelson and yet "died on the battlefield singing with his last breath, 'Nearer, my God, to Thee.' It might fairly be called the most popular hymn among all sorts and conditions of men in America."

It was also the favorite hymn of President McKinley, who supposedly used the words as a form of prayer as he lay dying after being shot by the anarchist Leon Czolgosz at the Temple of Music in Buffalo, New York, in September 1901. The song was sung at his funeral and at all the various memorial services that followed.

One of the most compelling pieces of evidence, though, for the use of "Nearer, My God, to Thee" was the fact that it was the best-loved hymn of Wallace Hartley and had been introduced to the Bethel Chapel by Wallace's father, Albion Hartley, when he was choirmaster. A friend from Colne told the *British Weekly*: "It was the custom of the Bethel church choir leader to choose the hymn or chant after prayer and Mr. Albion Hartley often selected 'Nearer, My God, to Thee.' The hymn was also a great favourite with his son, the bandmaster of the *Titanic*, for a cousin mentioned that he would often be kept waiting for Wallace to go and play cricket because he was practicing 'Nearer, My God, to Thee' in variations on the violin."

Ellwand Moody, Hartley's friend from the *Mauretania*, told the *Leeds Mercury* in April 1912: "I remember one day I asked him what he would do if he were ever on a sinking ship and he replied 'I don't think I would do better than play "Oh God Our Help in Ages Past" or "Nearer, My God, to Thee".'" In a statement attributed to Hartley, but not sourced and therefore dubious, he confirmed it as his favorite hymn but added: "I'm keeping that one reserved for my funeral." E. J. Elliot, president of the Musicians Union in Louisville, Kentucky, told the *Brooklyn Eagle* that it was a tradition for American musicians to play the music of the hymn at the graveside of departed colleagues. "I believe, knowing they were doomed as a result of their own heroism, the members of the ship's orchestra thus commended their own souls to their God, giving expression to their petition in the notes of their instruments."

In his 1986 book *The Night Lives On*, however, the follow-up to *A Night to Remember*, Walter Lord raised an interesting issue that questioned the validity of the story of the tune's use. He pointed out that although apparently both Americans and Britons recognized it, the hymn was sung to different tunes on either side of the Atlantic. The Church of England used a tune called "Horbury." The Methodists in England preferred a tune written by Arthur Sullivan (of Gilbert and Sullivan) named "Propior Deo" and Americans generally used a Lowell Mason tune known as "Bethany." He concluded: "Unless the band played all three versions (an absurdity), more than half of those who remembered the hymn must have been mistaken."[4]

This point has since been repeated over and over by various *Titanic* commentators, leading to the belief that the story of the band playing "Nearer, My God, to Thee" must be a myth. Lord didn't take into account, however, that Hartley wasn't just a Methodist, he was an Independent Methodist, a branch of Methodism mostly concentrated in the northwest of England. In the *Independent Methodist Church Hymnal* of 1902, "Nearer, My God, to Thee" is #529. In the accompanying music book, two tunes are suggested—#256, which is Arthur Sullivan's "Propior Deo," and #258, which is Lowell Mason's tune "Bethany," here referred to as "Bethel." Therefore it's fairly certain that Hartley, as the choirmaster's son, would at least have been aware of the two tunes and, as he would very likely have worshipped at Methodist churches in New York during his many visits involving weekend stopovers, would have heard the tune played.

The *Primitive Methodist Hymnal* of 1889, which Hartley may also have known, had both these tunes, plus "Horbury." Lowell Mason's tune had become well-known in England because it was featured in songbooks by the American musician Ira Sankey, which became very popular in the late nineteenth century when Sankey toured Britain as music director and singer with evangelist Dwight Moody.

Another point worth making is that "Bethany" (or "Bethel") and "Propior Deo," although in different time signatures, can sound very similar. What may have aided the process of recognition is the fact that passengers began singing along, both on deck and in the lifeboats. Even if the tunes were different, anyone knowing the words would have been able to join in without too much difficulty. The differences in the tunes could have gone unnoticed beneath the torrent of familiar words.

A Night to Remember featuring Charles Belchier as Wallace Hartley (1958).

The final timing question is—were they actually playing "Nearer, My God, to Thee" during the very last moments of the *Titanic*? An English passenger, Ada Clarke, made the case that they were. "They were brave and splendid, all the men. They died like brave men. At the last, all the men were kneeling and there floated out across the water the strains of 'Nearer, My God, to Thee.' I could hear it and saw the band men kneeling, too." Her story has been questioned because she left the ship fifty minutes before it went down and is unlikely to have been able to see such physical detail from her position when it sank.

Annie Martin, a stewardess who had previously been on the *Olympic*, was approached by the *Liverpool Daily Post* when she arrived back in England and was asked: "It's true that the band was playing as the ship was sinking, isn't it?" Her answer was: "Oh yes. They were playing. When we left the side of the ship [in lifeboat 11 at 1:25] the men were sitting on the companionway on the A Deck forward with lifebelts by their sides. They were making no attempt to put the belts on. Many of them were smoking. Others were beating time to the music with their feet. Even then, they thought they were safe. Everybody thought everybody would be saved."

One of the most dramatic accounts of the final moments came from thirty-four-year-old coal trimmer Thomas Patrick "Paddy" Dillon, who was interviewed by a local newspaper in Plymouth, England, after arriving back on the Red Star Line ship *Lapland* on April 28. He said he was one of the last to leave the ship and that the poop deck was by then at an angle of around sixty degrees and after a second explosion the bow "seemed to bob up and then break clean off like a piece of carrot." The musicians had been playing on the deck, he said, but they then slid off the deck along with Captain Smith.

"There was one musician left," he said. "He was the violinist and was playing the air of the hymn 'Nearer, My God, to Thee.' The notes of this music were the last thing I heard before I went off the poop and felt myself going headlong into the icy water with the engines and machinery buzzing in my ears." He estimated that he dropped two fathoms in the sea and when he came back up he was picked up by lifeboat 4. Another survivor interviewed at the same time said: "They began to render hymn tunes and continued to do to the last. While playing 'Nearer, My God, to Thee' the water was washing over their feet, and in a very short time they disappeared beneath the waves."

There were several other survivors who swore the musicians played until the very end and didn't pack their instruments away in order to dive into the water. American Caroline Brown, who left on collapsible D at 2:05, said: "The band played marching from deck to deck, and as the ship went under I could still hear the music. The musicians were up to their knees in water when last I saw them." American Alice Leeder, who left at 1:15 on lifeboat 8, wrote a letter the next day on the *Carpathia* in which she said: "I shall never forget the sight of that beautiful boat as she went down, the orchestra playing to the last, the lights burning until they were extinguished by the waves. It sounds so unreal, like a scene on the stage."

Another survivor claimed that at the end they played nothing but the hymn: "Suddenly the band stopped. The leader moved his baton and in slow, solemn tones the air 'Nearer, My God, to Thee' was wafted across the water to our ears. The band played the hymn continuously until their instruments were choked off by the swirling water." Charlotte Collyer, who had to leave her husband on the ship, said: "They kept it up to the very end. Only the engulfing ocean had power to drown them into silence. The band was playing 'Nearer, My God, to Thee.' I could hear it distinctly. The end was very close."

The evidence for "Nearer, My God, to Thee" being the band's final song seems overwhelming. A reporter from the *Witney Gazette*, who interviewed many of the 167 survivors brought back to Plymouth on the *Lapland*, concluded: "Practically all of the survivors agree that the band played hymns and not 'ragtime' tunes. After his fellow musicians had been washed away the violinist continued playing 'Nearer, My God, to Thee' until he went under with the ship."

Speaking to the *Daily Sketch*, the *Titanic*'s chief steward Edward Wheelton, who was rescued by lifeboat 11, said. "It was only just before the liner made her final plunge that the character of the programme was changed, and then they struck up 'Nearer, My God, to Thee.'" An unnamed survivor interviewed by the *Western Daily Mercury* said: "I shall never forget hearing the strains of that beautiful hymn as I was leaving the sinking ship. It was always a favourite hymn of mine, but at such a time and under such tragic circumstances it had for me a solemnity too deep for words. No praise could be sufficient for those courageous musicians whom we left behind. They were heroes to a man."

The only report of anyone from the band speaking to someone during this time was one of a musician "with a French accent" helping a woman into a lifeboat and another of Hartley giving Florence Ware, a second-class passenger from Bristol, his silver pocket flask with a drop of whiskey in it to keep her warm. The flask, made by James Dixon & Son of Sheffield in 1900, was auctioned in 1993 by Onslows, the British auctioneers. Doubts were subsequently raised about the authenticity of this story because Hartley was a known teetotaler and also because Mrs. Ware didn't mention this outstanding story when interviewed by the *Bristol Times* immediately after the sinking.

One can only guess what was going through the musicians' minds as hopes of rescue disappeared. While they were playing, the music would have acted as a mental safety rail and given them a purpose; but once they put down their valuable instruments, the true gravity of the moment they were facing would have rushed into their overly alert minds. They would have thought of parents, girlfriends, nephews, nieces. Hume would have thought of the child he now knew he'd never see. Brailey would have thought of the warning his father had given him.

Carlos Hurd left behind two pages of notes that were neither in his hand nor his wife's, but appear to be a timetable of events on the *Titanic* possibly collected by someone he had recruited to help him on the *Carpathia*. At the end it says the "band had been playing rag time, now playing 'Nearer, My God, to Thee.'" It mentions Hartley tapping on the bulkhead "as water swirls about his feet" and refers to Captain Smith "on bridge. As water comes to it steps forward to meet it." At 2:17 it says the lights went out. At 2:18: "band plays in darkness." At 2:20: "Ship sinks in white wake . . . One long continuous moon."

The final dive of the ship, as the bow lay submerged and the stern rose out of the water, was truly horrendous for all who witnessed it. This object of great beauty—even in its stricken condition—went down with a terrifying roar as all the boilers and internal machinery came away from their anchoring bolts and plunged through the shell of the ship, destroying everything in their way. The crashing of the machinery combined with the hissing of hot coals meeting the cold water created a sound that survivors later described as the most bloodcurdling they had ever heard. There was nothing they could compare it to.

The only sound left now was the crying of those who'd jumped into the icy water when they realized all hope of rescue had gone. Most of them would die not from drowning but from hypothermia and shock. By keeping them afloat, the life jackets designed to save them actually prolonged their agony. One survivor initially said that it was like hearing the screams of children in a playground but then corrected herself. She said it was far more horrific than that because these were the screams of adults who were fully aware of what was happening to them. The screams had nothing of the anticipation of a child. They were undiluted fear and desperation.

The rich died alongside the poor, the millionaire philanthropist alongside the impoverished Italian immigrant. No doubt the cries were in many languages and addressed to many gods. Benjamin Guggenheim and Thomas Andrews were lost, as were James Clinch Smith; Dr. Ernest Moraweck; Robert Norman; Archibald Butt; Jacques Futrelle; and Francis Davis Millet; Jack Phillips, the courageous radio operator; and Edward Smith, the captain, were never seen again.

Those fortunate enough to be in lifeboats had no idea when rescue would come or even if it would come. They didn't know which ships had been called or how close they might be. As it was, the first survivors to be picked up by the *Carpathia* weren't reached until 4:45 and the last wouldn't be rescued until 8:00. Until that time they just had to float, and to wait, and to try to keep warm, many of them after having lost parents, husbands, wives, and other relations. "I knew that no man could save me," Kate Buss wrote in her journal. "I was alone with God, and whatever happened must be for the best. I felt as I have felt before when death has stared me in the face, that I had to do nothing but wait on God's will."

12

"It Is with Great Sadness That I Have to Give You the Painful News."

Cunard's *Carpathia*, so recently home for Theo Brailey, was the first ship on the scene of the disaster. Its wireless operator, Harold Cottam, had been on his way to bed in the early minutes of April 15, when he put the headphones on for one last time and noticed there was no signal from the *Titanic*. Cottam tapped out a message: "What's wrong? Should I tell my captain?" Jack Phillips on the *Titanic* responded immediately: "Yes. It's a CQD, old man! We've hit a berg and are sinking." (The CQD signal was predecessor to the SOS.) The *Carpathia* was then around sixty miles away and at 12:45, after speaking to Captain Arthur Rostron, Cottam told Phillips that his ship would be there in around four hours. "We're turning around and steaming full force toward you."

It was a bold decision by Rostron to alter direction to meet the *Titanic*. He immediately prepared by turning the saloons into reception centers, putting the doctors on duty, and getting his ship's lifeboats ready. Never before having dealt with a disaster, he was imagining the more straightforward task of drawing alongside the stricken vessel and taking on board its passengers and crew. He never envisaged that by the time he arrived the *Titanic* would have completely disappeared.

By cutting off heating for the cabins and working the boilers to their capacity, Rostron was able to get the *Carpathia* to sail faster than she had ever sailed before, reaching the position given by Phillips less than three hours from the time of the last message. At first there was nothing to be seen, but then at 4:00 a green flare sent up by a lifeboat was seen and ten minutes later the first *Titanic* passenger from lifeboat 2 was hoisted up on a bosun's chair. The last lifeboat, number 12, came alongside at 8:00 and the last survivor came on board at 9:00. A total of 710 had made it, although 5 were to die before landfall. "Our decks and dining rooms were swarmed with the rescued, and such a pitiful sight I hope never to have to behold again," wrote Carlos Hurd's wife, Katherine, in a letter to her mother on April 18. "When we look upon the broken families all around us it makes us feel as if we would like to chuck the whole trip and run back to our own. But I suppose we will go on. Europe has certainly lost its savour to us now."

Rostron had to decide whether to head for the nearest land or head back to New York. "There was talk of turning back to Halifax, a run of about 36 hours," wrote Katherine Hurd, "but this plan was abandoned, I think because of the icebergs which were unusual in size and number for that latitude and time of year." Rostron chose the safest option, New York, and later that day Cottam sent a list of all survivors to officers on the *Olympic*, who would then pass them to White Star in New York. This was the first time that anyone on land had any inkling of the extent of the disaster. None of the musicians was on this list.

On the night of April 14, Martha Woodward woke in her bed in Headington, Oxford, convinced something had happened to her son Wes. At least, this was the story passed down in the family. As with all tragedies of this nature, the tales of warnings offered beforehand, sensations felt during, and visitations experienced afterward, have to be listened to with skepticism. A Scottish Salvation Army captain would later swear that on the fourteenth he was tending to a dying orphan girl who told him that she could see a big ship sinking with a person called Wally playing the violin coming toward her. Unknown to the child, the captain had apparently known Wallace Hartley as a boy.

The first that Britain knew about the sinking came from the evening editions of newspapers on Monday, April 15, when the story was that all had been rescued. On Tuesday, April 16, the news was bleaker. "Disaster to *Titanic* on Her Maiden Voyage" was the headline in the *Daily Sketch* with news inside that 655 were known to have been saved but 1,700 lives were feared lost. The next day it was 1,500 lost with 868 saved.

Part of the problem for the newspapers and for White Star was that no one was certain that the *Carpathia* was the only ship carrying survivors. There were vague hopes that other ships in the vicinity had rescued people. Then on April 18 came the news from White Star in Liverpool that the captain of the *Olympic* had announced: "Please allay rumours that *Virginian* has any *Titanic* passengers. Neither has the *Tunisian*. Believe only survivors on *Carpathia*." As the *Daily Sketch* put it: "The worst fears have now received official confirmation."

For the families of the musicians, the wait for final confirmation was tormenting. Hope was continually interrupted by grief and then grief was temporarily interrupted by hope. On April 17 the *Dumfries Standard* reported that among those on the *Titanic* was "Mr John Hume, son of Mr Andrew Hume, music teacher, George Street, Dumfries." It added, "No news has yet been received as to whether he is among survivors." The next day Andrew Hume visited the White Star Line office in Liverpool to find out what had happened. On April 20 the newspaper wrote: "Fears regarding the fate of Mr. John Hume, Dumfries . . . have now been practically confirmed." The next day a memorial service was held for him at the Congregational chapel he'd attended as a boy.

It was also on April 20 that Charlie Black sent handwritten letters to each set of parents announcing the loss of their sons.

It is with great sadness that I have to give you the painful news of the death of your son in the wreck of the White Star Line steamer *Titanic* this past Monday April 15th. During the time that he was employed by us we have been in every way extremely satisfied with him both for his musical talent and his excellent character. It may be a comfort for you to know to know that he died a hero having had the courage to play as the ship sank. His name has been published today in all the newspapers where he is considered to be a hero. I would be grateful if you could acknowledge receipt of this letter. I share in your grievous loss and send you my sincerest sympathy.

Charles W. Black

Ronald and Amy Brailey had been distraught at hearing no news whatsoever about their only son but then were told that he had survived. They sent a telegram to Teresa Steinhilber in Southport saying there was "no cause for despair." A few hours later they discovered that the report was wrong. Their son Theo was not among the survivors. They sent a second telegram telling Teresa of his death. She reacted so badly to the news that her parents sent her to Southport Convalescent Home to recover from the shock.

Letters and cards began pouring into the homes of the musicians' bereaved families. Ronald Brailey published a letter of thanks in the spiritualist magazine *Light* in which he quoted from Shakespeare's *Troilus and Cressida*:

> Permit me to ask that the many correspondents who have sent to our home their sympathies over our great, great loss, will accept this acknowledgement, as it is impossible for me to reply to them individually. Truly we have found that "one touch of nature makes the whole world kin," for from all over the British Isles we have received letters filled with expressions of deepest sympathy. The writers are of all shades of religious belief, and out of the oneness of hearts they have poured balm upon our sorrow for the physical loss of our earthly light and joy.

Soon after the sinking was confirmed, White Star contracted the Commercial Cable Company to collect any passengers' bodies floating in the Atlantic. The CS *Mackay-Bennett*, one of its ships used to lay and repair transatlantic telegraph cables, was converted into a floating morgue for the task. On April 17 it set out from Halifax, Nova Scotia, with a search crew, hastily built coffins, an Anglican priest, an embalmer, and a team of undertakers. The job was to bring back as many bodies as possible for identification and burial.

Once the debris field was reached, search parties went out in small cutters and hauled the bodies aboard with nets and poles. On April 22 cable engineer Frederick Hamilton wrote in his journal:

> We steamed close past the iceberg today, and endeavored to photograph it, but rain is falling and we do not think the results will be satisfactory. We are now standing eastwards amongst great quantities of wreckage. Cutter lowered to examine a lifeboat, but it is too smashed to tell anything, even the name is not visible. All round is splintered woodwork, cabin fittings, mahogany fronts of drawers, carvings, all wrenched away from their fastenings, deck chairs, and then more bodies. Some of these are fifteen miles distant from those picked up yesterday.

In seven days they found 306 bodies, far more than they had anticipated, and 116 of these were buried at sea because of lack of identification. All of the bodies were numbered, were cataloged by description and personal effects, and had tags attached to their toes. Only three of the musicians were found and, although their numbers are close together, suggesting they were found near each other, they would appear to have been picked up on three consecutive days—Hume on April 23, a day that Hamilton described as full of "rain and fog"; Clarke on April 24, which was "cold, wet, miserable and comfortless"; and Hartley on April 25. It was a harrowing job for the seamen. As Hamilton reflected, "Even the most hardened must reflect on the hopes and fears, the dismay and despair, of those whose nearest and dearest, support and pride, have been wrenched from them by this tragedy."

Body number 193 was Jock Hume. He was judged to be around twenty-eight (actual age twenty-one); had light, curly hair; was five feet nine inches; and weighed 145 pounds. He'd been wearing a light raincoat, a purple muffler, and his bandsman's suit. He appeared to have lost his socks and shoes and was wearing a silver watch. In his pockets were a cigarette case, an empty purse, a knife with a carved pearl handle, a mute, a brass African Royal Mail button, and an English lever watch. When these items were sent back to his parents, they were valued by the postal service as being worth $5 (Canadian).

Body number 202 was Fred Clarke. His estimated age was thirty-five (actual age twenty-eight) and he had black hair and no marks on his body. He was wearing a gray overcoat and gray muffler over his uniform. His socks were green, and he wore an initialed gold ring on one finger, a gold watch on his wrist, and a crucifix around his neck. In his pockets were a diamond pin, keys, a knife, a sovereign case, a pocketbook, a memo book, and eight shillings in cash.

Wallace Hartley was body 224. He looked to be twenty-five (actual age thirty-three), had brown hair, and was wearing a brown coat over his uniform. On his feet were green socks and black boots. On one of his fingers was a diamond solitaire ring. In his pockets were a gold fountain pen (initialed); a silver cigarette; a silver matchbox given to him by the staff at Collinson's Café in Leeds; a nickel watch on a gold chain; a gold cigar holder; a collar stud; a pair of scissors; an insignia cut from an old uniform; German, English, American, and French coins; a key; the letter from his friend Bill; and a telegram sent to him on board the *Titanic*. The earliest reports specifically noted that he was found with "his music case strapped to his body" and that "this will be forwarded to the White Star Company" (*Daily Sketch*, May 3, 1912, and other papers). This item, however, which presumably contained his violin, was never listed among the effects signed for by his father and its disappearance has long puzzled *Titanic* historians.

The items found on their bodies offer a tantalizing snapshot of the three musicians but raise as many questions as answers. Jock Hume's purple muffler and light raincoat suggests someone more concerned with appearance than comfort and warmth, an impression that confirms what is already known about him. But was the African Royal Mail button taken from a previous uniform, and did it mean that he had also traveled to Africa? Was the mute from his violin or another instrument?

Were Fred Clarke's notebooks connected with his work or were they personal journals? His mother signed for them, but no one in the family knows what happened to them. Tantalizingly someone wrote the word *Communicate* beneath the typewritten list of his effects and then wrote two names and addresses: Grechten Bechtel of Stapleton, New York, and Thomas Graham of Chryston, Glasgow. These must have been names found in the memo book that the medical examiner felt should be contacted. Grechten

Bechtel was the maiden name of an American girl who by 1911 was married and living in New Brighton on the Wirral, but who later moved back to America. Was Clarke planning to visit her or stay with her family in Stapleton on Staten Island?

Wallace Hartley's belongings indicate his senior position—plenty of gold, silver, and diamonds—but was the loose change his collection of tips for the night? The varieties of currencies suggest so, because, as far as we know, he had never traveled to France or Germany. The fact that he had almost exactly twice as much sterling as Clarke may indicate that they'd already carved up the evening's earnings in accordance with the contract signed with Charlie Black—one portion to each bandsman and two to the leader. If this was so, the bandsmen could have made £2 a crossing, the bandleader £4, which, taken over a month, would far exceed their wages.

Hartley and Clarke were easy to identify because they had items bearing either their names or initials. Clarke had a business card with his old address in Lowther Street, Liverpool, scored through and his new address, 22 Tunstall Street, added in pen. Hume had no such clues and so a photograph was taken of him in his coffin and sent to the White Star Line for identification. On July 16, Harold Wingate of White Star in New York wrote to Nova Scotia's deputy provincial secretary, Frederick F. Mathers, saying: "Our Southampton office has been able to identify no. 193 as John Law Hume a bandsman of the *Titanic* from the photograph. We expected this body to be identified as the uniform and effects indicated that it was one of the bandsmen."[1]

Next of kin were given the choice of having their loved ones buried in Canada after the *Mackay-Bennett* arrived back on April 30 or having the body returned. A letter from the White Star Line auctioned in 2002 revealed that at least one of the passenger's relatives was asked to pay £20 to ship a body back to England. The letter read in part:

Business card of Fred Clarke found on his body

We regret that we do not see our way to bring back home the bodies of those recovered free of expense, and in cases where it is desired for this to be done, it can only be carried out provided the body was in a fit state to be returned, and upon receiving a deposit of £20 on account of the expenses. The remains of those not returned to England we are arranging to have buried at Halifax, each in a separate grave, with a suitable headstone, and we hope this latter arrangement will commend itself to you.

It was said that White Star paid for Hartley's body to be returned to Britain, but this may have been because his story was so exceptional. Possibly White Star didn't charge for the Atlantic crossing, but Albion Hartley paid for the coffin, the embalming, and the transportation from Halifax to Boston. It's hard to imagine that the Clarke and Hume families turned down the offer of the repatriation of their sons' bodies for free. As it was, on May 3, John Frederick Preston Clarke was buried at Mount Olivet Catholic Cemetery after a service at St. Mary's Catholic Church and on May 8, John Law Hume was buried at Fairview Cemetery, each of their graves marked by a simple granite stone with their name, date of death, and body number. No relative was present at either of the funerals or burials.

The arrival of Wallace Hartley's body became a focal point of national grief. This young man not only represented all who had died on the *Titanic*, but also the values that the British feared were in decline. Here was someone, they thought, with a sense of duty, someone who had laid down his life for others. The fact that he exhibited all these traits while playing the tune of one of the country's best-loved hymns was a point of national pride.

Hartley's embalmed body was sent by train from Halifax to Boston and from there it was put on the White Star liner *Arabic*, which set sail on May 7. The *Arabic* was due to arrive in Liverpool on Friday, May 17, so Albion Harley arranged for the funeral to be held the next day at the Bethel Chapel in Colne with the burial to be in the family vault in Colne Cemetery, where his two young brothers had been interred. The coffin would be taken the sixty miles from Liverpool to Colne by road in a horse-drawn hearse.

The *Arabic* arrived at South Canada Dock on the morning of April 17. Albion waited in a nearby shed with the relatives of two other bereaved passengers to carry out the grim task of identifying his son from his discolored and bruised face, signing for the effects that had been saved in a white canvas bag, and walking with the undertakers as they took the large polished wood casket with brass mountings to the awaiting hearse and its two horses.

A reporter from the *Liverpool Daily Post and Mercury* wrote that Albion seemed "a pathetic figure . . . suffering from intense mental agony . . . as he signed the receipt for the delivery of the body his hands quivered with emotion . . . he walked away broken with grief." Albion told the reporter that a friend of his who traveled regularly on the *Lusitania* had heard his son play "Nearer, My God, to Thee" on that ship several times. This seemed to console him. In his life's defining moment, Wallace Hartley had behaved in a way that would bring pride to any Methodist Sunday school superintendent or choir leader.

The long slow journey of the hearse took ten hours, passing through the Lancashire towns of Preston, Blackburn, Accrington, and Burnley, before arriving in Colne during the early hours of Saturday morning. Away from the eyes of prying observers, the casket was taken into Bethel Chapel where Hartley's musical career had started more than twenty-five years before, and was met by around twenty of the family's relatives and friends. It was only when daylight came that Elizabeth Hartley, her three daughters, and Maria Robinson took their final look through the coffin's small glass window at Hartley's face. The *Colne & Nelson Times* described a scene filled with pathos. "Grouped around the coffin, from which they tore themselves away only by a great effort, they gazed steadfastly for several minutes. Then over the glass panel was screwed the strong coffin lid and human eye had seen the last of Wallace Hartley."

The funeral service began at one o'clock, by which time the chapel designed to seat seven hundred was filled with one thousand people— family and friends on the ground level and others in the balcony. Colne itself was crammed with more people than had ever been in the town at any one time, lining the mile-and-a-quarter route from the chapel to the cemetery that the hearse and mourners would embark on at two o'clock. Badges, posters, and postcards had been selling on the streets for at least a week and, according to the *Leeds Mercury*, "The theme for street singers for several days has been 'Nearer, My God, to Thee.'" Newspaper estimates put the size of the crowd at anywhere between thirty thousand and forty thousand.

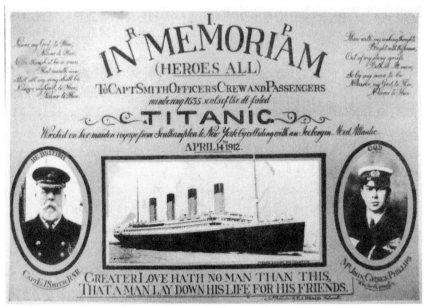

Titanic memorial postcards

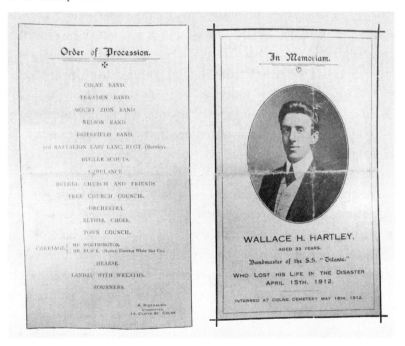

In the chapel Albion and Elizabeth sat with their daughters and Maria Robinson directly facing the coffin, which was on a draped catafalque.

Screwed on its lid was a brass plaque bearing the words "Wallace H. Hartley, Died April 15, 1912, Aged 33 years. 'Nearer, My God, to Thee.'" In front of the catafalque were piles of wreaths and flowers that had been placed there during the morning. Perhaps the most poignant was a floral cross of deep red roses given by Maria, which had the attached message: "O teach me from my heart to say 'Thy will be done.'"

The service began with Mendelssohn's "O Rest in the Lord" played as an organ voluntary, followed by the Issac Watts's hymn "Oh God Our Help in Ages Past," one of the two hymns Wallace had cited as his favorites. During the singing of it, Albion appeared to be close to collapse. Then came a prayer, the hymn "Lead, Kindly Light," and a message by the Independent Methodist preacher Thomas Worthington, a friend to the Hartley family whom Wallace had last met on the *Mauretania* in September 1911.

The gray-bearded Worthington gave an eloquent and deeply personal sermon. Captain Smith, he had read, had called on his men to "Be British," but whereas there were many good things about being British, there was something even more inspiring about being Christian. Worthington continued:

> From the bridge today I have a still more noble, more inspiring call to utter—"Be Christian"—and in this, too, I can associate our friend, Wallace Hartley. His sea faring, no doubt, had given him many experiences. There must have been many times when doubts would be raised as to whether nature or steam would prevail. Report gives an actual conversation on the point. What would he do in the face of wreck? Look for his lifebelt? That would be natural. Jump into number 1 lifeboat? Well, all that a man hath will he give for his life. But no! If report is correct—and there is every reason to believe it is—he said, in effect: "I should cling to me my old violin which has given so much pleasure to many, and often to me, and instead of playing to please or amuse or pass time I should play to inspire. Amid storm and wreck I should play "Nearer, My God, to Thee."
>
> And so it was. The unexpected happened, the unthinkable occurred. The ship that everyone thought could not sink is now two miles at the bottom of the Atlantic. But our friend kept his word. The inevitable command to get the boats ready in the middle of that dark but clear Sunday night, with the subsequent order "Women and children first" found

those hands now stiff in death gliding along the strings of that beloved violin and guiding the companion stick, producing the tune that at once became articulate and interpreted the desires of many hearts as they were lifted to heaven. This was done until the waves claimed both him and his violin. Yes, it is brave to be British. It is both brave and noble to be Christian. In fact, it is easier to be British when we are Christian.

We are glad as his family must be that his body has been recovered and embalmed that we may pay the respect due today. We offer our sympathy to his parents and family, who have lost a dear son in a most tragic way. We can do little to lighten their load. It will, however, be some consolation to them that their home has not only produced a brave British musician but a strong Christian, testified to by this vast concourse of people, and re-echoed by thousands throughout the length and breadth of the land. This product of the home life is such of which any parents may be proud.

> Oh may we triumph so
> When all our warfare's past;
> And dying find our latest foe
> Under our feet at last.

Hartley's coffin nearing the family vault in the cemetery.

The final hymn, inevitably, was "Nearer, My God, to Thee" with the music played by the Colne Orchestra and the voices led by the church choir. "Thoughts innumerable and grievous indeed chased each other across the mind," reflected the reporter from the *Colne & Nelson Times*. "A month ago the hero, whose body they knew to be in the coffin so easily visible, produced those strains on the precipice of death. Now a world was echoing those notes and he was soon to go on his last journey. Scarcely a soul in the congregation but shed tears as the hymn was sung."

The mourners were played out to the sound of "The Dead March" from Handel's opera *Saul*. Before she left, Maria stepped forward to the mass of floral tributes, picked out her cross, and carefully laid it on the brass plaque of her fiancé's coffin. It took more than an hour for the quarter-mile-long funeral procession to make its way through the crowds lining Burnley Road, Primet Hill, Albert Road, Church Street, Keighley Road, and into the cemetery. The blinds of shops were drawn down, flags were at half-mast, and men solemnly took off their hats as the cortege passed. There were nine carriages; eight brass bands; troupes of scouts; church groups, representatives of the Amalgamated Musicians' Union, the Refuge Assurance Company, and the YMCA; local dignitaries; policemen; St. John Ambulance Brigade volunteers; choirs; and local musicians. Charlie Black

Hartley's grave at Colne.

was there as the only representative from the White Star Line and traveled to the burial in a carriage with Thomas Worthington.

Twelve bearers took the coffin from the cemetery gates down the grassy hill to its final resting place in the family vault. Thomas Worthington spoke the last rites, the Bethel Choir sang "Nearer, My God, to Thee" to the accompaniment of a local village band, and as the remains of Wallace Hartley were lowered into the grave, a group of scout buglers played "The Last Post." Later the words "Nearer My God to Thee, Nearer to Thee" would be added to the gravestone, along with the opening bars of Sullivan's tune "Propior Deo."

There were already plans to establish a memorial for Hartley in Colne's main street and there was similar talk in Eastbourne and Headington about doing something for Wes Woodward and in Dumfries for Jock

Hume. In London, New York, Liverpool, Boston, and Southampton there were those who wanted to remember the entire band with a plaque, tablet, or statue.

None of the other musicians would have a send-off to match Hartley's. For the families of Theo Brailey, Georges Krins, Roger Bricoux, Wes Woodward, and Percy Taylor, there was the agony of never knowing what happened to the bodies of their loved ones. Had they been killed instantly because of the ship's suction dragging them down or had they frozen to death after time in the water pleading for help? Had they been on the deck when the ship went down or had they been trapped beneath as the machinery tore through the ship's innards and the lights finally went out? Were their bodies lost, or picked up but never identified?

Memorial to Wallace Hartley in Colne, Lancashire.

Leon Bricoux had obviously pondered these questions and had written to Charlie Black to try to elicit more information. On May 1, Black wrote back:

In response to your letter I have the sad task of letting you know that the body of your son has not been found. If it was to be found the

White Star Company has told me that it would be necessary for you to deposit 500 francs with them for the expense of having it embalmed in New York. The company has agreed to transport the body from New York to Southampton or Liverpool. In this case you would have to go to one of these two towns and transport it to France at your own expense . . . In the event that the body was found and buried in New York the company will arrange to give a separate burial space and a stone cross to each one.

Enclosed was a postal order for nineteen shillings, presumably Roger Bricoux's wages for the five days he served on the *Titanic*.

There had been a memorial service for Jock Hume led by the Reverend James Strachan, who had known him since childhood. Strachan noticeably didn't praise Jock for his strong Christian faith as Thomas Worthington had praised Wallace Hartley. Reading between the lines it would appear that Strachan was unsure whether Hume had continued in the faith and was unwilling to make false claims. In an interview at the time, he'd rather pointedly said he'd known Jock intimately for "fifteen of his twenty years," implying a break with the church after Hume left for the sea. In his sermon he made no claims about Christian faith in action nor did he offer any promises about heaven. Instead he concentrated on Hume's cheerfulness and the grief of those left behind.

"We are here to drop a tear on the watery grave of one who for years sat within these walls as a member of the Sabbath school and as a member of our Band of Hope," he said.

We knew him as a child, a boy, and a youth. His presence, up to the time of his leaving for the sea, was a familiar one here. We see him again with the violin rendering assistance in the conduct of the service of prayer in the sanctuary. We see on his lips and in his eyes the smile which was a striking characteristic of his familiar countenance. Through our tear-dimmed eyes we see him as he leads his bandsmen [*sic*] in the last of their and the vessels life, in the sweet holy strains of the music of the well known hymn "Nearer, my God, to Thee."[2] Thus he dies. We weep for him. We weep for his friends.

The minister at St. Antholin's Church in Peckham, where Percy Taylor had been a chorister and where his brother Frederick was still the organist, spoke about the tragedy. He said that Percy had been "one of that great-hearted company of musicians which played 'Nearer, My God, to Thee' in those awful moments of direst need, as the company went down, in their council, into the profundity of the immutable sea."

In the May 11 edition of *Light*, the journal of the College of Psychic Studies, someone by the name of Mr. H. Blackwell claimed to have been at a séance in London on April 24 where both W. T. Stead and Theo Brailey made appearances. Blackwell said he wrote down word for word what was said:

> I am Brailey. I am so happy to be with you. I thank God that I knew something of this [referring to what Stead had just communicated]. Dear Mr Stead was speaking on the subject frequently on board to numbers of people. He went to bed very late. It was at his suggestion that we played "Nearer, My God, to Thee," some moments before the boat went down. We had no suffering, only cold for a few moments. My father did not wish me to go on this voyage, but I thought it would be a good thing. I must go now. God bless you. Please let Father know.

The Brailey family's friend Clifford Buttle went one further. He had a visitation. On June 19, 1912, he was at his boot mender's shop in East London, when be began to feel an extreme chilliness, despite the weather being hot. Fearing the onset of flu, he left his assistant in charge of the shop and went home to lie on his bed. He then felt the room fill with mist and heard the sound of dripping water. "I was lying on my right side, and I saw the mist part like the halves of a curtain," he told *Psychic News*.

> Then, distinctly, I saw young William Brailey standing before me, water apparently cascading from his clothing to the floor.
>
> William Brailey held forth a crucifix, and I saw that it was beautifully made in nickel and ebony. According to my judgment it was about six inches long. Young Brailey spoke quite distinctly. He said to me, "Send it to Dad." This he repeated three times as if to impress me that the matter was most urgent. Then, still holding the crucifix out towards

me, he . . . retreated into the mist and vanished from my sight. A cool breeze came into the room and dispersed the mist. Gradually the icy chill left my limbs. I arose from my bed. I was alone.

He reurned to his shop, he said, and once inside noticed a sickly man looking through the window. The man came into the shop and tried to sell Buttle something. It was a nickel crucifix, but Buttle's mind was so distracted that he didn't make the connection and sent the man away. When he came to and realized the crucifix was a replica of the one he'd seen the apparition hold out to him, he sent his assistant to find the man and buy it from him.

> It was soon in my possession. It was a perfect twin to the one the young musician had brought to my bedside. The same night I wrote a record of this, my experience, and sent it, with the crucifix, by registered post to Mr. and Mrs. Brailey. Some time after my amazing experience I called on Mr. Ronald Brailey to ask him to explain the enigma of the crucifix. He told me that William, at the time of the *Titanic* disaster, was engaged to a young woman who was a Catholic. William Brailey was not a Catholic, so in all probability the crucifix was brought to convince his fiancée of his life after death.

Thousands of Sunday church services were turned into memorials for the *Titanic* victims and the story of the band was used as an illustration of the Christian quality of self-sacrifice, as well as an example of the hope of immortality in the face of death. At the Cathedral of St. John the Divine in New York, Bishop Greer preached a sermon that dwelt on the musicians.

> From those who have gone not to return a message has come, which throughout the world has already been voiced, and I can but repeat it. It is the message of a courage, of a heroism, of a sacrificial bravery of the finest and highest type, not the courage of the soldier on the field who is facing physical danger or facing physical death, and to whom such courage has come through the discipline of war, but a courage greater than that—the courage of those facing death, the courage of those who were feeling then the anguish of separation from all that made their lives of earth dear and

precious to them, who saw that precious freight lowered into the boats, drifting and floating from them, beyond their reach and call.

Where on all the famous battlefields of history do we find a finer and greater courage than that? And if what is reported be true, how fitting were then music strains which floated then about them! For were they not at that moment, while standing bravely on that sacrificial duty, standing nearer to God! Shall not their example teach this twofold lesson to us, that in spite of all their lacks and all the limitations, the men of this generation and the women are not lacking in courage, and that they do not need the training, the discipline, the experience of war to teach it or to give it?

Dr. Ernest Stires, preaching at St. Thomas's Church on Fifth Avenue, and with at least one *Titanic* survivor in the congregation, said: "The disaster has made of the whole human race a sorrowing family. The band played 'Nearer, My God, to Thee' on its knees, sinking down into the depths. Today I hear from them the heights, for they died a death worth dying, to teach us how to live a life worth living."

This sort of talk was too much for the novelist Joseph Conrad, who believed that newspapers had framed the whole disaster in sentimental terms that had then been adopted by public and clergy alike. He didn't think there was anything "heroic" about dying involuntarily because of the greed and incompetence of others. He also didn't think that the decency of many of those drowned was anything special. It's what he would have expected of any group from any section of society when confronted with peril.

His words about the band sounded one of the few dissenting notes in the coverage of their actions.

I, who am not a sentimentalist, think it would have been finer if the band of the *Titanic* had been quietly saved, instead of being drowned while playing—whatever tune they were playing, poor devils. I would rather that they had been saved to support their families than to see their families supported by the magnificent generosity of the subscribers. I am not consoled by the false, written-up, Drury Lane aspects of that event, which is neither drama, nor melodrama, nor tragedy, but the exposure of arrogant folly. There is nothing more heroic in dying very much against your will, off a holed, helpless, big tank in which you bought your passage, than in dying of colic caused by the imperfect salmon in the tin you bought from your grocer. And that's the truth. The unsentimental truth stripped of the romantic garment the press has wrapped around this most unnecessary disaster.

The other notable dissenter was playwright George Bernard Shaw, who wittily and acerbically expressed his view that the whole *Titanic* story had been created in the press to fit a rigid formula, which he called "an explosion of outrageous romantic lying." The band playing on deck was, according to Shaw, part of the preordained story. He didn't deny that it happened but offered a different interpretation of events. Possibly, he suggested, the music produced complacency rather than courage and therefore was in part responsible for the high death toll. What he referred to as "the romantic demand" was that "Everybody must face death without a tremor, and the band, according to the Birkenhead precedent,[3] must play 'Nearer, My God, to Thee.'"

> It was duly proclaimed that it fell out exactly thus. Actual evidence: the Captain and officers were so afraid of a panic, that, although they knew the ship was sinking, they did not dare to tell the passengers so—especially the third class passengers—and the band played Rag Times to reassure the passengers, who therefore, did not get into the boats and did not realize their situation until all the boats were gone and the ship was standing on her head before plunging to the bottom.

The public was largely unswayed by this suggestion of manipulation by the press and there was massive sympathy for the victims and respect for the musicians. Several music concerts raised money for the families of the bandsmen. Two orchestras performed for Fred Clarke on May 20 at Liverpool's Philharmonic Hall "in aid of the bereaved family, which depended in a large measure upon the financial results of Mr Clarke's art." The *Birkenhead News* commented: "If any glory at all attaches to the awful tragedy of the sea about which the world is still talking, it circles round the heads of these heroic bandsmen who played the mighty vessel to its doom. Materialists may scoff, as Mr Bernard Shaw has done this week, but there was something in the last scene, a pitiful grandeur, that makes all mankind kin, and defies hard reasoning."

In New York, Sara Regneas, wife of the American musician Joseph Regneas, organized a fund-raising musical soirée at her home on the Upper East Side that raised $1,000, and pupils of the Music School Settlement on East Third Street performed a concert that raised $800 for the families. By far the biggest memorial concert was on May 24 at London's Royal Albert Hall, where the largest orchestra ever assembled—five hundred musicians—played an afternoon concert for an audience of ten thousand. Thomas Beecham, Sir Henry Wood, and Sir Edward Elgar were among the guest conductors.

At least nine memorials were unveiled to the band during the next two or three years, almost all of them quoting from "Nearer, My God, to Thee" and mentioning the fact that the men had gone to their deaths while playing.[4] They were remembered at the Philharmonic Hall in Liverpool, where Fred Clarke had been an orchestra member; at St. Mark's Church in Dewsbury, where Wallace Hartley had worshipped in his final years when not at sea; and at places they had never visited. The most unusual of these was in the town of Broken Hill, New South Wales, Australia, where

Memorial plaque to Jock Hume at St. Michael's School, Dumfries, Scotland.

a monument was dedicated on December 21, 1913: "Erected by the citizens of Broken Hill as a memorial to the heroic bandsmen of the steamship *Titanic* who, playing to the end, calmly faced certain death whilst women, children, and their fellow-men were being rescued from the wreck of that ill-fated vessel off the coast of Newfoundland, on April 15, 1912."

A granite obelisk "in memory of John Law Hume" and steward Thomas Mullin was unveiled in Dock Park, Dumfries, by the town's provost on May 31, 1913. A brass plaque "to the glory of God and in memory of John Wesley Woodward" was installed in the nave of All Saints Church in Headington, Oxfordshire, and on October 24, 1914, a granite tablet with bronze plaques "to the self-sacrifice and devotion of John Wesley Woodward" was unveiled on Eastbourne's Grand Parade, close to the bandstand and facing the sea. On February 17, 1915, there was a ceremony in Colne for a bronze bust of "Wallace Hartley, bandmaster of the R.M.S. *Titanic*, who perished in the foundering of that vessel." The bust stood on a stone pedestal outside what was then the local library. In Spa, Belgium, architect's drawings were being made for an elaborate memorial in honor of Georges Krins—plans that were literally shelved once war broke out.

John Wesley Woodward memorial at Eastbourne.

⊷━━⊶

It was a beautiful summer day when the memorial to Jock Hume was unveiled close to the banks of the River Nith. Buglers from the Special Reserve had sounded the "Last Post" for the occasion, which was attended by hundreds of local people, including Andrew Hume and one of his daughters. When it was all over a band played the national anthem and church bells rang out. Yet all was not well with the relatives of the bandsmen. The recognition of those in power and the sympathy and generosity of the public were welcomed, but these expressions did nothing to settle the grievances that began to mount once the initial attention began to ebb.

Memorial to Jock Hume and Titanic steward Thomas Mullins on the river front in Dumfries.

13

"If You Think You Have
a Legal Claim."

On April 30, 1912, the day before writing to Leon Bricoux, Charlie Black had written a letter to Andrew Hume in Dumfries regarding his late son John Law Hume:

Dear Sir,

We shall be obliged if you will remit to us the sum of 5s– 4d, which is owing to us as per enclosed statement. We shall also be obliged if you will settle the enclosed uniform account.

Yours faithfully,

C. W. and F. N. Black

The account was for the alterations and cleaning needed to get his uniform ready for the *Titanic* after arriving back in Liverpool on the *Carmania*. The total was nine shillings and threepence. Hume had signed a receipt at the shop of J. J. Rayner permitting C. W. & F. N. Black to deduct the sum from his wage account. Presumably, as the *Titanic* voyage was incomplete, the Blacks didn't consider him eligible for full payment. This left him in their debt. Incensed by the callousness of the demand, Andrew Hume forwarded it to the Amalgamated Musicians' Union (AMU), who published it in the

June issue of the *Musicians' Report and Journal*. Beneath it the editor added the single line: "Comment would be superfluous!"

The full implications of the new hiring arrangements instituted by the Blacks were now being felt. No longer employees of the shipping line, the musicians were not covered by insurance taken out for employees, nor were they covered by the Workmen's Compensation Act (1906), which generally gave a worker "a right against his employer to a certain compensation on the mere occurrence of an accident where the common law gives the right only for negligence of the employer."

The AMU, which had already been at loggerheads with the Blacks over their wage decrease and monopoly of the shipping lines, fought hard for the musicians to be remembered and for their families to be given adequate welfare. Instead of raising money for "useless" plaques and memorials that "in six months' time . . . will be taken no more notice of than any other memorial stone, and everyone will forget the deed that caused the memorial to be erected," it channelled donations to a convalescent home for musicians, believing this to be a more fitting memorial. One of its most effective fund-raisers was a poster with pictures of all eight musicians beneath the inscription "The Heroic musicians of the *Titanic* who died at their posts like men—April 15, 1912" and with a verse from "Nearer, My God, to Thee." Priced at threepence and printed on art paper, more than eighty thousand copies were sold in the first month.

Anxious relatives turned to the AMU when they became frustrated. In June, Percy Taylor's wife, Clara, wrote: "I have not yet received anything from any fund." Martha Woodward, Wes's mother, claimed to be in the same position. Ronald Brailey wrote to Charlie Black on May 24 raising the issue of compensation and Black replied: "I cannot advise you in the matter of compensation. If you think you have a legal claim, will you please give me notice in writing of that, and it will in due course be dealt with by our insurance company, but under such awful circumstances it is practically impossible for the alleged claims to be settled for several months." The AMU couldn't imagine why "awful circumstances" could impede the speedy settlement of a legitimate claim. Weren't insurance companies in the business of "awful circumstances"?

Poster created by Amalgamated Musicians' Union.

The only policy covering the musicians was one the Blacks and White Star took out jointly from the recently established (1907) Legal Insurance Company, but it soon transpired that the insurers were quibbling over the scope of the word *dependent.* Wives and children were obviously dependents, but could working fathers, such as Andrew Hume and Ronald Brailey, honestly describe themselves as such? This meant that neither of the two main parties—White Star and the Black brothers—was making immediate contributions to the families. Outraged by this, three of the fathers—Leon Bricoux, Andrew Hume, and Ronald Brailey—mounted a legal case against C. W. & F. N. Black in June 1912, arguing that as workers who had lost their lives while carrying out their duties and through no fault of their own, their sons should be covered by the strictures of the Workmen's Compensation Act. There had never been any suggestion that they'd brought about their fate through negligence or misbehavior.

The case came to court on November 1 at Liverpool County Court, where Judge Thomas concluded that since the musicians were not signed to the ship's articles they were not legally crew members. Therefore, they were not employees of White Star. They were employees of C. W. & F. N. Black, but they couldn't successfully sue the Blacks because there was no evidence of negligence on their part. Thomas declared: "The ship owners did not treat the bandsmen as members of the crew. Their duties on board were in the nature of supplying a luxury, and their engagement was not directly by the owners. In these circumstances it would be a wrong application of the word 'seaman' to say they came within the act."

It was clearly with a heavy heart that Thomas decided in favor of the respondents. At the end of his summary he said:

> I wish to add this observation. Although I have felt compelled to hold that the Workmen's Compensation Act does not apply to the bandsmen, yet I cannot forget that these brave men met their death while performing an act which was of the greatest service in assisting to maintain discipline and avert panic. I hope the committee which is administering the *Titanic* Relief Fund may consider whether it is possible for them out of that fund to give such relief as may prevent the dependants from suffering from the fact that they have no legal claims under the Act.

Auguste Krins and his wife, Letitia, filed a claim for $25,000 against the Oceanic Steam Navigation Company, owner of the White Star Line, as it petitioned for its liabilities to be limited. In common with other passengers and relatives of passengers, they employed the New York attorneys Hunt, Hill, and Betts. Their argument was that the company should not be spared having to pay compensation for the death of their son because it was caused "by the wrongful acts, neglect, fault and negligence" of the company and its agents and servants. Part of their claim read:

Georges Krins in 1908.

> In failing to make said vessel seaworthy and properly manned, equipped and supplied, and in failing to provide sufficient life boats and in failing to man such life boats as were provided with sufficient and properly drilled crews, and in failing properly, after said collision, to take proper measures for the rescue of said Georges A. Krins, and other persons on board the *Titanic*, and otherwise, and such loss and destruction of lives and property was with the privity, faulty and knowledge of the petitioner, and occurred without fault on the part of the said Georges A. Krins.

The claim was submitted in April 1914 but, according to the family, was unsuccessful.

Andrew Hume tried other ways of obtaining compensation. He managed to get £92 from the Mansion House Fund, set up to help families of those killed, but a personal letter to J. Bruce Ismay elicited nothing. He then wrote to the U.S. Commissioner's office requesting a $2,500 settlement. In a three-page letter he detailed the liabilities he'd been left with. His son had gone on the *Titanic*, he said, with two violins—a G. B. Gaudagnini[1] valued at £200 and a Tomaso Eberle[2] at £125—taken on approval "with the purpose of choosing one of these as a life instrument. Neither violin was insured." Then there was the matter of the £500 house at 42 George Street, Dumfries, the mortgage of which had been bought with Jock in 1909, Jock expecting to bring in at least £100 a year in wages. There was still £300 of the mortgage remaining unpaid. "As I am now 50 years of age it is most unlikely that [I] can hope to clear it off without some assistance, the £92 paid being such a small portion." What he didn't mention was that he'd offered his house as security to the owner of the violins.

Andrew Hume's situation was further complicated when on October 18, 1912, Jock's fiancée, Mary Costin, gave birth to a daughter she defiantly named Johnann Law Hume Costin. Johnann automatically became a *Titanic* dependent and this weakened any claim Andrew may have had to being the legitimate recipient of any monies due.

Midway through her pregnancy Mary applied to the Mansion House Fund for help and her request was passed to the *Daily Telegraph's Titanic* Relief Fund. She filled in the right forms and was told to enter the child's name on the register of dependents as soon as it was born. She did this on the day of Johnann's birth. Two months later she went to court to request a settlement from the estate of John Law Hume. The court found John Law Hume to be the father of the child and said that Mary Costin was entitled to recover 2 pounds, 2 shillings expenses, plus 6 pounds, 10 shillings per annum for ten years from the estate.

However, according to Andrew Hume, his son had not only died intestate but in debt. Mary sent the figures to the *Titanic* Relief Fund who passed them to the Liverpool office that dealt with Scottish cases. Her plea was regarded sympathetically and in January 1913 it granted her the total amount, 67 pounds, 2 shillings. Unfortunately, the check was mailed to Andrew, who'd given the fund the impression that he had already paid her out of his own pocket and therefore needed reimbursing.

By April 1913 Mary had heard nothing from the fund, so her solicitor, Mr. Hendrie, whose office happened to be beneath the Costin's flat in Buccleuch Street, contacted it only to discover that Andrew Hume had the money. Percy Corkhill, of the *Titanic* Relief Fund in Liverpool, reassured Hendrie that "definitely the money was intended for the benefit of pursuer and her child, and not in any sense for defender's own benefit."

Andrew Hume, who had already been given more than £230 from various relief funds, including the Boston Musicians' Relief Fund based in Brookline, Massachusetts, didn't want to lose his grip on this money. He initially argued that he had paid Mary, then asserted that she had no legitimate claim. When asked whether his son was engaged to marry Mary Costin, all that his solicitor would volunteer was, "Not known and not admitted." When she eventually sued him for the money plus expenses at 5 percent per annum, he wouldn't give in and by the logic of his own argument had to take action against her on the grounds that she was "fraudulently attempting to appropriate the said money."

The "*Titanic* Fund Case," as the local paper referred to it, was a messy one that dragged on until February 1914, with Andrew Hume emerging as a venial character who had taken advantage of public goodwill for personal gain. A century of inflation means that the amounts involved appear small, so it needs to be borne in mind that the £230 that he had received was almost sixty times his son's monthly salary as a musician and almost half the cost of his house in George Street, Dumfries.

The transcripts of the court case show that he knew the *Titanic* Relief Fund money was owed to Mary Costin, but that once he had banked it, he was loath to pass it on. His excuses for not doing so were decreasingly plausible; at one point he even claimed to have a letter from his son (never produced in court) in which Jock argued that he was not the father of the child.

The judge decided in favor of Mary Costin and Andrew Hume was ordered to pay expenses. There was an appeal but this ended dramatically when Hume's lawyer, faced with evidence from a minute book that his client had specifically told the *Titanic* Relief Fund that he'd already paid Mary and therefore needed the money as reimbursement, had to withdraw from the case. If he'd known of this evidence, he said, he wouldn't have put up a defence. The judgment against Andrew Hume stood.

Not all of the musicians died penniless. Percy Taylor left 164 pounds, 4 shillings to his wife, Clara; Wes Woodward left an estate worth 1,195 pounds, 3 shillings, and 5 pence to his mother, Martha; and Fred Clarke left 128 pounds, 13 shillings, and 6 pence to his mother, Ellen. Oddly enough, in light of the number of years he'd spent at sea, Wallace Hartley hadn't made a will. He died intestate and administration was granted to his father, Albion, to give him access to his son's 656-pound estate.

Money from the *Titanic* Relief Fund was distributed according to need, a dependent wife with children naturally being awarded more than the parents of an unmarried person. In the case of the families of the musicians, Ellen Clarke got the largest amount (£151) because she had been reliant on her son's income and had no husband. Auguste Krins and Martha Woodward each got £150, and Leon Bricoux and Clara Taylor were given £100 each. Albion Hartley and Ronald Brailey took £70 each, and Andrew Hume got the smallest amount (£50).

They may have benefited from other independent sources. The American Federation of Musicians sent $1,000, many AMU branches stipulated that 50 percent of the money they'd raised was to go directly to the families, and there were fund-raising efforts in cities as far apart as San Francisco and Salisbury, Brooklyn and Bedford. Music halls all over Britain took collections.

Charlie Black, to his credit, tried to make amends by raising money. In a letter published in the *Cork Examiner*, he explained what his agency had done:

> Sir—In justice to all concerned, we shall be grateful if you would kindly give publicity to the following: These men [the band] were insured with the Legal Insurance Company Ltd, who took steps to ascertain the dependents, and in two cases where dependency was evident settlements were immediately made. They were compelled to repudiate certain claims on the grounds of "doubtful dependency," and matters were delayed in consequence. Although the court held that no legal liability held at all, the company have generously made *ex gratia* payments to the amount of nearly £700. [The wording makes it unclear whether "the company" referred to is C. W. & F. N. Black, White Star, or Legal Insurance.] In addition to the above, £1555 has been distributed from a fund organised by ourselves for the benefit of the relatives, and to our knowledge they have further benefited by a sum of over £1200 raised by concerts and from other charitable sources, making an approximate total of £3450. We are further in a position to state that their needs will be still further

sympathetically considered by the distributors of the National Fund. We wish to give publicity to these facts to refute the suggestion in various papers that the dependents of these brave men have been in any way badly treated.

The AMU used the strength of feeling against the Blacks after the *Titanic* disaster to challenge the agency. An executive committee resolution was passed on June 22, 1912, that "the price for ocean liners be £6.10.0 per month and 10/- towards the cost of uniforms. To become operative from September 1, 1912." Material in the AMU magazine indicates that this demand was not met:

> Messrs. C.W. & F.N. Black have, we understand, given our members the choice between leaving the Union and leaving their service on the liners. Those members who are loyal have nothing to fear. The Union will support any member who is victimised. In the meantime, members are warned against playing for Messrs. Black until they pay the proper rate, £7 per month. It may be necessary to warn members against playing for them at all, no matter what the price, if they decline to come to terms with the Union. Members having any information to give that will be useful in this campaign should write to the General Secretary.

There was no further mention of the issue in either the executive committee minutes or the AMU journal, but passenger and crew lists show that contemporaries of the *Titanic* musicians, such as Seth Lancaster and Edgar Heap, were no longer entering America as passengers after October 1912. The First World War would have interrupted their business for at least four years and the final blow to their supremacy came when Cunard shifted its transatlantic operations from Liverpool to Southampton in 1919.

Patrick Stenson, author of a biography of Commander Lightoller, tried digging around for information on Charlie Black in 1985 to help his friend Walter Lord who was writing *The Night Lives On*. By then there were only a few very old musicians who could remember him, but with these men there was lingering resentment over the way he gained a stranglehold over the entertainment industry of the big ships. "If you wanted to take your cello to sea you had to go through Charlie," Stenson reported back. "If you were not already an established musician on his books you would be auditioned and if suitable would be found a berth in one of his many sea-going orchestras. He wasn't quite 'Mr Ten Per Cent' as, once taken on, you worked for him and he paid the wages. I'm told that for reasons relating to this arrangement he wasn't always a man who saw eye to eye with his musicians."

14

"A Natural Fruit
of the Evil of the Age."

Why did the *Titanic* sink? Was it God punishing humans for their arrogance and pride or an inevitable result of a series of individual human blunders that combined for one horrendous moment? Was the lesson to be learned one of increased vigilance, improvements in shipbuilding, and closer attention to safety measures or one of increased humility, improvements in moral character, and closer attention to the needs of the poor, weak, and needy? In the world of 1912 these were not mutually exclusive concerns. Senator William A. Smith, of the Senate Investigation Committee, could just as easily talk about improving the moral caliber of merchant navy seamen and of *Titanic* victims being swept "before the Judgment Seat," as Dr. Ernest Stires of St. Thomas's Church on Fifth Avenue in New York could talk about the need for extra lifeboats and regular ice patrols in the Atlantic. There was no expanse separating the temporal and the eternal.

Inquiries were set up in both Britain and America and almost no one, from the White Star Line executives to the sailors on the *Titanic*, escaped blame. The ship was going too fast in an area known to be strewn with floating ice, and in ignoring repeated warnings from other ships, Captain Smith had shown an "indifference to danger." Once the ship had struck ice, he hesitated before sounding the alarm. The crew was poorly coordinated during the rescue operation; the lifeboats, which weren't adequately equipped, were also not filled (only 712 of 1,084 available spaces were taken up); the nearest ship, the *Californian*, had ignored distress signals.

There were practical lessons to be learned. New safety regulations would be enforced. Ships sailing in and out of America, for example, would have to register with the Bureau of Corporations and be checked by the Steamboat Inspection Service. There would need to be adequate lifeboat space for all passengers and crew and each lifeboat would have to be tested and have a canvas cover, mast rigging, a bailer, a compass, oil, water, and food. Ships would require wireless equipment capable of transmitting messages over at least one hundred miles, both night and day. Auxiliary power to cope in cases of main generator failure would be compulsory.

Two years later, the British Board of Trade introduced a bill based on recommendations from the International Convention for the Safety of Life at Sea. This included improved safety training for crews, additional lighting and "internal arrangements" on ships, fresh safety certificates, wireless telegraphy on all ships carrying fifty or more people, a clarifying of different levels of distress signals, patrols of dangerous sections of busy sea routes, and penalties for ships that did not send warnings of ice or other hazards.

The Senate Investigation Committee asked for changes in ship construction and testing. The bows of ships should be stronger, it said, and the bulkhead compartments should be genuinely watertight. There was criticism of the way the *Titanic* had been rushed into service after such a short time of sea trials. In the view of the committee, the boilers, bulkheads, equipment, and signal devices had been insufficiently tested before the maiden voyage.

In addition to these matters of construction, safety, training, vigilance, and improved communication, there was the issue of morality. Leaving aside the unanswerable question of whether God had allowed the catastrophe in order to shake the West out of its complacency, there was the unavoidable fact that the tragedy owed a lot to greed, indifference, pride, carelessness, irresponsibility, and neglect of duty. It wasn't hard for people to see the *Titanic* as a metaphor for Western civilization's obsessions with speed, wealth, and conquest at the expense of contemplation, sharing, and the well-being of one's neighbor. "One cannot read the details without having it very forcibly suggested that some of the besetting evils of our present day life are at the root of it," said Rev. E. J. Pulsford of Bath, in a sermon preached on April 21, 1912. "If, as seems likely from all the information available, safety was made a secondary consideration to speed and luxury, from a desire to outstrip others in the race for dividends, then the calamity is but a natural fruit of the evil of the age."

G. K. Chesterton, the influential commentator and observer of human foibles, took a similar line in a column in the *Illustrated London News*: "Quite apart from the question of whether anyone was to blame, the big outstanding fact remains: that there was no sort of sane proportion between the extent of the provision for luxury and levity and the extent of the provision for need and desperation. The scheme did far too much for prosperity and far too little for distress—just like the modern State."

The German press was quick to take the opportunity to bash Germany's main European rival. The disaster to them was an outcome of British decadence. "Sport, betting and arrogance all had a disastrous influence on the *Titanic*'s fate," declared the liberal Berlin newspaper *Vossische Zeitung*. Another paper, *Germania*, was convinced that it was the judgment of God. "It recalls the fate of the Tower of Babel—a punishment for the presumption of the builders in trying to build a ship to defy the elements."[1]

Some thought that we were already heading for a fall. There was a growing unease about the supposed lack of strength, courage, and self-discipline in young men. The Senate Investigation Committee said as much about the British crew and this caused London's *Evening Standard* to leap back in defence, saying: "During most of the nineteenth century England was well-accustomed to the habit of war. The habit of war produced bravery. In these days we have no practice of this kind. Mercifully we are spared the discipline of our grandfathers. Our nerves are weaker than theirs. Yes, but do we subdue them of necessity?"

In her book *The Titanic Tragedy: God Speaks to the Nations*, Mrs. Alma White, a Pentecostal from New Jersey, attacked not only "the overbearing spirit among those to whom money and birth have given rank" but also the "rapid physical degeneration of England's manhood." In her view the country had ignored God and was given over to "pride and the love of display." Among the things that seemed to her to indicate its godlessness were strikes, poverty, drunkenness, impure air, "indulgences of the flesh," a weak established church, and women who clamored for the right to vote. "God has given the world an awful warning through the *Titanic* disaster," she wrote. "Woe be unto them if they fail to profit by it."

She'd visited England and concluded that its official church offered "absolutely no spiritual food" to its people. She was distressed to discover clergymen with shares in breweries and distilleries, benefiting from the problem, as she saw it, rather than offering a solution. To her the *Titanic* represented "the wealth, pride and presumption of Britain" and she had a particularly stinging rebuke for J. Bruce Ismay, who, when confronted by a passenger who suggested cutting the ship's speed while in the ice field, had apparently answered, "We will go faster, and get out of the reach of them." Mrs. White believed that this was the language of someone intoxicated on worldly success. "He had drunk the Babylonian cup to the dregs," she said, "and God's rebuke was at hand."

Rather than seeing the disaster as a retribution for general moral decline, most Christian commentators and preachers of the time saw it either as a reminder of our insignificance when confronted with the power of nature or of our need to prioritize care for individuals over opulence, gluttony, and pride. "We're so sure of ourselves," said Canon White-Thompson in a sermon given in a church in Croydon, Surrey.

> We do such wonderful things. We conquer time and space. We subdue the elements. The winds and the sea obey us. We put a girdle around the earth and like a flash of light send our words through space. So we think that we have mastered Nature . . . Then, Nature, the silent, the inscrutable, having submitted to all this mastery, just puts out her finger and at her touch man is reduced to a helpless pygmy and all his works are swallowed up in nothingness.

Dr. Ewing, preaching at Rye Lane Baptist Chapel in Peckham, South East London, considered that it might be a wake up call to a spiritually slothful nation. "Perhaps we had grown proud," he said. "Perhaps we had grown intent upon our material success. Perhaps we were beginning to forget God, and he has spoken in the midnight hour and said: 'I am near. Remember me.'"

At the Church of the Ascension in New York, Rev. Percy Strickney Grant condemned the White Star Line in a sermon: "We must not forget the race for commercial supremacy which brought on this disaster," he said. "The White Star Line forgot the human element in its race. It placed the commercial before the human. It should not be necessary for us to wait the shriek of the Avenging Angel before we realize we are children of the Father and heed His care and the care of our fellow men."

It didn't escape attention that the largest percentage of those rescued was from first class (62 percent) and the smallest percentage was from third class (25 percent) and crew (23 percent). Lives were not considered to be equally valuable. Nor were they even equally valuable in death. When bodies were collected by the *Mackay-Bennett*, those identified as first class, even if their names were as yet unknown, were put in coffins, whereas second and third class were sewn into canvas bags and crew members were kept in an ice-filled hold. The bodies of poorer unidentified passengers had to be thrown back into the sea with weights strapped to their legs because of lack of space.

Almost all of the immediate news coverage, both in Britain and America, concentrated on the fate of what were then called "prominent persons." The shock was not just that the world's biggest liner had gone down, but that some of the world's richest people had gone down with it. Yet the obvious question was, why shouldn't the rich perish alongside the poor? Why should wealth entitle someone to more protection than poverty?

A further lesson to be learned from the *Titanic* was from the quiet selflessness of so many. If character is shown by the choices we make under pressure, then the character of most Britons, northern Europeans, and Americans was shown to be good. (Southern Europeans, Arabs, and Asians were generally portrayed as untrustworthy, self-interested, and quite possibly violent.) Mrs. Ada Clarke, one of the first to tell the story of "Nearer, My God, to Thee," left her husband behind because he urged her to get into a lifeboat even though she wanted to remain with him. She saw him standing on the deck as the ship sank. Ida Straus, wife of the multi-millionaire philanthropist Isidor Straus, elected to stay by her husband and they both calmly faced death together, seated and holding hands. W. T.

Stead apparently remained in his chair as though the next life was merely a last-minute change of destination.

It was the hundreds of similar stories of stoicism, charity, and self-sacrifice that heartened people, encouraging them to think that they weren't such a bad lot after all. Despite never having to display their best selves in the heat of war, a randomly selected cross section had managed to face life's most intense moment and emerge from it with glory. "We are rearing a self-reliant race—a race of men and women well equipped for the battle of life," roared an editorial in the *South London Observer* on April 24. "The heroism on the ill-fated *Titanic* shows conclusively that we have not degenerated since the days of Nelson. It was the same old British pluck which in the past often carried the Union Jack to victory."

Henry Van Dyke, professor of English literature at Princeton, believed that the very procedure of putting women and children first was an instinctive application of a Christian principle. If earning power, physical strength, or social standing had prevailed, it would have been men first, women second, and children last of all. He asked where this rule originated. "It comes from God, through the faith of Jesus of Nazareth," he argued in the *New York Times*. "It is the ideal of self-sacrifice. It is the rule that 'the strong ought to bear the infirmities of those that are weak.' It is the divine revelation which is summed up in the words: Greater love hath no man than this: that a man lay down his life for his friends. It needs a tragic catastrophe like the wreck of the *Titanic* to bring out the absolute contradiction between this ideal and all the counsels of materialism and selfish expediency."

Even those who didn't see specifically Christian values emerge were at least pleased that Western civilization's codes of behavior had survived amid the chaos. Van Dyke continued:

> There was no disorder, no rioting, the rule of the sea prevailed over the first law of nature. With the band playing and the lights of the sinking ship still burning, the doomed company awaited the end. They died like heroes, they died like men. It is a tragic and dreadful story, but it tells us how civilisation conquers the primal, savage instincts and brings into being and dominance the higher and nobler qualities of man's nature.

There is not in history a more splendid and inspiring example of self-control, of sacrifice, of courage and of manliness.

This was why the band emerged as such heroes. Not only had they behaved dutifully and without apparent concern for their own safety, but they also offered the hope that not all of the younger male generation were venial, lazy, proud, irreligious, inconsiderate, self-indulgent, weak-willed, and timorous. The example of the band suggested that the doom mongers may have got it wrong because, unlike soldiers, they hadn't trained to face danger and had come straight to the deck from the heart of early-twentieth-century splendor and luxury. If eight random men could display such strength of character in unison on the spur of the moment, the chances were that any other eight men randomly selected would react in the same way.

There was an element of truth to this, but it overlooked the vital role played by Wallace Hartley as bandmaster. Although it's not known whether the band played voluntarily or under orders, the men were under Hartley's command and his influence set the tone. He left behind no written confession of faith, but all the indications are that the faith of his childhood had continued into adulthood.

His moral character and his personal assurance that death was not the end must have stirred his bandsmen, all of whom had at least grown up in the church. The choice of "Nearer, My God, to Thee" was almost certainly due to Hartley's familiarity with the hymn and love for its message, something he had already confirmed to friends. Would the band have behaved in the same way under a dissolute and immoral leader or would someone not raised on the music of the church have chosen a hymn to restore calm amidst tragedy?

In the absence of detailed information on each bandsman's life, it's hard to pass judgment on the development of their moral character. In speaking of them as heroic, it's tempting to think that in childhood each of them was unafraid of pain and displayed unique signs of self-control and willingness to sacrifice, but the chances are that some were quite naturally brave and others just as naturally fearful. As has been wryly observed: "A hero is just a coward who got cornered." Yet together as a band under Hartley's leadership, they transcended their personal limitations.

The music itself played a major role in boosting their nerve. It's long been known that music can alter moods. In the seventeenth century the Restoration playwright William Congreve wrote the lines: "Music has charm to soothe the savage breast. To soften rocks, or bend a knotted oak." If the quote attributed to Wallace Hartley is anything to go by, he would have concurred with this sentiment: "I've always felt that, when men are called to face death suddenly, music is far more effective in cheering them on than all the firearms in creation."

George Orrell, bandmaster on the *Carpathia* in 1912, told Herman Finck, Musical Director of the Theatre Royal, Drury Lane, and author of "In the Shadows," which the band allegedly played on deck, that the musicians on any ship at the time were accustomed to the idea that they would be asked to play at any time that passengers were distressed.

"The ship's band in any emergency is expected to play to calm the passengers," he said.

> After the *Titanic* struck the iceberg the band began to play bright music, dance music, comic songs—anything that would prevent the passengers from becoming panic-stricken. The ship was so badly holed that it was soon obvious that disaster was ahead. Then various awe-stricken passengers began to think of the death that faced them and asked the bandmaster to play hymns. The one which appealed to all was, "Nearer, My God, to Thee."

Orrell got his information not from news reports but directly from the rescued passengers he spoke to on the *Carpathia*.

The effect of the music on passengers awaiting rescue appears to have been one of reassurance. When everything else on the *Titanic* was being turned upside down, the music remained the same. In the midst of mind-jarring abnormality, it was the one thing that retained its familiarity. For those out on the water it provided a bizarre soundtrack to a sight that so many would only be able to describe as "like watching a moving picture." It also appears to have inspired singing in the lifeboats. Passengers spoke of "Nearer, My God, to Thee" being sung by the survivors as they drifted on the water, but it's not clear whether they were singing along to the band or whether what the band had played had stayed with them.

It was a perfect media package—ordinariness to connect them with the common reader, bravery to act as an inspiration, and a piece of music that could become a signature tune for the whole event. Whenever there was a funeral, a memorial service, or a fund-raising event, "Nearer, My God, to Thee" would be played and the story of the band's final stand automatically brought to mind.

During the next two years, the immensity of the *Titanic* tragedy would be pored over in many books, magazines, and newspaper specials, but in the summer of 1914 came the start of the First World War and deaths on a previously unimaginable scale. On the first day of the Battle of the Somme, more than twenty thousand British troops were killed—the equivalent of thirteen *Titanic* disasters. By the end of the conflict, almost six million soldiers fighting against Germany had lost their lives. The war helped push the *Titanic* to the back of people's minds as words such as *tragedy* and *disaster* took on new and deeper meanings.

15

"THE SWEETS OF NOTORIETY."

If they had not died on April 15, 1912, almost all the musicians would have had to fight in France and perhaps half of them wouldn't have returned. When Roger Bricoux didn't respond to the French call-up in 1914, he was registered as a deserter even though he had been dead for two years. At the age of thirty-six, Frederick Nixon Black of C. W. & F. N. Black found himself in the British army, first with the Royal Defence Corps in Hereford, and then after the war, with the Manchester Regiment handling German prisoners. Theo Brailey, had he lived, would have been called back to the Lancashire Fusiliers.

Passenger ships continued crossing the Atlantic during the early part of the war in the belief that they were of no strategic value to the enemy. That view changed on May 7, 1915, when a German U-boat sank the *Lusitania* off the Irish coast, with the loss of 1,198 lives, an action that helped drag America into the war. The *Arabic*, the ship that had brought Wallace Hartley's body back from Boston, was torpedoed in August 1915. The great liners were repainted in dull grays or with dazzle camouflage and put to military use. The *Olympic* became a troop ship, as did the *Megantic*. The *Mauretania* at first carried troops during the campaign in Gallipoli, and then became a floating hospital. The *Oruba* was scuttled in Greece to create a breakwater, the *Carmania* became an Armed Merchant Cruiser fitted with eight 4.7-inch guns, and a U-boat sank the *Carpathia* off the east coast of Ireland in July 1918.

Some of the musicians' relatives initially stayed in touch with each other, united by the cause of getting the right financial recompense. Leon Bricoux and Auguste Krins met up in Paris with survivor Pierre Maréchal to try and make some sense of what had happened to their sons. Clara Taylor and Martha Woodward were in correspondence over the *Titanic* Relief Fund, and Andrew Hume, Ronald Brailey, and Leon Bricoux had contact over the case against C. W. & F. N. Black.

THEO BRAILEY

Ronald Brailey continued his work as a clairvoyant. The International Congress of Spiritualists, which met in Liverpool in July 1912, announced that the loss of Theo Brailey and W. T. Stead on the *Titanic* "would do more for Spiritualists in the spirit than in the flesh." He eventually moved to Shoreham by Sea, in Sussex, where in 1923 his home was burned down, destroying many of his private papers and photographs. The house was uninsured, so he had literally lost everything. He and his wife were forced to move back to London and live with their daughters. He died in February 1931, leaving an estate of £105 15s. 6d. Amy Brailey died in 1942.

Teresa Steinhilber never really recovered from the loss of her fiancé, Theo. He had been, she would later say, the love of her life. While recovering from the initial shock at Southport Convalescent Home, she noticed a group of women talking about her. When she queried them, one of them asked to read her palm and, as a result, predicted that she would marry and give birth to twins.

To a recently bereaved girl it seemed unlikely and became even less likely as the First World War reduced the population of eligible bachelors. Spinsterhood would become rife among her generation of British women and every young person, it seemed, had a maiden aunt. By the end of the war she was almost thirty years old and there were still no marriage prospects. She had started working in railway catering, initially as a hotel housekeeper and then as an administrator.

In 1924 the company she was working for, the Caledonian Railway Company, built a stunning hotel with its own station in a remote part of the Scottish Highlands. Called the Gleneagles Hotel it was the height of luxury and appealed to a wealthy clientele used to accommodation standards set by hotels on the French Riviera. It had not only first-class catering and splendid rooms, but a top golf course. It was here that Teresa met Alexander "Sandy" Crawford, a forty-nine-year-old jute merchant from Glasgow, who was rich, charming, handsome, and single. They married in October 1928 and in 1931 she gave birth to twins— a daughter, Margaret, and a son, Alistair.

It wasn't a happy marriage. Sandy spent a lot of his time in India, showed little affection, and had an alcohol problem. When the jute company he worked for hit financial problems, he tried to save it by pouring in his own cash. It proved to be a bad investment. The company collapsed and he was left penniless. The family was forced to downsize dramatically and take in lodgers. During the Second World War, when he was over sixty, Sandy became a military censor and then disappeared for two years without explanation. His whereabouts were only discovered when the police found him unconscious at the foot of a flight of stairs he'd fallen down while drunk. They contacted Teresa.

Teresa Steinhilber as an old woman with her son, Alistair Crawford.

Following Sandy's death Teresa lived in Leicester and then Southport before making her final home in Scotland where she died in 1985 at the age of ninety-six. Although her family knew of her engagement to Theo Brailey, she rarely ever spoke of it and left behind no letters, photographs of them together, or mementos. According to her son, it was as if the pain was too deep and she felt that the marriage she made was never as good as the one she had imagined with Theo.

WALLACE HARTLEY

Maria Robinson, Wallace Hartley's fiancée, never married. She moved to a house on the seafront at Bridlington, the town where Wallace had played in the Municipal orchestra, and died there of stomach cancer on June 28, 1939. Her estate of £739 10s. was left to her sister Margaret, who was with her when she died. Although her death was noted in the local papers— "Robinson: On June 28, 1939, at Marine Drive, Bridlington, Maria, eldest daughter of the late B. L. H. Robinson, of Thorp Arch, Boston Spa"—there was no obituary or news story. Her connection with Wallace Hartley had either been forgotten or was something she kept to herself.

Elizabeth Hartley, Wallace's mother, died in 1927, but Albion Hartley, who already looked old at Wallace's funeral, continued until January 1934, when he died in Harrogate, Yorkshire, at the age of eighty-three of "senile decay." Only one of the Hartley children, Mary Ellen Hartley, had children. Her marriage to Thomas Sellers in 1897 produced sons Ernest, George, and Frank, although George only lived until 1904. Ernest and Frank married but neither of them had children. So when they died, in 1984 and 1985 respectively, Albion Hartley's immediate line came to an end. The closest relatives to Wallace Hartley would become the descendants of Albion and Elizabeth's brothers and sisters.

PERCY TAYLOR

Clara Taylor, Percy's widow, remarried in August 1918, after returning to live with her parents in Dulwich. Her third husband, forty-seven years old at the time, was an accomplished singer named Albert Pearce, who worked initially in light opera and then in the music halls. He'd been in the chorus of the D'Oyly Carte Opera Company when he was seventeen, appearing in the 1887 premier of Gilbert and Sullivan's *Ruddigore* at the Savoy Theatre, and went on to become resident tenor for the Edison Bell Recording Company.

By the time he married, Albert's best days as a vocalist were over and he performed in music halls with Clara as Talbot and Pearce. In the 1920s the couple moved to Weston-super-Mare in Somerset to be near her sister Minnie, who had married Percy's brother, George. The four of them banded together to buy a restaurant in the town center, which they called Margaret's Grill.

Clara didn't discuss Percy Taylor. As far as she was concerned it was a relationship that hadn't worked and she left it at that. She was very happy with her marriage to Albert, which lasted until his death in 1946. George Taylor died mysteriously in 1955 during a walking holiday in South Wales. He went out one day but never returned. There was no news for several days and then local fishermen in Bridgend found his body in the sea, a tragic echo of Percy's death. Foul play wasn't suspected. It was assumed that he suffered a heart attack or a stroke while on the beach and that his body had subsequently been washed away. Clara died just over a year later at the age of eighty-four.

FRED CLARKE

Ellen Clarke, Fred's mother, was the most financially disadvantaged of the dependents. As a single mother since the disappearance of her husband, John Robert Clarke, she was reliant on her only son's income. She was working as a fruiterer and no doubt there had been hopes that the sorting out of John Robert's estate in America would benefit the family. She died in 1935.

WES WOODWARD

Although Martha Woodward was also a widow, she had six children who married and she was well looked after. Thomas remained at Magdalen

College until December 1925, his daughter Eleanor marrying an agricultural expert who went to work in Ceylon and Phyllis marrying the world-renowned luthier Alfred Charles Langonet. Neither Eleanor nor Phyllis had any children.

GEORGES KRINS

As well as his parents, Georges Krins left behind a brother, Marcel, and two sisters—Anne and Madeleine. Anne died as a teenager in 1917 and Madeleine married Englishman George Dustow, with whom she had two children. Marcel married Lucie Moreau in 1919 and had a son, Georges Henri Krins, two years later. Georges died in 2006. Madeleine died in 1981 and her children, Marcelle and George, in 1999 and 2008 respectively.

In 1978 Madeleine Dustow, facing a difficult time financially, wrote to the Charity Commission to find out what became of the money from the *Titanic* Relief Fund.

That some fund existed at one time is known to me as when my father was ill in 1937 I was living with my husband and son in London. He was paid a *small* sum of five shillings a week by the association [from] funds resulting from the concert given in the Albert Hall for the men who were in the band of the *Titanic* and who went down with the ship. I have in my possession the programme of this concert.

I would like to know if this association or any other organisation [that] has been set up to administer a memorial fund still exists and, if not, to what use any residue money was put. I have had a life long interest in this matter as my brother was a member of the ship's orchestra. I am an old woman of 83 years of age and I can assure you that my father, apart from the five shillings he had for about three months, never had any assistance from the association.

Yours faithfully,

Mrs. M. Dustow (nee Krins)

Roger Bricoux

A few days after receiving official confirmation that his son hadn't been rescued, Leon Bricoux had cards printed that he then mailed to friends and family:

> Mr and Mrs Bricoux and their son Gaston have the sad duty of informing you of the cruel loss that they have come to experience in the person of their son and brother
>
> ### Roger Bricoux
> *Violinist*
>
> Aged 20 years and eleven months, victim of the sinking of the Titanic.
>
> A mass will be said for the rest of our loved one, on Thursday May 2nd at 9:00 in the morning at l'Eglise Sainte-Devote in this parish.
>
> Rest in peace.

Leon maintained an active interest in the official inquiry and the battle for compensation. He dutifully collected cuttings that made reference to his son and carried on correspondence with everyone from C. W. & F. N. Black to the French consul in London and with an American company planning a souvenir edition of "Nearer, My God, to Thee" and wanting to include photos of the band.

Charlie and Frederick Black continued their business without any obvious repercussions from their involvement with the *Titanic*. In 1916 Charlie even made a trip across the Atlantic, sailing on the *St. Louis* from Liverpool to New York. By this time the brothers had moved home from Heron Road to a house called Ness Acre in the village of Willaston. The company stayed at 14 Castle Street until 1924, when it moved to 37 School Lane where it initially shared premises with the well-known Liverpool musical instrument manufacturers Crane & Sons Ltd.

Entrance to 14 Castle Street, Liverpool, former office of the Black Brothers.

The agency was still a going concern in 1934, when Frederick drew up his will and bequeathed to Charlie his "share of the profits, capital (if any) and goodwill in the firm known as C.W. F. N. [*sic*] Black Music Directors of 37 School Lane, Liverpool," but appears to have been wound up between 1939 and 1942. There was no mention of the business in the will that Charlie updated in 1946 when he was living at his final home on South Parade, West Kirby, overlooking the River Dee.

The wills of the two brothers offer a rare insight into their connections and interests. Frederick was the first to die, on October 14, 1945, and his will took up less than half a page. He was clearly the junior partner and his final wishes betrayed no outside interests or concern for posterity. The freehold of the house belonged to Charlie. Other than his share of the agency, all he had to leave was five hundred B shares in Central Equipment Ltd. (which he left to a friend named Andrew Orr) and a gross worth of £27,090 6s. 4d.

Charlie died less than a year later, on September 16, 1946, and his detailed will covered eight pages. His home and furniture were to pass to his sister Elizabeth, then living in Llandudno, North Wales, and the value of the rest of his possessions, along with his bank balance of £56,906, was to be put into a trust fund, the income of which would go to Elizabeth. On her death, £1000 would be paid to two cousins and the rest would be divided among a number of charities, including the National Sea Training School, the Children's Convalescent Home in West Kirby, the Halle Orchestra Pension Fund, and the Liverpool Radium Institute. He seemed particularly keen that he and his brother shouldn't be forgotten in the musical community and provided £10,000 to the Royal Academy of Music in London to establish the Charles

William Black Trust Student Fellowship (which is still awarded), £2,000 to the Musicians Benevolent Fund in memory of Frederick Nixon Black, and £1,500 to the Royal Manchester College of Music for the Frederick Nixon Black Scholarship.

When Elizabeth Alderson Black died on January 14, 1955, she specified that £100 of her money (she left £47,380 gross) should be invested by the Parish Church of Roby, Lancashire, to maintain the graves of her parents, William and Emma, and her sister Florence; and £100 similarly invested by the Parish Church of West Kirby, Cheshire, for the upkeep of the churchyard "and particularly the grave therein of my brothers Frederick Nixon Black and Charles William Black."

St. Bridget, the Parish Church of West Kirby, is a short walk from the last home lived in by the Black brothers. Charlie and Frederick, along with their sister Elizabeth, lie beneath a plain, horizontal, gray-green stone in the southeast corner of the churchyard. Chiseled into the stone and faint from weathering are simply their names and dates. There is nothing to indicate their connection with the most famous shipwreck in modern history.

JOCK HUME

The most dramatically affected of the musicians' families was that of the Humes. Not only did Andrew Hume suffer the indignity of being taken to court by his son's fiancée, but he also lost his home because of the missing violins, which today would be valued collectively at more than £500,000.[1] Andrew, by now approaching fifty, felt desperate about his financial situation. Within such a short time he had gone from being a hero's father to a discredited music teacher with no home or savings. Two of his daughters got on so badly with their stepmother that they'd left home—Grace, twenty-three, to become a nurse in Huddersfield and Kate, seventeen, to live in a nearby lodging house. It appeared that things couldn't get worse. But they did.

Kate was working as a clerk at the office of a local electrical company when, on August 10, 1914, she claimed, a nurse calling herself Miss Mullard came in and asked to speak to her. The woman, whom she had never seen before, said that she had worked with her sister Grace at a military hospital at Vilvorde, near Brussels, and was bringing the sad news that Grace had been murdered by German soldiers who had subsequently burned down the hospital. She gave Kate a handwritten letter supposedly composed by Grace as she died. A separate letter, written by the woman, explained the background. Miss Mullard's letter read:

> I have been asked by your sister, Nurse Grace Hume, to hand the enclosed letter to you. My name is Nurse Mullard, and I was with your sister when she died. Our camp hospital at Vilvorde was burned to the ground and out of 1517 men and 23 nurses only 19 nurses were saved, but 149 men managed to get clear away.
>
> I expect to pass through Dumfries about the 15th September but am writing this in case I should not see you. Your sister gave me your address, so, as I know Dumfries well, I shall send it to your office, if I do not see you. As there is a shortage of nurses in at Inverness, 15 of us are to be sent there. Grace requested me to tell you that her last thoughts were of Andrew and you, and that you were not to worry over her as she would be going to meet "her Jock." These were her words.
>
> She endured great agony in the last hours. One of the soldiers (our

men) caught 2 German soldiers cutting off her left breast her right one having already been cut off. They were killed instantly by our soldiers. Grace managed to scrawl this enclosed note before I found her. We can all say that your sister was a heroine. As she was a "loose nurse"—that is, she was out on the fields looking for wounded soldiers—and on one occasion when bringing in a wounded soldier a German attacked her. She threw the soldier's gun at him and shot him with her rifle. Of course, all nurses here are armed.

I have just received word this moment to pack for Scotland, so will try and get this handed to you as there is no post from here, and we are making the best of a broken down wagon truck for a shelter. Will give you fuller details when I see you. We are all quite safe here now, as there have been reinforcements.

> I am, yours sincerely,
> J. M. Mullard
> Nurse, Royal Irish Troop
> (Am not allowed to say which
>   special troop.)

The letter signed by Grace was dated September 6. The writing slanted on the page and the words were spidery. The last sentence appeared unfinished and the signature gave the impression of having been written by someone who was torn away as she wrote.

Dear Kate,

This is to say Goodbye. Have not long to live. Hospital has been set on fire. Germans cruel. A man here has had his head cut off and my right breast taken away. Give my love to Goodbye Grac x

According to Kate, as soon as she read the letter she broke down. Within hours the story had spread through the small town. When a policeman visited Andrew Hume's home, his wife allegedly muttered that Grace had "got the death she deserved" but Andrew remained suspicious, first because as far as he knew she was still in Huddersfield and, second, she wasn't qualified to work on a battlefield. To the policeman he said, "Grace couldn't nurse nobody."

Journalists from the *Dumfries Standard* interviewed Kate on September 14 and on September 16 a story headlined "Terrible Death of a Dumfries Nurse" appeared in the paper. National newspapers in London subsequently picked up the story. When Grace read news of her own tragic death, she immediately sent her father a telegram that read: "Reports untrue. Safe in Huddersfield."

On September 17 she wrote to him in more detail:

I am sorry you have been made miserable by the false report. I knew nothing about it until yesterday when I saw placards in town "Terrible Murder of Huddersfield Nurse." I bought a (Huddersfield) *Post* and saw the report. On arriving home I found a reporter waiting. I gave him details . . . Then I thought I'd better wire you straight away.

You say you heard about it on Saturday. It is an absolute mystery to me. I neither know, nor yet have I heard of such a person as Nurse Mullard. Neither have I been out of Huddersfield since war was declared. I certainly volunteered to go. Will you please forward any particulars regarding this affair? I have been informed this morning that the police may take it up. I hope they will. I should like very much to find out who this Nurse Mullard is . . .

I am again very sorry that you should be put to any trouble and inconvenience at all but I hope you will understand that it is as much a worry and trouble to me as well. The person who concocted the tale evidently knows all about us. I am trusting you will send me these particulars. Yours, Grace.

The tragic story of torture and murder had rapidly become the mystery of a hoax. Suspicion immediately fell on Kate but she persisted with her version of events, giving a detailed description of Nurse Mullard and suggesting that her father faked the letter from Grace. The police obtained copies of Grace's handwriting and quickly realized that it didn't match the letter said to have been sent from Belgium. At Kate's workplace they found notepaper that matched the paper of Grace's letter.

Kate was arrested for "forgery and uttering" and was taken into custody in Dumfries. Later she was transferred to a jail in Edinburgh where at the end of December she went on trial before the Lord Justice General, Lord Strathclyde. She pleaded not guilty, arguing that when she wrote the letters she was not in control of her emotions. As her counsel explained: "When the alleged offence is said to have been committed, her mind was so unbalanced that she could not, and did not, understand what she was doing and the effect thereof, and was not responsible therefore."

The question for the court was—if it was a hoax, what could the possible motive be? Grace, dressed in a fashionable fur stole and blue serge jacket, appeared totally composed as she stood in the dock. She said:

I had no intention of causing any sensation or alarming my father, step-mother or anyone else. I do not know why I wrote it, but I fancied what I said would be the way Grace would have written of herself in her last minutes. I could fancy the whole thing as it was written, but I had no idea that anyone would see the letters. I cannot say what made me do it, except the cruelties the Germans were committing. I was seeing and imagining the things I wrote. I cannot think why I wrote the name of Mullard, except that I believed a man of that name went down on the *Titanic*,[2] and perhaps it got into my head, which at the time seemed to be turning around. I firmly believed what was in the letters was true and that Grace had been killed. I had worked myself into that belief. I did not think I was doing anything improper.

While in prison she was examined by two physicians who found her to be alert and intelligent, although perhaps a bit shallow and easily given to fantasy. The death of her mother, the bad relationship with her father and stepmother, the outbreak of war, and her sudden departure from home were all cited as possible reasons why she might have taken refuge in the world of make-believe. Neither doctor believed that she had criminal intent. "The story was a mere childish device to create sensation and draw attention to herself," concluded Dr. Robertson, physician superintendent at the Royal Asylum, Morningside, and a lecturer in mental diseases. "Having once made up the story, she naturally stuck to it, and possibly was led into what appears to be criminal by the circumstance that she was asked to publish the letters."

Crucial to this mental confusion, in the opinion of both doctors, was the death of John Law Hume. It wasn't just the loss of someone she loved, but the sense of self-importance that resulted from the newspapers' attention. "Her favourite brother was lost in the *Titanic* and that made the first strong impression on her mind in her life," reported Sir Thomas Clouston, an expert in mental and nervous diseases. "She used to dream about him. There was a lawsuit about his affairs too, which went on for long and kept up her distress. Two tablets were put up to his memory, at the unveiling of which she was present and was much upset." Dr. Robertson concurred: "She at this time tasted the sweets of notoriety arousing through being related to a person connected with a public event. No doubt to a person of her temperament there would be a great temptation to put herself in the same position again."

At the end of two days the jury delivered a verdict of guilty but with a recommendation of leniency. The judge agreed. Three months in custody was already enough for a seventeen-year-old girl who'd done something foolish as a result of unique pressures. At the end of his summing up he turned to her and said: "Kate Hume, I am very willing to accede to the recommendation of the jury, who have given the most careful and anxious consideration of your case. In consideration of the fact that you have already been three months in prison, and having regard to your precious good character and to your age, I consider that you may be released now on probation."

Kate married Thomas Terbit in 1919 and had four children. She named her youngest son John Law Hume Terbit. She never told her children about the court case. Andrew Hume left Scotland in 1915 and moved to Peterborough where he lived for four years before going on to an address in Brixton Road, London. In 1920 he moved to 34 Great Portland Street in the West End of London where he carried on making violins until his death from a brain hemorrhage on March 24, 1934, at the age of sixty-nine. His obituary in the *Strad* read: "Mr Hume was born in Edinburgh [*sic*], of Scotch parents, and studied violin making in Germany, where he worked from 1880 to 1888. On his return, he carried on the business of violin maker at Dumfries. Later he moved to London. His instruments gained an award at the Wembley Exhibition of 1924–25." He left £811 5s. 8d.

Johnann Law Hume Costin, the only authenticated child of a *Titanic* bandsman, had the most extraordinary life of all. Her mother, Mary, died of tuberculosis in 1922, leaving Johnann an orphan at the age of ten. Mary's mother, Susan, took over her care but two years later she, too, died and Johnann was passed to an uncle. Perhaps uncomfortable with the unusual first name given to her by her mother, she changed it to Jacqueline and later became known as Jackie.

On paper her chances of making anything of her life were slim. She'd lost both her parents and her guardian grandmother by the time she was twelve, was raised in a less-than-rich town, and carried what was then the stigma of having been born illegitimate. Yet, in her midteens she came to London where she worked as a salesgirl in a shop and in 1937 married a distinguished Fleet Street crime reporter named John Ward and had two children, Cherry and Christopher. John Ward died in 1945 and she was left to raise her children alone. In the 1950s she worked in a noneditorial capacity for the *Daily Mirror*, then Britain's best-selling newspaper, and then got a top job in the British film industry working in publicity for producer Herbert Wilcox and his glamorous actress wife, Anna Neagle. In a short time she had moved from the suburb of Kew to Hampstead, then to Holland Park and finally Knightsbridge.

She became a friend to journalists, directors, producers, and film stars and carried on working in PR well into her seventies. Both of her children in turn became writers. Cherry, who married a French cardiologist, moved to Paris and became a stringer for many Fleet Street papers, including the *Evening News*, *Daily Mail*, and *Daily Mirror*. Christopher was a popular columnist on the *Daily Mirror* for thirteen years, edited the *Daily Express* from 1981 to 1983, and then, in the 1980s, cofounded what became Britain's leading contract publishers, Redwood Publishing, which specialized in magazines for clients such as American Express, British Rail, Marks and Spencer, Woolworths, and Sky.

Still chairman of Redwood but semiretired, Christopher lives in a spectacular Grade-A-listed early-nineteenth-century mansion surrounded by sixty-eight acres of rolling countryside in the Scottish Borders. He is a successful and wealthy man whose entry in *Debrett's People of Today* lists his recreations as walking, photography, and shooting. He has been a trustee of the World Wildlife Foundation and was chairman of WWF-UK for six years.

He's only an hour away from Dumfries by car but his life couldn't be more different from that of his grandmother Mary Costin or even his grandfather John Law Hume. He's conscious that he is the result of a tough struggle for survival and with more time on his hands he has started to research his remarkable family, traveling to Halifax, Nova Scotia, to discover his grandfather's grave, contacting violin experts to see if he can find out the stories behind the Eberle and the Guadagnini that were lost at sea, and sifting through crew records to nail down the ships that his grandfather served on.

Johnann Law Hume Costin, by then better known as Jackie Ward, died in 1996 at the age of eighty-three. She was living in Kensington Church Street, not too far from the Royal Albert Hall where her father was celebrated in music in 1912. "After the worst possible start," says Christopher with obvious pride, "she made a great success of her life."

16

"I Should Cling to My Old Violin."

As I neared the end of writing this book, I was talking with a contact who had helped me with information about Wallace Hartley. Suddenly she said, "Have you heard about Wallace's violin?" Of course I knew about the violin inasmuch as it was one of the great mysteries surrounding his death and the discovery of his body by the *Mackay-Bennett*. Press reports immediately after the discovery made specific mention of the fact that he had been found with his violin case strapped to his chest. It may have been these that led Thomas Worthington to say at his funeral that Hartley had in effect said: "I should cling to me my old violin which has given so much pleasure to many, and often to me, and instead of playing to please or amuse or pass time I should play to inspire." The reports also said that the violin, its case, and other material, were being sent to White Star for forwarding to England.

But nothing ever arrived, or at least nothing that was reported on. Unusually, the violin wasn't mentioned on the official list of effects that Albion Hartley signed for. Nor were its case and the other loose items. In her 2002 book *A Hymn for Eternity*, Yvonne Carroll wrote: "Wallace Hartley's violin was found strapped to his body but disappeared before his body was sent back to England." The suspicion was that somone had spirited it away shortly after it was brought to land.

Maybe it was because of this loss that Arthur Catton Lancaster, a musical instrument maker from Colne, who had played alongside Hartley in the Colne Orchestra, decided to make a violin in honor of his friend. Lancaster had played at the funeral and lived close to the old Hartley home on Albert Road. He engraved the words "Nearer, my God, to thee, nearer to thee" on the tailpiece of the tribute instrument, had a color image of the *Titanic* painted on the back, and had a small varnished photograph of Hartley fixed beneath it. The intention was that it would be competed for each year by violinists in the Colne Orchestra and kept by the winner.

The painting of the *Titanic* and photo of Wallace Hartley on the back of the tribute violin made by Arthur Lancaster.

The violin was mentioned in *Strad* magazine at the time, and then in the second edition of Rev. William Meredith-Morris's classic book *British Violin Makers* (1920) where it was described as having "a large and telling tone." Lancaster was praised in general for his beautiful workmanship. At some time after the 1920s the violin was no longer with the Colne Orchestra, its whereabouts unknown. In 1955 it was bought and repaired by Eric Voigt of Manchester and eventually sold on. Then, in 1974, an anonymous bene-factor appeared at a rehearsal of the East Lancashire Youth Orchestra one Saturday morning and handed over the violin as a gift, requesting that it be played once a year in honor of Wallace Hartley.

The East Lancashire Youth Orchestra became the Burnley Youth Orchestra and the violin was traditionally kept by the leader but through-out the years had been badly treated. In 2010 the Lancashire Sinfonietta took the instrument to David Vernon Violins of Manchester, where it was completely restored by Paul Parsons.

I thought this was the violin that my contact was referring to, but it wasn't. I was shown a collection of color images, some of them featuring a violin in a large brown leather bag, others of sheet music, black-and-white photos, and scribbled notes in what looked like a diary. I assumed it was all part of a single collection. "What is it?" I asked. My contact replied: "This is supposed to be the violin and case that Wallace Hartley was found with after the *Titanic* went down."

As far as the band on the *Titanic* was concerned, this was the Holy Grail. As far as the *Titanic* in general went, it must rate pretty close, next to having a chunk of the ship raised or discovering a safe full of unposted letters writ-ten on board. If this was what it purported to be, it contained the answers to many questions that had perplexed *Titanic* historians during the past century. If this was the actual violin that once played "Nearer, My God, to Thee" as the *Titanic* went down, it must be valued at millions of dollars. It's hard to think of another musical instrument that would raise as much money.

Questions began tumbling through my mind. Was it genuine? How was it possible to know whether it was real or not? Who had been holding on to it? Who had taken the photographs and why? The answer to the last question was easy. They had been made by someone intending to put the instrument up for auction. The photos had existed for at least five years and had been shown to a select few people who it was thought could assist with the authentication.

Although I was looking at photographic evidence rather than the physical collection of objects, everything about what was in the pictures struck me as being the real deal. If this wasn't genuine, it was a highly elaborate and well-researched fraud. Regardless of the objects' immediate source, all the evidence pointed to their having once belonged to Maria Robinson, Hartley's fiancée. On the July 14 to 26 pages of a 1912 diary was what looked like the draft of a letter written to a Mr. F. Walters or Walthers at the Office of the Provincial Secretary, Nova Scotia. It read: "I would be most grateful if you could convey my heartfelt thanks to all who have made possible the return of my late fiancé's violin. May I also take this opportunity to express my appreciation to you personally for your gracious intervention on my behalf." Beneath this was the remark, "A. H. informed," surely a reference to Albion Hartley.

If this was a draft of a letter, it indicated that Maria had made a direct appeal to Nova Scotia's provincial secretary for the return of the violin and that by July 1912 it had been received by her without the event ever being publicized. All queries about effects were dealt with by the deputy provincial secretary, who was named Frederick F. Mathers. Either I had misread Maria's handwriting or she had made a small spelling error.

The question of why she wanted to have the violin rather than allowing it to go to his family was answered when I looked at its details. The tail-piece, a V-shaped piece of silver stretching from the bottom of the strings to the lower edge of the violin's body, had been carefully inscribed with a message. "For Wallace on the occasion of our engagement from Maria." It not only made sense that Maria would have wanted to cherish it and felt she almost had a right to claim it, but also offered a possible explanation as to why Hartley strapped it to his chest, next to his heart, and went into the water with it rather than jettisoning it to allow him more freedom of movement.

The violin itself had been photographed deep inside the case, which was not a normal violin case but a thick brown leather bag that looked more like an old-fashioned family doctor's bag. It had a handle but it also had two straps, possibly two inches wide, that could easily have been put over his shoulders. On the side it was initialed in black letters W. H. H. The violin looked golden brown and was in good condition apart from some minor erosion on the tailpiece. It had perhaps been restored because included in the belongings was a copy of a 1903 book, *The Repairing and Restoration of Violins* by Horace Petherick, which had been signed to "Miss Robinson" by one "J. Griffin" on December 8, 1915.

The other material had been kept either in or with the case. Some of it, like the sheet music to a song called "The Ship That Will Never Return" by F. V. St. Clair[1] and the violin book given to Maria in 1915, obviously weren't part of Hartley's collection, but other material could have been. There was some sheet music dated April 1911 from the Will Rositer Band and Orchestra Club and, most significantly, sheet music to "Nearer, My God, to Thee."

What was interesting about this sheet music for "Nearer, My God, to Thee" was that the music was not Arthur Sullivan's "Propior Deo," Lowell Mason's "Bethany" (or "Bethel"), or even the Church of England's "Horbury,", but a 1902 tune by Lewis Carey that was performed by the Australian contralto Ada Crossley, who would later appear at the memorial concert for the *Titanic* musicians held at the Royal Albert Hall. She first appeared in London in 1895, played five times before Queen Victoria, and toured in America. This version of "Nearer, My God, to Thee" was one of her signature tunes.

It raised the question as to whether this was the version, or *a* version, that the band played on August 15, 1912. Was Carey's music, made popular by Ada Crossley, the setting that most people at the time were familiar with because it had been taken around the world? If it was the one played, could this explain why so many people from different countries and church affiliations instantly recognized it? If it was added to the music case after Hartley's death, it still could be because Maria knew that he played this tune.

Other material appeared to be family memorabilia with no obvious connection to Hartley: a postcard to a Miss Laura Crocker in Upper Clapton, a First World War medal given to a Thomas Robinson, a Bible containing the family tree of a William Davies who married Eleanor Young on the island of St. Helena in 1849. There was no sign of music composed by Hartley, which was rumored to have been in the case when he died.

Through making inquiries I was able to establish that this violin did exist. The photos weren't the result of digital manipulation. However, everyone connected with it was bound to a vow of confidentiality. This was partly because the instrument was still being subjected to historical and scientific tests and partly because the optimum sale date would be the *Titanic*'s centenary year. Tens of thousands of UK pounds had already been spent attempting to verify its authenticity as the actual violin used by Wallace Hartley on his final voyage. All that I could deduce for certain was that it had come down through the family of Maria Robinson and that the present owner was a man.

If this object was what it appeared to be, it made an extraordinary story. If it wasn't what it appeared to be, it was still an extraordinary story, but this time one either of forgery or incorrect attribution. It could, for example, have belonged to Hartley but not have been taken on the *Titanic* or have been commissioned by Maria after his death to replace a real one that was lost. I took the photo of the violin to David Rattray, who is a luthier, instrument custodian at the Royal Academy of Music, and author of *Masterpieces of Italian Violin Making*. His guess was that the violin was of German origin, probably from the late eighteenth century, and that in 1910 it could have been bought for £30 to £40.

Although I didn't mention Hartley's name, for fear of leaking the story, he was skeptical that a wooden musical instrument could have survived the sinking. Any contact with water and the glue would have dissolved, leaving the violin to fall into its constituent parts. He mentioned the well-attested case of the "Red Diamond" Stradivarius, which was swept into the Pacific Ocean on the California coast in the 1950s and was painstakingly reconstructed by master craftsman Hans Weischar.

Paul Parsons, who had restored Arthur Lancaster's tribute model, also didn't believe a violin could last in such inclement conditions. First, there was water, then salt, then movement, and finally freezing temperatures. Hartley's body floated for ten days and we know that by the time the *Mackay-Bennett* arrived, there was rain, dense fog, and a heavy swell. "It would have disintegrated," Paul Parsons told me. "The glues that are used on an instrument are water soluble. Even in very cold temperatures the glue would eventually turn to gel within a very short space of time."

Yet reports by the rescue team suggest that because of the way the life jackets were made, the upper portions of the bodies were kept well above the waterline. I was surprised to discover that Fred Clarke's business card, which had been with his body in the water for eight days, had only a small watermark on the lower edge. Similarly, the letter that Wallace Hartley had from his friend Bill looked remarkably undamaged and, significantly, the ink hadn't even run. It appeared to have had less contact with water than a letter accidentally dropped in a bathtub.

The violin's possible price of £30 to £40 at first appears expensive for an engagement present around 1910, bearing in mind that it represented up to ten months' pay for a ship's musician and that Maria Robinson had no job. How could she have afforded such a gift? The clue may be in her father's death in 1909, close to the time of the engagement. He unexpectedly fell into a diabetic coma and died three days later at the age of only fifty-one. Although he left no will, his work as a cloth manufacturer would have left him wealthy and his money would have been passed to his four children. In the 1911 census both Margaret and Maria were listed as being women of "private means."

If Maria did get the violin back, what would have happened to it subsequently? There was no mention of it in her will when she died unmarried in 1939, so she may already have passed it on, possibly to her sister Margaret who was also unmarried. From there it could have gone either to Mary, the youngest sister, who married John Wood in 1910 and had a son, also John, in 1911, or to her brother William, who married Florence Noble in 1908 and had Helen in 1913 and Margaret in 1915. John Wood, Mary Robinson's son, married Pauline Longstaffe in 1957, but they don't appear to have had children, so the most likely inheritor would be a son of William's daughters.

It could be that for years the violin was considered to be of sentimental rather than commercial value. It has been only in the last two decades or so that prices for *Titanic* memorabilia have rocketed. The record for a single item so far is £101,000 and for a collection of pieces £235,000. The owner of this instrument must have thought they would be better off with a cash reward than an old violin in a leather case languishing in a cellar or attic.

The primary question must be—even if it is shown to be the right age and to have had contact with seawater—how can it be definitively proved to have been the violin that Hartley played on the deck of the *Titanic*? There are no photos of him on that trip that can be blown up for detail.

The most compelling evidence is the diary with the draft letter. This suggests a feasible story of a violin rescued from the *Titanic* being returned to Maria Robinson. Other names on the same page can be verified as people who were alive at the time and living in the Leeds area: Arthur Roberts, of 10 Eldon Street, was a twenty-three-year-old shop assistant; "St Johns Adel" was a reference to St. John's Church in Adel, a district of Leeds. The note "letter from Mary" most likely refers to Mary Hartley. Unfortunately, there are no letters between Maria and Frederick Mathers in the Nova Scotia Archives to corroborate the diary draft.

If the violin turns out to be Hartley's *Titanic* instrument, it will be a huge media event and, one hundred years after their deaths, will bring the band back into the limelight. People will again be asking the question first asked in 1912: "Who were these musicians?" Those close to this unfolding story hope that the tests will be completed in time for it to go on a world tour before being auctioned in 2012. If it is proved to be what the vendor believes it is, it will be the most expensive *Titanic* artifact ever auctioned.

In June 2010 British composer David Bedford premiered *The Wreck of the Titanic*, a large-scale work for orchestra and choir, at the Liverpool Philharmonic Hall. Commissioned by the Lancashire Sinfonietta and three music services in Cheshire and Lancashire, it featured the band playing the tunes of the era along with new music based on such influences as the rhythms of hammers beating in a shipyard and the tapping of the Morse code. The leader of the Liverpool Youth Orchestra played with Arthur Lancaster's tribute violin.

No one associated with this violin appears to have been aware of the fact that Arthur Lancaster's son was Seth Lancaster, the twenty-year-old cellist who was offered a job on the *Titanic* back in December 1911. It was only during the first week of April 1912 that he learned the Black brothers had moved him to the *Mauretania* to take the place of Roger Bricoux. He had fully expected to be playing alongside Wallace Hartley on the *Titanic*. When the *Titanic* sank, he was three days behind it on the *Mauretania*, which had left Liverpool on April 13, and he arrived in New York on April 19, the day after the *Carpathia* arrived.

When Arthur set about making his tribute violin, he was no doubt not only grieving for his friend Wallace Hartley but keenly aware that but for the late switch he could also have been mourning the death of his own son. When news of the sinking was first received in Colne, anxious friends deluged the Lancaster home at 5 Smith Street to find out what had become of Seth.

A measure of Hartley's stature among his contemporaries and of the affection that Arthur Lancaster had for him only came to light in 2010 when Paul Parsons began restoring the violin. After carefully removing the back, he noticed there was writing on the inside at the upper top that wouldn't have been seen for almost one hundred years. It was in such a position that it could only have been put there as it was being made. Part of this was Lancaster's name, address, and the date of the work—June 29, 1912. The rest of it was a moving tribute to the man who by word and example had led the *Titanic*'s band to play on.

> In memory of my friend Mr Wallace Hartley, the heroic leader of the ill-fated *Titanic*. Life is dear to those we love. Hoping that this violin will be as pure in tone as my friend was pure in heart.

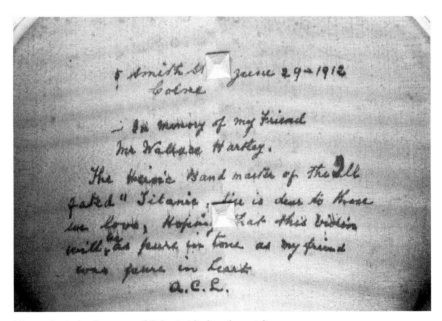

Message by Arthur Lancaster of Colne inside the tribute violin.

Sources

I used the following libraries and archives: Birkenhead Central Library; Brooklyn Public Library; Compton Estate Office, Eastbourne; Devonshire Collection, Chatsworth House; Colne Library; British Library; British Newspaper Library; Bristol Record Office; Magdalen College, Oxford; College of Psychic Studies, London; Royal Northern College of Music, Manchester; American Federation of Musicians; Companies House, London; Conservatoire Royal de Liege; Chicago History Museum; Sotheby's of London; East Riding of Yorkshire Library Service (Bridlington Local Studies Library); East Sussex Library, Eastbourne; General Register Office for Scotland; the National Archives of Scotland; Dumfries Archive Centre; Dumfries Public Library; Harvard Theatre Collection, Houghton Library, Harvard University; Liverpool Philharmonic; the Hymn Society of the United States and Canada; Performing Rights Society, London; Gloucester Cathedral; McMaster University Library, Hamilton, Ontario; London Metropolitan Archives; Lambeth Archives; University of Stirling, Scotland; Maritime History Archive, Memorial University of Newfoundland; Lancashire Sinfonietta; National Library of Jamaica; Merseyside Maritime Museum; Francis Hurd Stadler *Titanic* Collection, Missouri Historical Society Archives, St. Louis; Special Collections, Mitchell Library, Glasgow; National Art Library, Victoria & Albert Museum, London; Nova Scotia Archives & Record Management; Special Collections, Royal Academy of

Music, London; Royal College of Music, London; Ritz Hotel, London; Prudential Insurance, Stirling, Scotland; Halle Orchestra, Manchester; Royal Society of Musicians, London; Southport Library; Lancashire Fusiliers Museum; Royal Military School of Music, Kneller Hall, Twickenham; UK Documents; National Maritime Museum, Greenwich; Royal Bank of Scotland; the Grand Hotel, Eastbourne; Government Register Office (UK); National Archives, Kew, Ulster Folk and Transport Museum, Holywood, Northern Ireland.

The following people helped me with information about their relatives connected with the *Titanic*'s band; Shirley Brailey, Priscilla Clarke, Lesley Chapman, Beata Dustow, Grace Dalton, Alistair Crawford, Mary Gambell, Alex Glass, Liz Hiddleston, Yvonne Hume, Judith Jeremy, Dorothy Kiely, Ros Meeson, Margaret Mills, Graham Osborn, Jeanette Osborn, Anne Osborn, Jack Osborne, Annette Percival, David Powner, Christopher Price, Annette Robson, Doug Semple, Bobbie Seymour, Katherine Shone, Jeremy Steinhilber, Sue Steinhilber, Helen Turner, Peter Vannozzi, Christopher Ward, Bill Winton, Beverley Wolstenholme, Jeanette Woodward, Lilli Woodward.

I also had help from writers and researchers with expertise on the musicians. Olivier Mendez was generous in sharing his passion for Roger Bricoux. Yvonne Carroll answered my repeated questions about Wallace Hartley. Both Jean-Marc Haugustaine and Philippe Delaunoy sent me valuable material about the life of the fellow countryman Georges Krins, Robert McDougall gladly shared information and photographs relating to Wallace Hartley, and Christian Tennyson-Ekeberg, although writing his own book, kept me in touch with developments. Sally Wood translated some letters from French to English, Kelley McRae researched the Brooklyn Eagle (in Brooklyn) and Diane Eliopoulos Montgomery told me that Roger Bricoux was quoting from Balzac.

General Bibliography

Ballard, Robert. Titanic: *The Last Great Images*. Toronto: Madison Publishing, 2008.

Ballard, Robert. *Robert Ballard's* Titanic. Toronto: Madison Publishing, 1987.

Barratt, Nick. *Lost Voices from the* Titanic. London: Preface Publishing, 2009.

Bryceson, Dave. *The* Titanic *Disaster: As Reported in the British National Press*. New York: W. W. Norton, 1997.

Gibbs, Philip. *The Deathless Story of the* Titanic. London: Lloyd's of London Press Ltd., 1912.

Haas, Charles A. and John P. Eaton, Titanic *Triumph and Tragedy*. Yeovil: Patrick Stephens Ltd., 1986.

Hansen, Erik Fosnes. *Psalm at Journey's End*. New York: Farrar, Straus & Giroux, 1996.

Hyslop, Douglas (with Alastair Forsyth and Sheila Jemima). Titanic *Voices: Memories from the Fateful Voyage*. New York: St. Martin's Press, 1999.

Lord, Walter. *A Night to Remember*. New York: Holt, Rinehart & Winston, 1958.

Lord, Walter. *The Night Lives On*. New York: William Morrow, 1986.

Matsen, Brad. *Titanic's Last Secrets*. New York: Twelve, 2008.

Titanic *Historical Document Archive*, 2 discs, www.paperlessarchives.com.

Winocour, Jack ed., *The Story of the* Titanic *as Told by Its Survivors*. New York: Dover Publications Inc., 1960.

Printed Sources

Chapter 1

Books

Berger, Meyer. *The Story of the* "*New York Times.*" New York: Simon & Schuster, 1951.

Biel, Steven. *Down with the Old Canoe: A Cultural History of the* Titanic. New York: W. W. Norton, 1996.

David, Elmer Holmes. *History of the* "*New York Times*" *1851–1921*. New York: New York Times.

Fine, Barnett. *A Giant of the Press: Carr van Anda*. Oakland: Acme Books, 1968.

Heyer, Paul. Titanic *Legacy: Disaster as Media Event and Myth*. Westport, CT: Praeger, 1995.

Morris, James McGrath. *The Rose Man of Sing Sing*. New York: Fordham University Press, 2003.

Ross, Charles G. *The Story of the* "*St. Louis Post-Dispatch.*" Ann Arbor: UMI, 1992.

Ticehurst, Brian. *The* Titanic *Rescuers*. Southampton: B & J Printers, 2001.

Newspapers

"Latest News from the Sinking Ship." *New York Times*, April 15, 1912.

"Big *Titanic*'s First Trip." *New York Times*, April 15, 1912.

"*Titanic* Boilers Blew Up." *New York Evening World*, April 18, 1912.

"Women Go Mad in the Boats." *Daily Mirror*, April 19, 1912.

"Rescue Ship Arrives." *New York Times*, April 19, 1912.

"Thrilling Story by *Titanic*'s Surviving Wireless Man." *New York Times*, April 19, 1912.

"Rescue Ship Arrives." *New York Times*, April 19, 1912.

"The Story of the *Titanic*." *The Times*, April 20, 1912.

"Band Goes Down Playing." *Daily Mirror*, April 20, 1912.

"Band Played Solemn Hymn as Great Ship Sank." *Daily Sketch*, April 20, 1912.

"Sinking Ship's Band Chose Fitting Hymn." *New York Times*, April 21, 1912.

"Operator's Story Enthrals England." *New York Times*, April 21, 1912.

"England Proud of the Band." *New York Times*, April 21, 1912.

"Keep Your Mouth Shut: Big Money for You." *New York Herald*, April 21, 1912.

"The *Titanic's* Musicians." *New York Times*, April 22, 1912.

"Brave as the Birkenhead Band: The *Titanic's* Musician Heroes." *Illustrated London News*, April 27, 1912.

"The Tragedy of the *Titanic*—A Complete Story." *New York Times*, April 28, 1912.

"On the Other Side: *Titanic* Disaster Survivors in New York." *Illustrated London News*, May 4, 1912.

"The *Titanic* Band Memorial Concert." *The Times*, May 25, 1912.

"Capt. Rostron Guest of Mrs. J. B. Thayer." *New York Times*, June 2, 1912.

Dorrance, James French. "The Sea-Going Reporter: Tugging the *Titanic* Story." *Publishers' Guide*, October 1912.

Hurd, Carlos. "When the *Titanic* Sank!" *The Quill*, June 1932.

"The Press: News Judge." *Time*, February 5, 1945.

Stadler, Frances Hurd. "My Father's Scoop of a Lifetime." *Mature American*, Spring 1988.

CHAPTER 2

Books

Brinnin, John Malcolm. *The Sway of the Grand Saloon: A Social History of the North Atlantic*. London: Macmillan, 1971.

Herson, John. *Liverpool as a Diasporic City*. (Unpublished thesis.) Liverpool: John Moore's University.

Oldham, William J. *The Ismay Line*. London: Journal of Commerce, 1961.

Scarth, Alan. Titanic *and Liverpool*. Liverpool: Liverpool University Press, 2009.

The Shipbuilder & Marine Engine Builder, *Titanic* and *Olympic* Edition, June 1911.

Newspapers

"The New White Star Liners." *The Times*, September 1, 1908.

"Ireland: The Shipbuilding Industry." *The Times*, November 11, 1908.

"South Coast: Southampton Docks Reconstruct Trafalgar Dock." *The Times*, November 3, 1909.

"The Olympic and *Titanic*: Insurances Effected." *The Times*, January 6, 1911.

"The Transatlantic Service: Port Accommodation in America." *The Times*, January 26, 1911.

"Launch of the *Titanic*." *The Times*, June 1, 1911.

"Dock Works at Southampton." *The Times*, June 14, 1911.

"The *Titanic*." *The Times*, October 11, 1911.

"Shipbuilding." *The Times*, January 22, 1912.

"Dry-Docking the *Titanic*." *The Times*, February 5, 1912.

"Bandsmen Now Passengers." *New York Times*, March 24, 1912.

"The Largest Vessel Afloat." *The Times*, April 11, 1912

"Band Goes Down Playing." *Daily Mirror*, April 20, 1912.

"The *Titanic* Disaster." *Musicians' Report and Journal*, May 1912.

"The Sea-Going Bandsmen." *Musicians' Report and Journal*, July 1912.

"News." *Orchestral Association Monthly Report*, January 1913.

"The Truth." *Musicians' Report and Journal*, February 1913.

Babler, Gunter. "The Dinner at Lord Pirrie's." www.*Titanic*files.org, 2002.

CHAPTER 3

Books

Barczewski, Stephanie. Titanic: *A Night Remembered*. London: Hambledon, 2004.

Carr, James. *Annals and Stories of Colne*. Manchester: Duerdon, 1878.

Carroll, Yvonne. *A Hymn for Eternity: The Story of Wallace Hartley*. Stroud: Tempus Publishing, 2002.

Cryer, M. *Memories of Colne*. Blackpool: Landy, 2006.

McDougal, Robert. Titanic *Bandmaster Remembrance Book*. Blackpool: Robert McDougal, 2000.

McDougal, Robert. Titanic *Wake: Wallace Hartley Memoriam Tribute*. Blackpool: Robert McDougal, 1996.

Moore, Benjamin. *History of Wesleyan Methodism in Burnley and East Lancashire*. Burnley: Faxette Printing Works, 1899.

Vickers, James. *History of Independent Methodism*. Wigan: Independent Methodist Bookroom, 1920.

Wyatt, Ken. *The* Lusitania's *Musician: The Tale of a South Yorkshire Survivor*. Swinton: Babash Printers.

Newspapers

"Sale of Work at Bethel School." *Colne & Nelson Times*, March 22, 1884.

"Colne Musician Lost in the *Titanic*." *Colne & Nelson Times*, April 19, 1912

"Wallace Hartley." *Bridlington Chronicle*, April 19, 1912.

"Shock for Thorp Arch Young Lady." *Boston Spa News*, April 19, 1912.

"Band Leader's Last Hymn." *Leeds Mercury*, April 22, 1912.

"Remembering the Musicians." *Brooklyn Daily Eagle*, April 24, 1912.

"The Lost *Titanic*." *Colne & Nelson Times*, April 26, 1912.

"The Loss of the *Titanic*; Local References." *Bridlington Free Press*, April 26, 1912.

"That Brave Musician." *Dewsbury and District News*, April 27, 1912.

"Dewsbury's *Titanic* Hero." *Dewsbury and District News*, April 27, 1912.

"Mr. Wallace Hartley: Proposed Dewsbury Memorial." *Dewsbury Reporter*, May 11, 1912.

"The Late Mr. Wallace Hartley." *British Weekly*, May 16, 1912.

"Honouring a Hero's Death." *Bridlington Free Press*, May 17, 1912.

"*Titanic* Bandmaster." *Liverpool Echo*, May 17, 1912.

"The Dead Brought Home: Heroic Bandmaster's Father Interviewed." *Liverpool Echo*, May 18, 1912.

"*Titanic*'s Heroic Bandmaster." *Leeds Mercury*, May 20, 1912.

"Wallace Hartley: A Hero of the *Titanic*." *Independent Methodist*, June 1912.

"Robinson Obituary." *Bridlington Chronicle*, July 1, 1939.

"A Night to Remember." *Colne & Nelson Times*, June 22, 1956.

"Memories Are Stirred." *Colne & Nelson Times*. October 31, 1958.

Jack, Ian. "Further, My God, from Thee." *Independent*. September 26, 1999.

CHAPTER 4

Books

Latitude 41, No 29. Journal de l'Association Francaise du *Titanic*. France, 2004. (This 92-page edition was a mini-biography of Roger Bricoux written by Olivier Mendez.)

Newspapers

"La Catastrophe du *Titanic*: Notre Concitoyen Roger Bricoux." *Monaco-Revue*, May 12, 1912.

"Nearer, My God, to Thee: Two Leeds Musicians Go Down with the Ship." *Yorkshire Evening News*, May 20, 1912.

CHAPTER 5

Books

Aspin, Chris. *Dizzy Heights: The Story of Lancashire's First Flying Men*. Helmshore: Helmshore Local History Society, 1987.

Cousins, James H. and Margaret E. *We Two Together*. Madras: Ganesh, 1950.

Grasset, Joseph. *Marvels Beyond Science*. London, 1910.

The Lancashire Fusilier's Annual. 1902, 1903, 1904, 1906, 1907.

Oppenheim, Janet. *The Other World*. Cambridge: Cambridge University Press, 1985.

Smyth, Major B. *History of the Lancashire Fusiliers 1822–1903*. Vol. *2*. Dublin: Sackville Press, 1904.

Stead, W. T. *Hymns That Have Helped*. London: Stead's Publishing House, 1912.

Surtees, George. *A Short History of the XX Lancashire Fusiliers*. London: Malcolm Page, 1955.

Newspapers

"'Property' Ghosts at a Séance." *Daily Mirror*, March 9, 1906.

"Prehistoric Sacrifice: Scene Reconstructed by a Bayswater Seer." *Daily Express*, November 12, 1906.

"W. Ronald Brailey, Clairvoyant." (Advert.) *Light*, January 4, 1908.

"Is Spiritualism Declining?" *Daily Mail*, May 24, 1908

"Ronald Brailey's New Address." *Light*, April 23, 1910.

"Mr. C. C. Paterson's Biplane." *Flight*, May 28, 1910.

"Mr. Paterson Flies Across Country." *Flight*, August 13, 1910.

"Mishap with the Gaunt Monoplane." *Flight*, April 1, 1911.

"Southport Aerodrome." *Flight*, July 1, 1911.

"Another Local Victim." *Southport Visiter*, April 20, 1912.

"The *Titanic*: Another Local Victim." *Southport Guardian*, April 24, 1912.

"Acknowledgement from Mr. and Mrs. Ronald Brailey." *Light*, April 27, 1912.

"Message from Mr. W. T. Stead." *Light*, April 27, 1912.

"The Pianist of the *Titanic* Orchestra." *Brighton Advertiser*, April 27, 1912.

"Letter from H. Blackwell." *Light*, May 11, 1912.

"Nearer, My God, to Thee." *Light*, July 13, 1912.

"That Glorious Band." *Lancashire Fusiliers Annual*, 1912.

Jones, Laura. "100 Year Anniversary for Formby's Freshfield Beach." *Southport Visiter*, May 19, 2010.

Chapter 6

Books

Forvague, H. W. *Municipal Eastbourne 1883–1933*. Eastbourne: Sussex Printers Ltd., 1933.

Olympic *Collision with HMS* Hawke. The Official Enquiry.

Pugh, Peter. *Grand Hotel Eastbourne*. Eastbourne: Grand Hotel, 1987.

Taylor, Frank Fonda. *To Hell with Paradise: A History of the Jamaican Tourist Industry*. Pittsburgh: University of Pittsburgh Press, 1993.

Thomas, Edward. *The Playhouse on the Park*. Eastbourne: Friends of the Devonshire Park Theatre, 1997.

Willett, Mary. *A History of West Bromwich*. West Bromwich: Free Press, 1882.

Woodward, Reginald. *Boy on a Hill*. Gainsborough: G. W. Belton, 1984.

Young, Kenneth. *Music's Great Days in the Spas and Watering Places*. London: Macmillan, 1968.

Newspapers

"Devonshire Park." *Eastbourne & Sussex Society*. February 18, 1908; March 31, 1908; March 9, 1909; March 23, 1909.

"Music in Eastbourne." *The Strad*, 1908, page 405.

"The Duke's Orchestra." *Eastbourne & Sussex Society*, April 27, 1909.

"The Duke's Orchestra." *Eastbourne & Sussex Society*. May 4, 1909.

"The Giant Olympic: A Luxurious Floating Hotel." *New York Times*, June 25, 1911.

"Oxonians on Board the *Titanic*." *Oxford Chronicle*, April 19, 1912.

"Local Passengers on the *Titanic*." *Oxford Times*, April 20, 1912.

"John Wesley Woodward." *Eastbourne Gazette*, April 24, 1912.

"John Wesley Woodward." *Oxford Illustrated*, April 24, 1912.

"The *Titanic* Fund." *West Bromwich Free Press*, April 26, 1912.

"Oxford Victims in the *Titanic* Disaster." *Oxford Chronicle*, April 26, 1912.

"An Eastbourne Hero in the *Titanic* Disaster." *Brighton Advertiser*, April 27, 1912.

"Hero Musicians." *Eastbourne Gazette*, May 1, 1912.

"Bandsmen Who Were Known Here." *Daily Gleaner*, Jamaica. May 2, 1912.

"Mr. J. Wesley Woodward." *Daily Gleaner*. Jamaica, May 3, 1912.

CHAPTER 7

Books

Baptie, David. *Musical Scotland*. New York: Hildesheim, 1972.

Rattray, David. *Violin Making in Scotland 1750–1950*. Oxford: British Violin Makers Association, 2006.

Newspapers

Hume, Andrew. "On Violin Construction." *The Strad*, 1910, page 367.

Hume, Andrew. "Violin Construction." *The Strad*, 1910, page 447.

"Disaster to Grand Liner: Dumfries Man on Board." *Dumfries & Galloway Standard*, April 17, 1912.

"Local Men Missing." *Dumfries & Galloway Standard*, April 20, 1912.

"Sinking Ship's Band Had Chosen Fitting Hymn." *New York Times*, April 21, 1912.

"The Last Hymn." *Dumfries & Galloway Standard*, April 24, 1912.

"Memorial for *Titanic* Victims." *Dumfries & Galloway Standard*, May 1, 1912.

"John Hume." *Musical Mail and Advertiser*, May 1912.

"Dumfries *Titanic* Victims." *Dumfries & Galloway Standard*, June 4, 1912.

"Fund for Families of *Titanic* Bandsmen." *New York Times*, July 14, 1912.

Hume, Andrew. "Correspondence." *The Strad*, 1913, page 79.

Piper, Towry. "Fiddles by Living Makers." *The Strad*, 1915, page 402.

"Scottish Violin by Andrew Hume." *Sotheby's of London Catalogue*, November 12, 1987.

CHAPTER 8

Books

Germain, Jean Francois. *L'Echo du Naufrage du* Titanic *en Belgique*. Vol. *1*.

Mowbray, Jay Henry. *Sinking of the* Titanic. New York: Dover, 1998.

Musschoot, Dirk. *De Vlamingen up de* Titanic. Tielt: Lanoo, 2000.

Newspapers

"Dined with the Queen Sixty Years Ago." *Morning Leader*, November 8, 1897.

"A Guest of the Lord Mayor in 1837." *City Press*, November 6, 1897.

"Death of of Mrs. Wheeler." *City Press*, March 8, 1902.

"Liverpool Symphony Orchestra." *Liverpool Courier*, October 6, 1908.

"Akeroyd Symphony Orchestra Concert." *Liverpool Daily Post*, November 3, 1909.

"The Akeroyd Orchestra Concert." *Daily Post & Mercury*, December 1, 1909.

"English Singer Makes American Debut." *New York Dramatic Mirror*, May 21, 1910.

"Akeroyd's Symphony Orchestra." *Liverpool Evening Express*, January 18, 1911.

"Akeroyd Rhapsody Concert." *Liverpool Echo*, November 1, 1911.

"Un Liegeois parmi les Naufrages." *La Meuse*, April 16, 1912.

"An Argyle Theatre Bandsman among the *Titanic* Orchestra." *Birkenhead News*, April 20, 1912.

"*Titanic* Disaster." *Progress*. July, 1912.

"Camberwell and the *Titanic* Disaster." *South London Observer*, April 27, 1912.
"In Memory of Bandsmen." *Liverpool Daily Post*, May 4, 1912.
"Heroic Bandsmen." *Liverpool Daily Post*, May 13, 1912.
"Pour Nos Heros." *Le Cri de Liege*, October 26, 1912.
"Nos Heros." *Le Cri de Liege*, November 30, 1912.
"Pour Nos Heros." *Le Cri de Liege*, September 13, 1913.
"Il Etait un Grand Navire." *La Meuse*, September 16, 1925.
"Georges Krins: Le Hero du *Titanic*." *Liege M'etait # 67*, 1978.

CHAPTER 9

Newspapers

"Hatless Boycott." *Daily Mirror*, March 30, 1912.
"Long Hair V. Cambridge." *Daily Mirror*, March 30, 1912.
"Capt. Scott's Antarctic Message." *Daily Mirror*, April 1, 1912.
"L'Anglais Parisien." *Daily Mirror*, April 2, 1912.
"Capt. Scott's Own Story: Life Near the Pole." *Daily Mirror*, April 2, 1912.
"This Morning's News Items." *Daily Mirror*, April 3, 1912.
"The *Titanic*." *The Times*, April 3, 1912.
"*Oceana*'s Treasure." *Daily Mirror*, April 4, 1912.
"Strike Declared Ended." *Daily Mirror*, April 8, 1912.
"Three Weeks' Wait for Coal Supply." *Daily Mirror*, April 8, 1912.
"The Largest Vessel Afloat." *The Times*, April 11, 1912.

CHAPTER 10

Books

Gracie, Archibald. *The Truth about the* Titanic. New York: Kennerley, 1913.
Jessop, Violet. Titanic *Survivor*. Stroud: Sutton Publishing, 1998.
Jones, Victor Pierce. *Saint or Sensationalist? The Story of W. T. Stead*. East Wittering: Gooday Publishers, 1988.
McCaughan, Michael. The Birth of The Titanic. Montreal: McGill-Queen's University Press, 1999.
Palmer, Tony. *All You Need Is Love: The Story of Popular Music*. London: Weidenfeld & Nicholson, 1976.
Ticehurst, Brian J. Titanic *Passenger Miss Kate Buss of Sittingbourne, Kent*. Swaythling: B & J Printers, 1994.

Newspapers

"An Alarming Incident." *Daily Telegraph*, April 11, 1912.
Candee, Helen Churchill. "Sealed Orders." *Collier's Weekly*, May 4, 1912.
"*Titanic* Letter Expected to Fetch £25,000." *Guardian*, March 30, 2010.
"2ft Near-Miss That Sent the *Titanic* to Its Doom." *Daily Mail*, April 14, 2010

CHAPTER 11

Books

Beesley, Lawrence. *The Loss of the S. S.* Titanic. London: Heinemann, 1912.

Brimelow, William. *Independent Methodist Church Hymnal.* Wigan: Independent Methodist Bookroom, 1902.

Finck, Herman. *My Melodious Memories.* London: Hutchinson, 1937.

Hart, Eva. *Shadow of the* Titanic. Dartford: Greenwich University, 1994.

Howells, Richard Parton. *The Myth of the* Titanic. London: Palgrave Macmillan, 1999.

Lightoller, Charles Herbert. Titanic *and Other Ships.* London: Ivor Nicholson & Watson, 1935.

Machen, John Gresham. *Christianity and Liberalism.* New York: Macmillan, 1923.

Richards, Jeffrey. *Imperialism and Music.* Manchester: Manchester University Press, 2001.

The Wreck and Sinking of the Titanic. Chicago: Homeward Press, 1912.

Newspapers

"New York Mourns Its Dead President." *New York Times,* September 20, 1901.

"Tragedy of the *Titanic.*" *New York Times,* April 18, 1912.

"Woman Survivor of *Titanic* Tells of the Last Hours of the Ship." *Christian Science Monitor,* April 19, 1912.

"Bandsmen Heroes on the Sinking of the *Titanic* Play 'Nearer, My God, to Thee.'" *Daily Mirror,* April 20, 1912.

"Says Musicians Knelt as They Played Hymn." *Cleveland Plain Dealer,* April 20, 1912.

"Brave Musicians of Ship Meet Fate." *Worcester Evening Gazette,* April 20, 1912.

"Music on the Sinking Ship." *Daily Express,* April 20, 1912.

"Still Playing as Water Creeps Up." *Worcester Evening Gazette,* April 20, 1912.

"Musicians Knelt as They Played Hymn." *Cleveland Plain Dealer,* April 20, 1912.

"*Titanic* Survivors." *Western Daily Mercury,* April 29, 1912.

"Local Survivors." *Liverpool Daily Post,* May 1, 1912.

"Interview with Miss Sarah Stap." *Birkenhead News,* May 4, 1912.

"'Autumn' and Its Hymns." *New York Times,* May 12, 1912.

"Wreck of the *Titanic*: Little Girl's Account." *Leatherhead Advertiser,* May 18, 1912.

"Death Order to Bandsmen?" *New York Times,* May 31, 1912.

"The Author of 'Nearer, My God, to Thee.'" *New York Times,* September 30, 1912.

"Survivor of *Titanic* Disaster Tells of Grim Experiences." *Vineland Times Journal,* March 25, 1953.

Kerr, Jessica M. "A Hymn to Remember." *The Hymn,* January 1976.

Mills, Simon. "Play It Again, Sam." Titanic *Commutator,* vol. 24, no.149, 2000.

Music, David W. "The *Titanic* Hymn: A Conjecture." *The Hymn,* October 2001.

CHAPTER 12

Books

Behe, George. Titanic: *Psychic Forewarnings of a Tragedy.* Wellingborough: Patrick Stephens, 1988.

Hamilton, Frederick A. *The Diary of Frederick A. Hamilton, Cable Engineer of the Commercial Cable Company's Cable Ship* "Mackay Bennett." Greenwich, London: National Maritime Museum.

Newspapers

"Disaster to *Titanic* on Her Maiden Voyage." *Daily Sketch*, April 16, 1912.
"Funeral Service for *Titanic* Victims." *Toronto Globe*, May 4, 1912.
"Band Leader's Body." *Leeds Mercury*, May 9, 1912.
"*Titanic* Band Leader's Funeral." *Leeds Mercury*, May 17, 1912.
"The *Titanic*'s Bandmaster." *Daily Express*, May 18, 1912.
"*Titanic* Bandmaster Buried: 30,000 Mourn." *New York Times*, May 19, 1912.
"*Titanic*'s Heroic Bandmaster." *Leeds Mercury*, May 20, 1912.
"*Titanic* Bandmaster Buried." *Daily Mirror*, May 20, 1912.
"The *Titanic*: Bandmaster's Funeral." *Wigan Examiner*, May 21, 1912.
"Funeral of Mr. Wallace Hartley." *Colne & Nelson Times*, May 24, 1912.
"Find Joy in Stead's Death." *New York Times*, July 8, 1912.
Buttle, Cifford. "*Titanic* Victim Materialised Holding Crucifix." *Psychic News*, May 14, 1955.
"40,000 People Mourned a Famous Son." *Colne Times*, January 26, 1962.
"*Titanic* Owners Wanted £20 for Bodies." *Daily Telegraph*, February 24, 2002.

Chapter 13

Books

Conrad, Joseph. *Notes on Life and Letters*. London: Dent, 1921.
Eaton, John, and Charles Haas. *Titanic Triumph and Tragedy*. Wellingborough: Stephens, 1986.

Newspapers

"Memorial of *Titanic* Victims." *Dumfries & Galloway Standard*, May 1, 1912.
"Memorial for *Titanic* Dead." *Daily Gleaner*, Jamaica, May 2, 1912.
"Proposed Memorial to Dumfries *Titanic* Heroes." *Dumfries & Galloway Standard*, May 4, 1912.
Shaw, George Bernard. "Some Unmentioned Morals." *Daily News and Leader*, May 14, 1912.
"*Titanic* Bandsman's Heroism: The Benefit Concert." *Birkenhead News*, May 23, 1912.
French, E. B. "The *Titanic* and the Literary Commentator." *Bookman*, June 1912.
"Wills and Bequests: Mr. Henry Wallace Hartley." *The Times*, June 6, 1912.
"A.M.U. *Titanic* Convalescent Homes Fund." *Musicians' Report and Journal*, July 1912.
"*Titanic* Disaster Action Against Company." *Cork Examiner*, November 2, 1912.
"Tablet to *Titanic* Heroes." *New York Times*, November 4, 1912.
"The *Titanic*'s Bandsmen." *Glasgow Herald*, November 16, 1912.
"Letter from C. W. & F. N. Black." *Cork Examiner*, December 23, 1912.
"Why the Widows Receive No Insurance Money." *Musicians' Report and Journal*, December 1912.
"Tablet to *Titanic* Band." *New York Times*, January 5, 1913.

"Memorial Unveiled at Southampton." *Musicians' Report and Journal*, May 1913.
"Dumfries *Titanic* Victims: Memorial Unveiled." *Dumfries & Galloway Standard*, June 4, 1913.
"A Relief Fund Grant." *Glasgow Herald*, November 19, 1913.
"Dumfries *Titanic* Claim." *Glasgow Herald*, December 4, 1913.
Mary Catherine Costin v Andrew Hume, 1913. The National Archives of Scotland, CS 252/326.
"The *Titanic* Fund Case." *Dumfries & Galloway Standard*, January 21 1914.
"*Titanic* Fund Case." *Dumfries & Galloway Standard*, February 14, 1914.
"Memorial to the Late Mr. Wallace Hartley." *Colne & Nelson Times*, February 19, 1915.

CHAPTER 14

Books

Pulsford, Rev. E. J. *Divine Providence and the* Titanic *Disaster.*
White, Alma. *The* Titanic *Tragedy: God Speaking to the Nations.* New Jersey: Pentecostal Union, 1913.

Newspapers

Van Dyke, Henry. "Women First." *New York Times*, April 19, 1912.
"Many Creeds Pray for *Titanic* Dead." *New York Times*, April 22, 1912.
"Rule Britannia." *South London Observer*, April 24, 1912.
Chesterton, G. K. "Our Notebook." *Illustrated London News*, April 27, 1912.
"Memorial Service for *Titanic* Dead." *New York Times*, April 29, 1912.
"Dead of the *Titanic* Honoured in Church." *New York Times*, April 14, 1913.

CHAPTER 15

Books

"Ruddygore": A Booklet to Commemorate the Centenary of the First Performance. London: Sir Arthur Sullivan Society, 1987.
Precognition Against Kate Hume for the Crime of Forgery. National Archives of Scotland, AD/15/14/46.
Trial Papers Relating to Kate Hume for the Crime of Forgery. December 28, 1914, National Archives of Scotland, JC26/1914/113.

Newspapers

"Action Against Dumfries Violinist." *Dumfries & Galloway Standard*, August 9, 1913.
"Action Against a Music Teacher." *Dumfries & Galloway Standard*, January 10, 1914.
"Action Against a Music Teacher." *Dumfries & Galloway Standard*, January 28, 1914.
"Victim of Atrocity." *Glasgow Citizen*, September 16, 1914.
"The Dumfries Atrocity Hoax." *The Times*, December 29, 1914.
"The Atrocity Hoax." *The Times*, December 30, 1914.

"*Titanic* Hero's Father: Death of Mr Albion Hartley." *Colne & Nelson Times*, January 9, 1934.
"Cherry Ward: Veteran Paris Based Freelance Journalist." *Press Gazette*, July 9, 2004.

Chapter 16

Books

Morris, William Meredith. *British Violin Makers*. London: R. Scott, 1920.
Rattray, David. *Masterpieces of Italian Violin Making 1620–1850*. London: Royal Academy of Music, 1991.

Newspapers and Magazines

"Violinists at Home and Abroad." *The Strad*, 1912, page 153.
"*Titanic*'s Bandmaster: Found with His Music Case Strapped to Him." *Daily Sketch*, May 3, 1912.
"*Titanic* Violin Made for Wallace Hartley Plays in City." www.news.bbc.co.uk, July 2, 2010.
"Wreck of the *Titanic*." *Liverpool Daily Post*, July 2, 2010.
Sinclair, Fiona. "The *Titanic* Violin." www.thewreckoftheTitanic.com.

NOTES

Chapter 1

1. There has never been agreement on the number of survivors nor on the number of passengers and crew aboard the *Titanic*. The lowest number of survivors usually mentioned is 705 and the greatest, 713. Five survivors are believed to have died on the *Carpathia* before reaching New York.

Chapter 2

1. I am grateful to author Patrick Stenson for this information that he researched in 1984 on behalf of Walter Lord.
2. Sharing the third floor of 14 Castle Street with C. W. & F. N. Black were four firms of architects, two merchants, two solicitors, a timber company, a quantity surveyor, and a shipbuilder.
3. The crossing was made in 4 days, 19 hours, and 52 minutes. The average speed was 23.99 knots.
4. After the sinking of the *Titanic*, it was thought best not to give the ship such a boastful name, and it was renamed the *Brittanic*. Launched in February 1914, it was sunk by a mine on November 21, 1916.

Chapter 4

1. I am indebted to David Powner, the son of Laura Kelsall, for this family story.
2. *"L'amour dans la soie"* is a quote from Balzac's novel, *La Peau de Chagrin*, about the excesses of bourgeois materialism in which the main character, Raphael de Valentin, says he prefers love in silk as opposed to love in poverty.

Chapter 5

1. "Turn ye not unto them that have familiar spirits, nor unto the wizards; seek them not out, to be defiled by them: I am the Lord your God" (Lev.

19:31). "There shall not be found with thee anyone that maketh his son or daughter to pass through the fire, one that useth divination, one that practiseth augury, or an enchanter, or a sorcerer. Or a charmer, or a consulter with a familiar spirit, or a wizard, or a necromancer" (Deut. 18:10–11).

2. Like Yeats they were interested in the thinking of Madame Blavatsky (1831–1891) who attempted to synchronize elements of Hinduism, Buddhism, spiritualism, and the occult and was a cofounder of the Theosophical Society.

3. William Ulick Tristan St. Lawrence, 4th Earl of Howth, died March 9, 1909.

Chapter 6

1. Jones was quite an entrepreneur. In 1884 he had made a name for himself as the first person to import bananas into Britain.

2. John Wesley Woodward also played with the Eastbourne Municipal Orchestra at some point before taking up employment with the Duke of Devonshire.

3. Emeric Hulme Beaman's novels were *Ozmar the Mystic* (1896), *The Prince's Diamond* (1898), *The Faith That Kills* (1899), and *The Experiment of Doctor Nevill* (1900).

4. Simon Von Lier later changed his name to Herr Von Leer to appear German but was forced to become Van Lier when war started in 1914 and the Grand was assuring its patrons that "No German, Austrian, Turk, or Bulgarian (either naturalized or non-naturalized) is employed in any capacity in this hotel."

Chapter 10

1. No one can be certain how the accomodation was finally arranged but the original plans by Harland & Wolff indicated two cabins each capable of housing 5 musicians.

Chapter 11

1. Lightoller's comment was made some years later. The term "jazz" didn't come into use for another two or three years after the *Titanic* sinking, although music that would later be described as jazz was already being played.

2. The letters between Fred Vallance and Walter Lord are in the McQuitty-Lord Collection at the Caird Library, National Maritime Museum, Greenwich, London.

3. "Nearer, My God, to Thee" first appeared in William Johnson Fox's *Hymns and Anthems* (1841).

4. In the 1943, 1953, and 1997 films all named *Titanic*, the musicians are portrayed playing "Nearer, My God, to Thee" to the Lowell Mason tune "Bethany." In *A Night to Remember* (1958) it is set to the Church of England's favored tune "Horbury." The 1953 film wrongly showed the musicians playing brass.

Chapter 12

1. It's probable that the only reason Hume's body wasn't buried at sea as unidentified was because his bandsman's uniform was mistaken for an officer's uniform. Unidentified officers and first-class passengers were usually spared the indignity of being tossed back into the sea.

2. Andrew Hume appears to have wrongly assumed that his son was the bandmaster on the *Titanic*. Even after Hartley's funeral he persisted in this mistake.

3. The sinking of troopship HMS *Birkenhead* off the coast of Cape Town in February 1852 was frequently alluded to in accounts of the behavior of the musicians on the *Titanic*. The soldiers didn't play music as their ship went down, but they stood firm as women and children (the families of officers) were loaded into lifeboats. Out of 643 people on the ship, only 183 survived. The incident gave rise to the procedure of "women and children first" and the resolute behavior of the soldiers was referred to as "the *Birkenhead* Drill." The story of the event was frequently used as an illustration of fortitude, duty, and selflessness and the British musicians would have been aware of it.

4. A partial list of memorials and their original locations: The Orchestral Association, 13–14 Archer Street, London (July 17, 1912); Philharmonic Hall, Liverpool (November 4, 1912); Parish Church, Southampton (January 3, 1913); Southampton Library, Southampton (April 19, 1913); St. Marks Parish Church, Dewsbury, Yorkshire; Dock Park, Dumfries, Scotland. In memory of John Law Hume, (May 31, 1913); Broken Hill, NSW, Australia (December 21, 1913); Grand Parade, Eastbourne. In memory of John Wesley Woodward (October 24, 1914); All Saints Church, Lime Walk, Headington, Oxfordshire. In memory of John Wesley Woodward; Albert Road, Colne, Lancashire. In memory of Wallace Hartley (February 17, 1915); Symphony Hall, Boston, Massachusetts; Memorial Bandstand, Stuart Street, Ballaratt, Victoria, Australia (October 22, 1915); St. Michael Street School, Dumfries, Scotland. In memory of John Law Hume; rue de Donzy, Cosne-sur-Loire, France. In memory of Roger Bricoux (November 2, 2000); place Royale 21, Spa, Belgium. In memory of Georges Krins (September 14, 2002); Beacon Hall, Wavertree Road, Edge Hill, Liverpool. Additionally there are blue plaques on two homes formerly lived in by the Hartley family—90 Albert Road, Colne, Lancashire, and 48 West Park Street, Dewsbury, Yorkshire.

Chapter 13

1. Giovanni Battista Guadagnini, 1711–1786.
2. Tomaso Eberle, 1727–1792.

Chapter 14

1. The German-made 1943 film *Titanic* was similarly used to attack the immoral capitalism of Britain and America.

Chapter 15

1. According to David Rattray of the Royal Academy of Music, the Guadagnini, if in good condition, could fetch £400,000 and a similarly well-preserved Eberle, between £100,000 and £140,000.
2. She may well have been thinking of steward Thomas Mullin who attended St. Michael's Street School along with Jock Hume.

Chapter 16

1. Judging by other songs written by F. V. St. Clair, he was Canadian. The words to "The Ship That Will Never Return" are:

(V. 1) A big ship left port on its first maiden voyage,
The world gazed in wonder and pride
Old England was proud of the ship and its crew,
Whose Captain was trusted and tried.
The ship was a city of splendour and light,
Its rich and its poor side by side,
But when the shock came and the vessel went down
Rich man and poor man like Englishmen died.

(Chorus) Oh the ship that will never return
The ship that will never return
Brave words were spoken and brave hearts were broken
Ah, here's where true love you discern
Mothers they sobbed in prayer
As they parted from loved ones there
Husbands and sons, brave hearted ones,
On the ship that will never return.

(V. 2) Titanic its name and Titanic its size,
O'er the waves of the ocean she rode,
Four days had gone by since she'd left the old land,
With over two thousand aboard.
And then came the crash in the dead of the night,
But none on that ship were dismayed,
They trusted the Captain, they trusted the crew,
And even the women they were not afraid.

(V. 3) "Be British" the Captain cried out from the bridge
"Be British" and British were they,
The women and children the first for the boats—
And the sailors knew how to obey;
As long as old England sends ships over sea
The deeds of that night she'll recall
When rich man and poor man went down side by side
Where rank made no difference for Death levelled all.

Picture Credits

Steve Turner: pp. 19, 20, 36, 37, 38, 40, 41, 43, 62 (top), 64, 80, 81, 83, 93, 94, 95, 98, 104, 106, 112, 125, 167, 168, 174, 175, 176, 204, 205, 244

Steve Turner Collection: pp. v, vii, 10, 11, 14, 17, 30, 91, 115, 122, 124, 147, 150, 164 (top)

Missouri Historical Society Archives: p. 9

Lancashire County Library and Information Service: p. 166

Beverly Wolstenholme: p 21

Collection Bricoux Family/ Olivier Mendez: pp. 25, 49, 51, 52
Robert McDougall Collection: pp 33, 39, 118
East Riding of Yorkshire Library Service (Bridlington Local Studies Library): p 42
David Powner: p. 56
Graham Osborn: pp. 60, 62 (bottom), 63, 65, 69, 70
East Sussex Library and Information Service: p. 78
Jeanette Woodward: p. 75
National Archives: pp. 87, 88, 89, 127
Mary Gambell: pp. 102, 103, 201
Lesley Chapman: pp. 108, 109 (top and bottom), 181
Nova Scotia Archives and Record Management: p. 161
Colne Library: p 164 (bottom)
University of Stirling (Musicians' Union Archives): p. 179
Annette Robson: p. 199
Paul Parsons/Vernon Violins: pp. 214, 221

ABOUT THE AUTHOR

Steve Turner's previous books include *A Hard Day's Write: The Stories Behind Every Beatles' Song*, *The Man Called Cash*, *Trouble Man: The Life and Death of Marvin Gaye*, and *Amazing Grace: The Story of America's Most Beloved Hymn*. He is the author of several collections of poetry and contributes interviews and travel stories to various British newspapers and magazines. He lives in London.

INDEX